ESCAPING THE RUSSIAN ONSLAUGHT

TO MY PARENTS

RUTH AND HANS-RUDOLF MEISSNER

DISCLAIMER

I am pleased to acknowledge the kind assistance of the numerous people who helped me create this project. Foremost, my greatest gratitude goes to my family and friends for the excellent information they provided and the encouragement I needed to continue my journey.

The novel is a historical and human-interest story inspired heavily by actual events. However, the novel must be fiction since I cannot precisely know what occurred or was said. Names, persons, characters, locations and incidents are either products of my knowledge of my heritage and research or the recollections of stories told to me by my parents.

ESCAPING THE RUSSIAN ONSLAUGHT

A FAMILY'S STORY OF FLEEING THE RUSSIAN ARMY AFTER HITLER'S NAZI REGIME

DORLIES VON KAPHENGST MEISSNER RASMUSSEN

PEN & SWORD HISTORY

AN IMPRINT OF PEN & SWORD BOOKS LTD.
YORKSHIRE – PHILADELPHIA

First published in Great Britain in 2025 by
PEN AND SWORD HISTORY
An imprint of
Pen & Sword Books Ltd
Yorkshire – Philadelphia

Copyright © Dorlies von Kaphengst Meissner Rasmussen, 2025

ISBN 978 1 03613 063 3

The right of Dorlies von Kaphengst Meissner Rasmussen to be identified as Author of this work has been asserted by her in accordance with the Copyright, Designs and Patents Act 1988.

A CIP catalogue record for this book is available from the British Library.

All rights reserved. No part of this book may be reproduced, transmitted, downloaded, decompiled or reverse engineered in any form or by any means, electronic or mechanical including photocopying, recording or by any information storage and retrieval system, without permission from the Publisher in writing. NO AI TRAINING: Without in any way limiting the Author's and Publisher's exclusive rights under copyright, any use of this publication to "train" generative artificial intelligence (AI) technologies to generate text is expressly prohibited. The Author and Publisher reserve all rights to license uses of this work for generative AI training and development of machine learning language models.

Typeset in Times New Roman 10/13 by
SJmagic DESIGN SERVICES, India.
Printed and bound in the UK by CPI Group (UK) Ltd.

The Publisher's authorised representative in the EU for product safety is Authorised Rep Compliance Ltd., Ground Floor, 71 Lower Baggot Street, Dublin D02 P593, Ireland.
www.arccompliance.com

For a complete list of Pen & Sword titles please contact
PEN & SWORD BOOKS LIMITED
George House, Units 12 & 13, Beevor Street, Off Pontefract Road,
Barnsley, South Yorkshire, S71 1HN, England
E-mail: enquiries@pen-and-sword.co.uk
Website: www.pen-and-sword.co.uk

or

PEN AND SWORD BOOKS
1950 Lawrence Rd, Havertown, PA 19083, USA
E-mail: uspen-and-sword@casematepublishers.com
Website: www.penandswordbooks.com

CONTENTS

Acknowledgements vii
Prologue   Ruth Talks About Her Experiences During the
                 Second World War viii
Chapter 1   The Cavalrymen Came to Klein Pobloth 1
Chapter 2   Ruth's Plan to Escape 11
Chapter 3   Ruth's Resolve to Escape Heightened 15
Chapter 4   The Evening Before Ruth Escaped 25
Chapter 5   The Day Ruth Escaped 27
Chapter 6   Melding in With the Refugees 37
Chapter 7   Kolberg 44
Chapter 8   The Arrival of Their Train 56
Chapter 9   The Freight Train in Winter 63
Chapter 10   Güstrow 70
Chapter 11   Schloss Prüzen End of February and March 1945 74
Chapter 12   Tension Builds Farther 79
Chapter 13   Urgency Builds 84
Chapter 14   The Performance 87
Chapter 15   The Letters 89
Chapter 16   Byways 97
Chapter 17   The Parade 104
Chapter 18   On the Journey 107
Chapter 19   The Meadow 120
Chapter 20   The Horses 125
Chapter 21   Their Lieutenant 129
Chapter 22   A New Freshness 136

Chapter 23	May Sunshine	139
Chapter 24	Firestorm	144
Chapter 25	Shattered Dreams May 1945	148
Chapter 26	To Lübeck Occupied by the British	150
Chapter 27	The Beach House, 15 May, Vorrade	156
Chapter 28	Two New Men in the House	162
Chapter 29	After the War	168
Chapter 30	Quest to Find Rudi and Archim	171
Chapter 31	Hans-Rudolf Returns	174
Chapter 32	Achim Returns	180
Chapter 33	Winter Comes	183
Chapter 34	Registering the Horses	186
Chapter 35	To Osnabrück	190
Chapter 36	From Village to Village	196
Chapter 37	The Enormous Undertaking	198
Chapter 38	Eating Chicken	201
Chapter 39	Over the Bridge	203
Chapter 40	Beautiful Bathroom	209
Chapter 41	Schwege-Hunteburg	212
Chapter 42	January 1946	219
Chapter 43	Ruth Visits Her Mother	225

Epilogue ... 231
German Words and Definitions ... 233

ACKNOWLEDGEMENTS

It has been my good fortune to have a renowned German family tree. This history has been passed down orally and has inspired me to venture on a quest to bring forth my family's incredible tale.

I want to thank my parents, Ruth and Hans-Rudolf (Rudi) Meissner. I am greatly indebted to them, for they were willing to spend endless hours with me, tape-recording their stories and reminiscing about their life experiences. They also gave me the family's oral history. I am grateful to my sisters Susanne and Annerose and my brothers Hans-Georg (George) and Thomas for their firsthand knowledge and recollection of their experiences.

I appreciate my husband Duane's confidence, my children Daren and Dawnel, my son-in-law Steven Meyer and my granddaughters – Annelies, Brenna and Lauren – who have patiently spent their time with me, as well as Matthias Beulke and Martina Riesener, and their research of the Pomeranian area, Carol Gresky, Margaret Webber, Karen Spruill, Susan Dole Cole, and my cousins Klaus Hertel and Gunnar Nebelung with MyHeritage. Without their involvement and encouragement, I would not have been motivated to move forward. Their optimism and confidence allowed me to see the potential in this book.

For me, this book is not only a labour of love. It is a promise that I've carried throughout the years: to tell my parents' story.

Prologue

RUTH TALKS ABOUT HER EXPERIENCES DURING THE SECOND WORLD WAR
Ruth and Rudi's Tainted World

My mother, Ruth Clara Schläger Meissner, meticulously documented her recollections on tape recordings, drawing from her memories of the harrowing time when she waged her own battle, fleeing with her sister-in-law and four children, all under the age of six. As I listened, my mother's distress was such that she often had to pause because her accounts were too painful to recount. This meant that a significant number of events were open to my own interpretation. These tapes are a testament to her strength and resilience.

Seated at her 1950s table, its chrome legs gleaming and an orange and cream motif adorning its surface, my mother would nervously trace an imaginary spot as if trying to erase the haunting memories of those fearful times. As I listened, she would search for words, her impatience and pensiveness palpable. "After I was born in 1911, the world became a wretchedly rough place to live. Dorlies, how did we ever survive World War Two?" Her question, a refrain, was often accompanied by a gesture as if she could scratch a line through those war years.

I answered. "Mother, your everlasting tenacity carried your young family to safety."

"Oh, Dorlies!" Her faint voice was weak, locked within her, and could not be heard. It was difficult for me to discern her struggles.

"Mother, if telling me this story is too trying, we do not need to continue."

Suddenly, my mother's eyes, always full of life, had a more decisive, lively stare, alive with images, like a glass that would never overflow. She seemed filled with recollections and wouldn't utter them, not even to me. Then she began to talk.

"After the Great War ended in 1918, no one could have imagined what losing the war would mean for the German people, with the whole country devastated and in complete disarray.

"In the Treaty of Versailles, the victors of the war drew a new map of Europe and decided to punish Germany for starting the war," she recounted. "Germany was

Ruth Talks About Her Experiences During the Second World War

held liable for repaying 132 billion gold Reichsmark as reparations. The outrageous demands caused a breakdown in German society. How could an already broken nation survive with the demands of reparations placed on them by the Big Four?" my mother asked earnestly, "As they enforced the treaty's terms, these nations perpetuated the crisis in Germany. The humiliation and economic instability made the timing ripe for right-wing politicians vying for power.

"In 1922, the revolution in Russia ended with the formation of a new state, the USSR, with Lenin at the helm, the symbol of hope for all after the revolution. However, the Russian people gained nothing; the new state only worsened their trials. In Italy, Mussolini's rise to power inspired Hitler, so he decided to concoct a plot to seize power over the Bavarian state government. Ultimately, local militias stopped Hitler from taking power, and later, Hitler was convicted of treason and sentenced to prison. During this time, he was able to regroup and plan for his next move, which was to seize power. Lenin died in 1924, and Stalin took power. He ruled with an iron fist, as predicted by Karl Marx, who proclaimed Russia would be under Stalin's dictatorship. Lenin died in 1924, and Stalin took power over the country as a hardhanded dictator.

"I must continue telling you about my life story so that the generations to come can learn what happened in Germany in 1933. Everything transpired so rapidly that many German people did not know about or believe the atrocities and genocide perpetrated by Hitler's army. The Nazi Party was a secret society of thugs and madmen. In February of that year, the Reichstag (a building that housed the German Parliament) was set on fire. Hitler, a power maniac, blamed the communists and used the fire to enshrine himself with the title of Führer. He, along with his henchmen, overthrew the national democratic governmental system and turned it into a warring totalitarian state.

"Hitler abolished all other forms of government when he rose to power. Over Hitler's years in power, 370 politicians were murdered, and anyone who spoke out against the Nazi Party was shot or jailed. These times were frightening for those of us against Hitler because propaganda ran rampant, and you could not go anywhere without seeing the big, long red flags with the swastika waving at you. Informants were everywhere. Even your next-door neighbour could turn you into the Party, who would shoot you without question.

"It was terrible. So many people around the world did not understand what violence and fear we faced every day. Even the president of the United States, Franklin Delano Roosevelt, did not understand that the educated Germans and the former nobles despised Hitler and wanted him eliminated.

"After Hitler was elected in 1936, his recommendations seemed sensible to the German people: rebuilding Germany's infrastructure (which helped put the unemployed to work) and structuring the "Brown Shirt" programme for a stronger Germany. Hitler's charisma blindsided countless Germans, and many, even the nobility, fell under his spell during this time.

"However, the nobility posed a threat to his power. These people were educated, and thus, they questioned Nazi philosophy. By the time we realised what was occurring, it was too late for aristocrats to band together against Hitler's tyranny, and noblemen were required to serve in Hitler's army. Over time, the punishments for speaking out worsened. If someone spoke a word of disapproval against Hitler and the Nazi Party, they would be shot on the spot.

"You must bear with me while I digress. I want to tell you about when I first met your father and noticed his enticing, azure eyes. From the moment I first saw him, he was incredibly charming and had a sense of humour and an aptitude for storytelling like no one else I had encountered. When he made me laugh, it brought me back to life, and I could not resist when we first began our courtship because he had such integrity that I plunged my heart into the love affair and was ready to unveil my heart to this extremely outgoing man.

"Your father and I were married at the Kempen Estate, my family's estate, on 24 June 1938. However, we would not find one moment of peace together for many years because of the war. After we married, we moved to Cottbus and soon had your sister, Susanne. When the war began, Rudi and I felt it was a blessing that he had broken his right knee twice before the war began. His injured knee kept him from officer duty, and he dodged much fighting, saving his life.

"The people in the city became terrified of the radical Nazi dictatorship, which was filled with hatred for homosexuals, the mentally ill, the physically challenged, Freemasons, Catholics and Jews. To instigate hatred towards the Jews, the Nazis broke the glass in Jewish establishments and synagogues on what became known as the 'Kristallnacht' on 9-10 November 1938. The city of Cottbus was hit hard by these terrifying events. Yet, the German authorities did nothing.

"I stayed by Rudi's side as he and a doctor he worked for rushed into the streets to assist the wounded. We tried to help, but we were pushed back by Nazi thugs who were slashing their way to commit more atrocities. Rudi was injured during the fray. When I saw my husband's bandaged face, I wept bitterly. 'Please, let us leave this place,' I begged. 'We can move back to my parents' home, the Kempen Estate. They will take us in, I know they will.'

"Since his youth, Rudi had premonitions of things to come, and many of his predictions have come true. After his stint in Russia, Rudi knew that the adversaries would take their revenge.

"On 1 September 1939, your father, Susanne and I played beside one of my favourite Linden trees in Kempen's Park. I remember wearing a caramel-coloured red, printed, knee-length dress that day. I took a picture of Rudi and Susanne playing on a blanket and enjoying the sunshine. While Rudi tickled baby Susanne, our maid rushed to us and handed him a telegram. The Nazi insignia on the envelope took our breath away. The letter contained orders to join the Nazi Party and march off to war. I could not imagine life without Rudi, my loving husband and father. But

Ruth Talks About Her Experiences During the Second World War

now he was confronted with an impossible choice: go against his morals or face certain death. Thousands of Germans had already been imprisoned for speaking against the Nazi movement. Rudi knew disobeying orders meant our young family could be next.

"There have not been genuine moments of peace since your father and I became engaged. There were countless issues of outside interference in our lives over which we had no control. Will it ever stop?"

"Your father had just received his orders. I remember his hands trembling when he ripped the thin grey paper open and could see how devastated he was, but he was determined to put on a happy face. He embraced us and whispered, 'We shall get through this. We can get through anything together.' Despite the terrible news, he twirled Susanne and me in a wide circle. I giggled in delight as we plunged gracefully onto the green grass. He gazed at me hopefully, drew us closer, and said, 'Thank God, all the army wants is my motorbike. It will be tough to give it up since we used the bike for our honeymoon. The bike was registered when I took out my driver's licence. You know how well the Nazi record-keeping is. I must report to the Trampke train station within the hour.'

"We made a deal with your grandmother, Dolores. If we moved our family from my parents' estate of Kempen to Klein Pobloth, also in the country, she would remodel the first floor of the manor house. She kept her promise, so we moved in during the first week of July 1940.

"Rudi was drafted in the spring of 1941 to fight on the Eastern Front, which began on 22 June 1941. Because of his twice-injured knee, Rudi was ordered to drive an army truck in the spearhead of the Operation Barbarossa. After a horrendous winter in Russia, we were delighted when Hitler proclaimed that all soldiers who were the head of an estate in Pommern, the breadbasket of Germany, were to return to tend to their farms. Within five days after our reunion, Rudi received a telegram informing him that he must return to fight for our homeland to protect Germany from the heavy onslaught. We did not realise when Rudi was assigned to the Western Front, later known as the Battle of the Bulge, it would be one of the fiercest battles in history. Communication was challenging. Wiesbaden was the only post office address I could use as a general holding area. Letters from Rudi were few and far between. If a message did arrive, the censorship would be outrageous. The note could hardly be read, with bits and pieces cut out, only a few words left behind to reconstruct using my imagination.

"I saw so much death and horror during those years. My father died, and then my darling brother Joachim was killed while stationed near St Petersburg. My elderly uncle, Paul Schläger, remained imprisoned because he spoke ill about Hitler's regime to a neighbour. Worst of all is the story of my uncle, who was married to a Jewish woman. They had three children together. He came to believe that his family would be tortured in one of the camps, so he lured them into the nearest cemetery, shot them and then turned the Luger on himself after doing his 'merciful' deed.

"After we escaped from our home, I realised that there would never be closure with the loved ones I left behind. In 1941 on his last visit home, Rudi was on a five-day furlough from the Eastern Front in Russia before departing on what he felt would be his last deployment for Germany's Western Front. Rudi's loving warnings spoke volumes, reminding me of his premonition many months earlier while battling to survive the cruel Russian winter. He was confident our Fatherland was doomed.

"Once we were alone, Rudi spoke of the atrocities he witnessed in Russia. Each time he mentioned the Red Army, he flinched, with the pain of his time in combat still raw and his youthful charm remained buried behind the loss of life he had witnessed. When we first married, his eyes were bright and passionate. Now, that light was snuffed out by the horrors of war.

"Rudi was determined to keep his young family out of harm's way and did not wish us to experience, as he had, the carnage the Red Army left in its wake. His intense gaze would not omit any warnings to me. 'Remember, the Red Army does not take prisoners of war. Instead, they exterminate whoever and whatever they capture.'

"By 1944, we feared that Stalin's ruthless army would invade our borders. I hope you understand that these times were horrifying worldwide, not just in Germany."

"We also faced bombings from the British Royal Air Force. They were not supposed to target civilian areas, yet they still decimated cities such as Leuna, Hamburg, Lübeck, and Berlin throughout the war. The constant air attacks kept Rudi, me and the rest of Germany in perpetual fear. Rudi warned me about his visions of the black swarms of invading aeroplanes dropping bombs as if in a grisly black hail on the major German cities. I wished he could be spared the horrors of war, and then, in 1945, I found that I must place my little family in the same abominable situation.

"For months, essentials, such as gasoline and electricity, were to be used only in an emergency, and the postal service was interrupted. The over thirty plots of assassinations on Adolf Hitler assisted him and his henchmen in believing their Führer was invincible, thereby keeping World War Two raging until the spring of 1945. By the beginning of January 1945, my morale had deteriorated to breaking point.

"Your father was at war. There was little support for me in our home. The situation had become too dangerous to keep you, Susanne and Hans-Georg out of harm's way. I still remember when I had to make the most difficult decision of my life – to leave Klein Pobloth and take you, your brother and your sister to safety."

My mother closed her eyes, lost in the past and her memories.

Chapter 1

THE CAVALRYMEN CAME TO KLEIN POBLOTH

The small village was silent on this January evening in 1945, save for the jarring clatter of horse's hooves on the black cobblestone lane as they hastened through the ancient community of Klein Pobloth, which caused Ruth's window to vibrate. She snuffed out the candles beside her and knelt on the elongated windowsill but could not resist drawing the heavy, golden damask drapes from the casements of the three-story Meissner family's ancestral home. Her curiosity peaked. Ruth peered into the sleet, which blotted out her view. The snow afforded her poor protection from an oppressive, glacier-like wind from the nearby Baltic Sea creeping through the thirteenth-century building and carrying her anxiousness through her petite, chilled frame.

Outside the confines of the first floor of Klein Pobloth manor house, belligerent considerations were already bothering Ruth for wishing to escape to a safer haven. The mighty Nazi Party mocked small communities like hers, claiming that the women and children would have to dig ditches if attacked by the Red Army. Ruth grieved that her home in Pomerania would be next. Murderous, warring, communist factions were already rampaging within the Pommern borders, evident for months, and preparing the way to destroy her homeland. It was clear that Ruth was terrified, but she did not accept death as an option. Why was she the only one in the household who questioned and doubted the government that tore asunder the nation she loved so well?

Ruth's urgency to flee with her children was well-founded. A year earlier, Ruth had learned of the Nemmersdorf massacre on 21 October 1944. She had rushed to tell her mother-in-law, Baroness Dolores von Kaphengst Krause Meissner, and her sister-in-law, Anneliese Hertel, the news. "The Red Army has invaded Nemmersdorf. People are saying that the townspeople were tortured and killed. They have even shot and killed women and children. It's a massacre. What they have done is unconscionable," she declared. Still, Dolores and Anneliese refused to acknowledge the danger. Even when the ominous Red Army massacred numerous Germans as well as the French and Belgian prisoners of war, Dolores foolishly refused to give up on the possibility of peace. Trusting her intuition, Ruth chose

Escaping the Russian Onslaught

to save her family and escape Pommern instead. The authorities predicted that a steady stream of troops, weapons, tanks, munitions and vehicles would soon wreak havoc when they crossed the Pommern countryside.

The Red Army would draw nearer to Ruth's family home in Pommern if the gates were flung open. There would be nowhere to hide from the onslaught of the Russian war machine marching through Germany. They would slash her country to bits. How long before they all died?

Dolores, Anneliese and the flamboyant estate manager, Herr Risch, accused her of being a traitor to her husband Hans-Rudolf's impeccable aristocratic legacy. Ruth felt utterly betrayed by them and decided she could no longer bear such treatment.

In her despair, Ruth sought refuge from the others in her first floor dwelling in the mansion, practically barricading herself away from the three people she now wished to disregard. Walking a tightrope, Ruth imposed a self-inflicted moratorium on further contact with the remaining household members. There would no longer be peace in this place.

Ruth's gentle ways grieved the bitter silence of separation from the others in the home, leaving her to converse only with Emma, her maid and her three children: Susanne, who would be aged six in March; Hans-Georg, five in March; and Dorlies, who would be two in June.

Though the war interrupted Ruth and Rudi's passion, their love deepened with the separation. She kept hearing her husband's firm but calm voice and clung to his every tender word: "Ruth, do what you must to keep our family out of harm's way." Ruth knew it was her duty to follow Rudi's advice. When Ruth did not heed Dolores's words, Anneliese and Herr Risch placed extreme pressure on her.

Ruth considered an escape plan while waiting for the tea kettle to boil. She needed to discover a way to flee not only her in-laws but the increasing danger of the world outside. A piercing whistle startled her. The hot cup of diluted tea Ruth was placing on the table in front of her crashed onto the parquet floor, startling her three children playing on the multicoloured and red Persian carpet, who began weeping. Ruth frowned at her carelessness. "That will make a stain." She called for Emma to bring her cleaning supplies to help freshen up the mess.

On this cold evening in late January 1945, a sharp whistle rang out throughout the village of Klein Pobloth. Then the clattering of horses' hooves rang out, confirming that strangers were in the hamlet. Ruth pressed her knuckles against her petite mouth. Did she expect to be captured by the Russian thugs? However, Ruth was a realist. There would have been a warning from the surrounding estates. Earlier, warning sirens were set up in Gross Jestin and the churchyard at the Lübchow, Klara Schumann's estate across the road from the Klein Pobloth Estate. The estate manager also secured the entrance to Klein Pobloth. Pinnow, the night watchman, was assigned to ring the alarm bell when he heard the church bells at Schumann's sounding a warning.

The Cavalrymen Came to Klein Pobloth

The darkness of the evening crept further into her living area. Feeling uneasy, Ruth snuffed out the remaining candles. As she did, she looked out of the window once again. Less could be detected now. Her husband's prophecies about their country's destruction were being fulfilled. With Dolores and Anneliese out of the home, Ruth felt helpless but waiting for death's blow was not in her nature. Although Ruth's brown eyes filled with tears, she was determined not to allow terror to set in.

Leaving the children with Emma, Ruth slipped into Rudi's study adjacent to the living room. The shelves in the room housed the gun rack holding ten of Rudi's rifles he had kept hidden from the government. The rifles were only for hunting wild boar or red deer that rummaged through the potato fields. The family stored these bagged animals in the icehouse adjacent to the manor house for a festive dinner.

She reached for the .22 Long Rifle that Dolores purchased from the American Sears Roebuck Catalog years earlier for Rudi's twelfth birthday surprise. From hunting the great woodlands of Klein Pobloth, Ruth could handle this rifle with the most accuracy. Hoping it might keep the intruders at bay, she placed several copper and brass bullets into her green sweater pocket and securely tucked the gun under her arm.

The children were accustomed to seeing their mother and father with hunting equipment, but Ruth did not relish frightening them any further. She crossed between the two rooms, not wanting to strike more terror into the three little ones this evening.

Her hands trembled as she folded the puddled, golden, floor-length drapes away from the ancient, elongated window. Once more, Ruth peered beyond the large veranda and the weathered rose garden leading to the circular drive. The sound of countless horses anxiously pawing the cobblestones permeated through her supple, youthful skin and ears. She could not see how many wagons and horses came to a halt. A man's loud voice sounded a command. It was too far from her, and she could not detect the language. The racket of equipment, plus the other men chatting among themselves, echoed to the window. When the first man's voice ordered something, the chattering ceased.

Turning halfway back into the room, her face stark, she said, "Mutti must see who has come into the lane."

Her son drew her out of her thoughts. She felt his body tremble against her slender legs, and his tiny arms tightened about her brown and turquoise woollen skirt. Hans-Georg pushed his small hands through his fine baby brown hair. His timid, hazel eyes studied Ruth. "Mutti, I hear a man yelling orders. Mutti, do you know if the people are strangers?"

"Not yet, son, but I will know soon. You and your older sister, Susanne, can help finish feeding baby Dorlies her mashed carrots. Can you do this for your mother?"

Both Susanne and Hans-Georg were accustomed to obeying their mother. Little Dorlies still needed encouragement to feed herself. She was so petite, too small for her large blue eyes.

Through her uneven, six-year-old teeth, Susanne smiled and said, "Mutti, there are a lot of horses out there. Can we go out and say hello?"

"Not now, my sweet girl. I know you love animals, but this is not the right time to be outdoors." Ruth straightened her daughter's thick blond mane. "First, Mutti must see who these people are."

In the silence of the large room, her breathing slowed. Her petite body trembled, and her colour was ashen. Distracted by the quiet, bravery won over. Despite the danger that might await them, Ruth was adamant that she knew what was happening in the community. Kneeling on the freezing, cold windowsill, she caught a glimpse of the early season snow glistening in the dusty evening haze. Her mind was caught up in fear and anticipation but was soon relieved by the forty stylish German soldiers dressed in grey-blue woollen uniforms astride their mounts. They were kinsmen, not the Russians she feared the most.

When Ruth looked closer, steam was pouring from the horses' nostrils. Armed with some knowledge of horses, Ruth understood these animals had been working long and hard. Now, she could see that the men, horses, a wagon with equipment and one carriage carrying a woman with three children looked as though they had suffered much distress.

A man's faint grey shadow laboriously lifted one leg over his glossy, polished, brown leather saddle, and then both legs slid to the frozen gravel drive. Ruth pondered the three long strides as his black boots crushed the gravel stones of the circular drive carrying him forward. Sudden chatter from the men disrupted the still night air. Behind him, the wagons and horses were quieted by another voice's rawness which uttered a German curse. Once again, she heard, "Quiet!"

Ruth looked back to see her children. A pistol cocked. She listened closely, not remembering when the night had been so still. In three long strides, the man approached her front door. Her heart hammered in her chest – this mysterious man had a firearm. Ruth and her three small children were cut off from the community, which lay just beyond the park. In those lonely seconds, Ruth realised she and the children were the only ones in the house. These men were not siege engines that would hurl deadly warfare. She understood that tired soldiers were more susceptible to terror caused by hunger, for the war had been brutal on the German soldiers over the last years.

Within a stride, the silhouette grabbed one of the bronze horses adorning the right side of the door knockers on the twelve-foot-high green entry doors.

Before opening the heavy wooden door, Ruth looked through the side windows to study the entry to the circular drive to see a family with the driver controlling the animal. Fighting to keep her composure, Ruth shut her eyes to a possibly extremely

The Cavalrymen Came to Klein Pobloth

dangerous situation. She peered out between the drapes once more and then melted into calming relief when she saw an agreeable smile from the man in a blue-grey German officer's uniform.

Ruth hesitated before opening the door. Disturbed by the silence on the other side, she did not move immediately. What had become of the others who had been in the house? They must be out in the barns. The household staff would not have presumed to present themselves at the front door. It was time to answer the door, and she was the one who was responsible for receiving the stranger.

Her shoulders proud and steady, Ruth cocked the rifle and placed it at her waist as she stepped through the tall green doubled doors onto the terrace. The small firearm could leave several holes in the individual on the opposite side, but stopping the attacker's first blow was the extent of the damage it would accomplish. The enemy could carry their fury throughout Klein Pobloth and would keep her alive long enough to torture her in front of the children. If death were to come to Ruth, she would rather go down and let the children live.

As Ruth opened the door, the strong Baltic Sea winds thrust across the Pomeranian countryside, driving the salty taste into Ruth's mouth. Though it was still early evening, Ruth hesitantly stepped through the two Roman arches before closing the door behind her. As if for reassurance, she gazed back at her small children and saw Emma concealing one eye behind her chequered blue and white apron.

The village lamplights revealed a light film of powdery snow coating the shoulders of Ruth's brown coat. A shiver of uncertainty swiftly drew her mahogany hair into the trimming of the brown fox wrapping. With the rifle in hand and great deliberation, as she tried to conceal her worried smile, she inquired, "Yes, how can I assist you?"

Caked with brown sleet, the commander downed his grey cap. As was the custom to the Lady of the house, out of politeness, he bowed his head and clicked his tall black boots.

A light glimmer of hope caught the corner of his eyes. His reassuring voice showed a hint of the devastating horror he had witnessed. Grimacing, he wrenched his shoulders, "My dear Lady, we mean you no harm." The man dared to place his right hand on the muzzle. "Please relax your rifle and place it downward. My plea is urgent. May I speak to the mistress of the house?" Uncertain, she clung to his every word. Ruth asked him to be seated on one of the white metal chairs before acting any further.

She hesitated. If she were to fire a shot, the people left in the community would hear the racket and come to her aid, but there appeared to be no need to be an alarmist. By studying the darkness, Ruth could see more mounted soldiers close the gap behind the lieutenant. There was no hope now in lunging backward into the safety of her home. By doing so, she could jeopardise the safety of her children.

Escaping the Russian Onslaught

When she remembered that no one else was home, Ruth began to panic. Dolores and Herr Risch were in the barns, and Anneliese was visiting a neighbour. Ruth had no choice but to speak with the officer.

Her heartbeat drummed fast in her chest as she wished to whirl out of the darkness back into her home's security. As Ruth stepped a few paces into the light, her dark brown eyes met his smile. "Sir, I am Frau Hans-Rudolf Meissner. At present, I would be the one to speak with."

The lieutenant's situation soon became clear. The group's commander claimed his equestrian school and family were seeking lodging away from the marching Red Army.

At thirty-three, Ruth was in her prime, placing her among the beauties of the county of Gross Jestin. She studied the commander. The man's blue uniform was mussed, unusual for a German officer. Undoubtedly, his company had moved swiftly across a vast terrain. Throwing back his head, he drew in a sharp breath and exhaled politely.

Steadying his expression, his blue eyes met Ruth's. "Gnädige Frau, I am Lieutenant Robert Blank." He placed his cap under his right arm. "This time of great upheaval, my equestrian school with forty men requires lodging. Only for a few days," he explained, "only until two of my men recuperate. They were shot by Russian snipers while practicing for their next military parade. We lost one man killed who needs to be buried, but the ground was too frozen."

Shivering in her brown walking shoes, Ruth stepped back a few paces. His account so weakened Ruth that she could only lower her head. He looked dazed, with a chalky, staring face, absent eyes, and almost without voice, as if every means of communication had vanished. The shuffling of his black boots was the only sound present. Suddenly, he said, "My Lady, I am so very sorry to have spoken to you in such vulgar language."

Parched, the lieutenant licked his lips and smiled charmingly, causing her knees to buckle. "If you please, place your rifle back into the house. We are all so parched," shivers ran through his body, "and bitter cold, exceedingly hungry also. The young woman looked at him, her brown eyes full of fear, yet something in her heart melted with the young man's pleasant ways. Ruth stepped back into the house. *I must help!*

She had been in uncomfortable and dangerous positions before. Admittedly, with forty strapping young, hungry soldiers in the great park directly in front of her, Ruth hesitated to leave her three children with only Emma in attendance. She knew that weary and thirsty men were more susceptible to unleashing havoc for want of food and supplies.

She wished her husband was at her side in those lonely seconds. He had been conscripted into the war, and she often worried for his safety.

The steady trotting of hooves sent her back onto the veranda. Her shaking increased, and then, to her relief, a vague outline holding a lantern began to

The Cavalrymen Came to Klein Pobloth

materialise from the dusty air toward her right. Pinnow, the night watchman, came toddling their way to investigate the goings-on. Despite his ageing years, Pinnow dashed toward the commander, uttering a curse and pushing his pipe firmly into the man's chest. His tenseness indicated his demeanour. He grumbled through his peppered walrus moustache, "Wait here! You must wait here!" Then he spat the brown residue of his pipe into the snow.

Tipping his billed grey worker's cap, Pinnow smiled at Ruth, "My Lady, can I be of assistance?" Pinnow's request had a sharp force to carry his point home. The old, weathered man shook the head of his bitten wooden pipe vigorously at the younger man. "We must find your mistress before making any decisions," Pinnow insisted.

Pinnow waddled across the park as rapidly as his ageing body could and tottered toward the artillery. His curiosity crept up, so he stepped closer, lifting his trusty black metal lantern. The golden light flickered to reveal the outline of some of the men on their mounts. Ruth saw Pinnow fling back the green canvas cover and study the wagon's bed. When he spotted the frozen bodies, Pinnow gagged. Dazed, he marched closer to Ruth, "I will find your mother-in-law so we can provide the necessary accommodations."

Not surprised at her protector's comment, she pressed the commander no further, waiting for the decision to put the forty men and their horses in the unoccupied horse barn. "Wait here, sir." Ruth stepped back into her well-appointed parlour. "Emma, watch over the children. Give the gentlemen outside a bite to eat and some more milk. You can make a sandwich from the luncheon meat left in the refrigerator, or you might slather it with fresh butter and some of those homemade raspberry preserves from last summer." Already halfway out the door, Ruth called over her shoulder, "I will help where I can." She flipped on the outside light to illuminate the barns.

There were accommodations in the horse barn for the coachmen and chauffeur so the two injured men and several others could bunk there. Her body quivered from terror at the man's account, so Ruth followed the lieutenant to the three men's supply wagon. The further they walked, the more horrifying the carnage was painted in her mind. They hurried to the men, and the officer's face became grimmer as they walked. "My Lady, turn away. Do not look into the wagon. It is too frightening for a lady to view."

Nevertheless, Ruth caught a glimpse of the bodies lying inside and collapsed. Gingerly, the lieutenant supported Ruth's elbow and turned her back to the lights of the welcoming manor house. Moving sluggishly, sickened and terrified at what she saw, she heard the horses whinnying to be fed and watered. As she approached her home, her heart pounded harder and faster in anticipation of what lay ahead for her community. She could not hear clearly. She shoved her luxurious fox collar away from her chilled ears to listen to the lieutenant.

"My Lady, we have a stretcher. Can you provide shelter for both the horses and my men? Some iodine or other disinfectant, medications, bandages and warm blankets?"

Attempting to cover her nose from the cold, Ruth pushed her brown fox collar closer to her pale face. Her voice was weaker than she had hoped when she said, "I am versed in caring for the sick in my community. I will help tend to your men. Everything will be all right, sir. My family will help where we can."

The lieutenant closed his eyes and shuddered from relief. "Outstanding."

Empty car garages were available for the buggy and the equipment wagon. Without hesitation, the community harboured the horses and the forty young soldiers who accompanied them. Most adult women and men were forced to join Hitler's campaign against the rest of the world. Thus, there was no protection available for the remainder of the community. No mingling with the young girls left in the village would be allowed.

The lieutenant's wagon was a few steps away from the supply wagon. His ungloved right hand firmly stretched out to his wife. His deep blue eyes were alive. "May I introduce my family who is travelling with me?"

Feeling more at ease, Ruth laughed in relief. "Oh, having your family's company would be a pleasure. If it is agreeable with you, I have an ample living area. Your family can spend their time recuperating with us, my three little ones and me. Yours will have a bedroom they can share and plenty of toys to keep them occupied. You and your wife can occupy an adjoining guest bedroom suite if you like."

Despite the danger from the oncoming Russians, Lieutenant Robert Blank, Maria, his wife, and their children were invited to lodge in Ruth's apartment for the following three days. During their brief stay, Klein Pobloth cared for the cavalrymen and those injured with the help of Ruth, Pinnow and the farmworkers' wives.

Ruth and Maria focused on the wounded while Emma attended to the children. The commanding officer's children were ill then but no one knew their ailment. With six youngsters under eight, the home was filled with enough childish enthusiasm to last for days.

Rest was well warranted for all within. The first evening was spent in humble silence for those women and men already lost in the largest siege of its history. Holding Ruth's blue Angora woollen yarn about her arms, Maria twisted the thread into a softball. Ruth, Maria and the lieutenant chatted about trivial matters: anything but the previous years. After Hitler and his collaborators took power, they forbade German citizens to speak ill of him or the Nazi Party. If one wrong word were spoken to a staunch Nazi, they would report it or arrest them at gunpoint straight away.

The following morning, the children were ecstatic to have each other's company. While Emma was occupied teaching the youngsters board games, working puzzles and playing hide-and-seek in the rumpus room, the adults sat at Ruth's kitchen table, massaging cups of hot, makeshift coffee, savouring the flavors, and feeling more comfortable with one another. They were prepared to advise one another of the dangers that lay ahead.

"Gnädige Frau Meissner," he nodded courteously, "my wife and family thank you from the bottom of our hearts for our welcome at Klein Pobloth. My family has been travelling with me to remain out of harm's way of the large cities. We have not had farm-fresh, soft-boiled egg, butter and warm hard rolls for months. I will ensure the school thanks the Baroness when they meet her."

Ruth stood to replenish the three coffee cups, offering as much creamy milk as possible to hide the bitter taste from the acorn and grain mixture the community had learned how to roast. "Yes, she would appreciate speaking to your young men. Dolores Meissner has enjoyed young people all her life. With most young people out of the community, it will give her pleasure."

The commander's wife, a pleasant young, friendly woman, smiled. "The conflict in our country has been overwhelming for years. Then the outright hostility resulted in another war." Maria studied Ruth, hoping to inquire about her political stance, and discovering nothing from Ruth's demeanour, she fretted. Before she continued, Maria gazed at her husband, who gave his approval. The young woman continued, "Since Hitler and his collaborators gained power in March of 1933, the radios are packed with sugary propaganda."

As the commander spoke, the warm winter sun softened the depressing atmosphere hanging in the room. "Frau Meissner, please tell us your news first."

Waiting a moment to study these two strangers intently, Ruth could not afford to confide only to have them be pro-Nazi. Time and again, life had taught Ruth well that no one could be trusted. She must be as cunning as a cat, sniffing out if these people were ready to catch her in a plot against the Führer. However, she must not allow an opportunity to pass by to learn as much news outside the hinterland of Klein Pobloth as possible. It might never come again before a siege strikes from within her country or the borders surrounding Germany.

Pushing her unfinished cup to the side, Ruth said, "The resulting turmoil is not over, and uncertainty appears to be coming to us from every direction. With the intermittent radio broadcasts I receive, who knows what I can trust?"

Attempting not to reveal her feelings, Ruth sat motionlessly. "It is difficult to think of what may lie ahead, but I must keep my family safe. Customarily, I brought extra supplies to the farm families over the past years. Among the laypeople on the farm, the rumours ran rampant. While visiting the farm workers' homes, I was invited to sit at their tables. Over the past five years since moving to Klein Pobloth, Olga, the chicken maid, has become a trusted friend." Releasing the grip on her cup, Ruth relaxed.

"Originally, Olga is from Poland, but she has made her home on the farm since she was young. Over the years, she considered herself German and has been faithful to our government. However, she has had reservations and shares her thoughts with me. Like many other estates around here, we have young Polish prisoners of war working for us to do much of the planting and harvesting." Her birch kitchen chair caught the back of her shoulders. Relaxing further, she folded her hands on her multicoloured, small, printed housedress. Ruth smiled. "Because Olga enjoys speaking the language of her birth, she has gotten to know two other Polish workers who have decided to make Klein Pobloth their home." A sigh of trepidation followed. "Olga confided to me that she gained much information about the world outside when chatting with them." Her expression became tense. "They speak of how the opposition is drawing a tighter ring around Germany. The young women felt that Germany was being wrenched apart from within."

The news related by the lieutenant was too important not to listen intently. "Sometime in September, the first German town fell to the Americans. It was a little place called Roetgen, southeast of the vital city of Aachen. Belgium was practically cleared by this time, and the assault upon Germany was advancing."

The commander's face twitched as he said, "I heard it through the ranks that the siege on Aachen began on September sixteenth."

Ruth sank into her chair. Her heart skipped several beats when she realised her beloved Rudi was stationed near Aachen. After sharing her information with the lieutenant and his wife, both informed Ruth of what they had heard while travelling. The lieutenant said, "While the Americans and the British were liberating the Netherlands, the ancient forts of Metz, which had never been attacked since the year 451, were pounded by American guns and planes. Plus, the American Third Army levelled France's German defences. Some of my men who travelled to France in earlier years paid close attention to France, and they say the town of Nancy is under siege.

"You must understand Frau Meissner; we must move on at daybreak."

Ruth said, "I understand it is for your safety."

Chapter 2

RUTH'S PLAN TO ESCAPE

There was no hesitation or trepidation in Ruth's mind that she should make her escape on the morning of 27 February 1945. She and her children must not be detained from fleeing any longer. Ruth Clara Schläger Meissner determined it was no longer prudent to depend on anyone other than her own confidence for her family's safety. Her tenacity in making that decision would change the trajectory of the Meissner family's lives forever.

Observing the foggy, orange sunrise broaching the first floor grand portal in her husband's ancestral Klein Pobloth Estate, Ruth noted the uncertainties of life gathered below. As the bronze farm gong rang, she noted 4 a.m. She alerted the farm labourers along the black cobblestone street to see after the throngs of weary refugees. Troubled with the adversity of what lay ahead for her family's future, Ruth watched hordes of people torn from their homes in the easternmost province of Pommern striving to escape to the west. Ruth was anguished by the examples of these warnings before her. The Red Army was known for its savage atrocities as it attempted to spread its communist ideologies throughout Europe. The only thing standing in the way of world domination was the beleaguered war-torn nation of Germany.

After Rudi's tour of duty in Russia, he reported to Ruth that the Red Army was already slaying thousands of women, children and old men in Russia. The Jewish population was particularly vulnerable. Stalin deemed these people useless, and their food could be better used by feeding those who could fight for his cause. However, Stalin was too clever to allow this terrifying information to leak out. Unbeknownst to the rest of the world, Stalin slaughtered more Jews than any nation. Any prisoners of war attempting to return to Russia were ordered to be struck down so they could not pass on the good news of how other nations were free and educated. Determined to keep them under his thumb, he removed any political figure who got in his way. To Ruth and many other Germans, Stalin was more of a threat than Hitler.

Beyond her front entrance, damp, brown grass was trampled in the park. It was teeming with people rushing to gather their meagre belongings and arrange them on their pushcarts or sling the heaps over their backs. People did not have a plan to escape; the ebb and flow of refugees was constant, causing a gasp to escape Ruth's dry throat.

Escaping the Russian Onslaught

In the first light of morning, the folks loitered in the park just beyond the frostbitten rose garden leading to the circular drive. They waited only long enough to receive what might be their last morsels for the day. The chatter appeared abnormally turbulent. The people around the park grumbled about the damage from the ongoing degradation. There was a temporary lull, but hunger won out.

The previous night, Ruth helped to prepare a makeshift soup kitchen for hungry travellers. They began serving three-foot-long dense rye bread baked the previous Friday. Today, the dark rye slices were slathered with freshly churned butter. Fresh milk and strong makeshift coffee were divided into the tin cups dangling from their carts along with cold cuts from the estate's February 1944 butchering, but the meat was not as bountiful this winter in 1945 as it would have been.

Ruth recalled that a year ago, in February 1944, when she heard hysteria and then pandemonium, she wrenched backward, terrified. She kissed her children's foreheads and quickly asked Susanne to watch after Hans-Georg and Dorlies. She dashed through the French doors into the long hallway in three strides and onto the first floor veranda. For the remainder of the day, her heart drummed in her chest when she heard the harsh shouting of two German soldiers armed with machine guns ordering, "Halt! Halt!"

She peered out of the elongated window leading to the densely fogged park. A ghastly sight lay in front of her. Immediately, she saw that the two German soldiers were standing guard over some twenty bedraggled and starving Russian prisoners of war. While resting on the estate grounds, the soldiers had detected the raw meat's stench in the icehouse next to the manor house. Five frantic Russian soldiers broke loose, charged toward the snow-laden building dripping with icicles, and burst through the narrow entrance. The men smashed the door, snatched the carcasses from their hooks, and the Russians gorged on the bloody pig, wild boar, red deer and Hirsch corpses. The surroundings reeked of blood.

In the past, Ruth had always found the small icehouse enchanting, but now, the grounds around the icehouse were transformed into a ruby river of melted snow from the bloody carcasses ravenously strewn about. Ruth stepped onto the veranda's edge and turned to be sick in the withered century-old rose plant that led to the roof of the three-story manor house. When she became upright again, Ruth was horrified to have one of the Russian soldiers at her feet.

A hauntingly hoarse voice pitched forward. "My Lady! I speak a little German. Please do not let them send me back to Russia. Stalin's army will kill me! He will kill all of us prisoners who will be sent back home."

Ruth sidestepped his grasp and said, "I am sorry, there is no way I can help you. Surely," she added, "you will not be sent back."

As if resigned to his fate, the Russian soldier crept back to the park.

The German soldiers were farther down the lane, so they did not see the Russians' intrusion on the icehouse, the property, or Ruth herself.

Ruth's Plan to Escape

Moments later, Ruth saw that the shivering Russian soldiers who broke into the icehouse had joined the others without being detected.

Ruth gagged violently and struggled back into the house, then collapsed onto the red carpet, her eyes rimmed in terror, her face ice. She tightly clutched the chair near the door to avoid collapsing onto the floor.

The children were anxiously waiting for her, whimpering out of confused concern for their mother. "Mutti, what is wrong, Mutti?" her young son, Hans-Georg, questioned.

Breathing deeply before answering, she patted his soft baby hair. She could not bear to tell him of her decision to leave Klein Pobloth. Too much was uncertain. "My darling boy, all is going to be all right. There is nothing to worry about. A few men are resting in our park, so Pinnow and some other farmworkers are giving them food and some fresh milk to drink. They will be on their way soon."

Ruth felt sympathy for the starving men. She knew she was helpless to aid the poor soldiers in the park. The shivering Russians were moved on by the stern German guards within the hour. Outside her window, Ruth heard, "March on! March on!"

Her mind was made up – now it was time to flee their home. Yet, it occurred to Ruth that she needed to put some plans in place. She did not have enough cash ready when she first decided to leave Klein Pobloth, so she wrote to her bank asking them to send her several thousand Marks. She had received the verification, saying the money was dispatched. Regrettably, the money did not reach her because the mail service was already disrupted in all areas of Germany. Ruth could get to the money quickly because it was in her parents' home bank in Stargard. Risch's denial was too rapid to believe when questioned about the money. Suspicions ran rampant in her mind. Had Dolores given orders to stop the bank envelope from reaching her? How could she doubt her mother-in-law's sincerity? On second thought, coupled with Dolores's motherly jealousy and drive to keep her legacy alive, she had prevented Ruth at every turn from escaping. Dolores had commanded Ruth to stay at Klein Pobloth no matter what. Thus, Ruth and her children had an urgency to escape from underneath Herr Risch and Dolores's unjust demands. Their underhanded campaign fueled Ruth's drive and desire to escape.

Stress undermined her ability to make decisions clearly. Although Ruth had stopped smoking cigarettes before she became pregnant with Susanne, she yearned for the sweet aroma of tobacco. *It has been years*, she mused, w*hat I would not give for a long puff on one right at this moment.* Quickly, she searched her desk for a pencil to place in her mouth instead.

Although asking him made her skin crawl, she went to Herr Risch's office, planted her petite feet firmly on the wooden floor, and pleaded with the man she loathed above all other men. "Please help us," she begged. "Even a small sum of money would be of great use to us." Hoping to rouse fear in her, he laughed in a sinister voice and then spat, lashing out with the same bile that her mother-in-law had a few days ago.

"I do not have any money," he replied sarcastically. "Where do you think I would get hold of the kind of money you want?" Stunned that a petite woman like Ruth would stand up to him, Risch shook his head angrily and turned on his heels. He paused and turned towards Ruth again, wearing the same sinister smile. Ruth despised Risch for his attitude. She questioned why this healthy man had not been called to fight for the Fatherland when her Rudi was putting his life in danger every day on the frontlines. Perhaps his friendship with Hermann Göring excused him from his duties in the German military? In any case, he had the power to stop Ruth from getting her family to safety. Ruth saw unstoppable greed in his pitiless eyes. She would have to find another way.

When she saw the lecherous look in his eyes, she stopped breathing. She knew full well that Risch thought women were for one thing only, and Ruth was not about to give him what he desired. Ruth stiffened her back and walked away. She had listened to the gossip surrounding the Rischs' for some time and understood their continual greed where the community was concerned. Risch and his wife considered themselves too important to mix with the farm workers' families. The couple was sure that Klein Pobloth would be theirs and the farm's assets would be turned over to them after Dolores was gone.

Ruth's heart was swollen with the weight of her emotions, and she feared succumbing to despair after her battles with Herr Risch. But she refused to let fear paralyse her. She was determined to save her children and herself, no matter the cost. Her courage burned bright, and her resolve would be tested to its limits in the coming months.

Chapter 3

RUTH'S RESOLVE TO ESCAPE HEIGHTENED

It was up to Ruth Meissner to keep her children from the evil invading their country. The only choice left to her was to aid her family in escaping, and she had to find a way to make the escape happen soon.

Once Ruth stiffened her resolve with the realisation that fleeing was inevitable, she slipped through the twelve-foot-high, forest-green doors. It was still pre-dawn. Ruth did not wish to awaken her three children and softly closed the French glass doors to their part of the house behind her. She determined that if her plan was to work, she must act promptly. Stepping back into the spacious hall area, Ruth reflected on the legacy of history she would deeply miss. She quietly slipped into her spacious first floor of the manor house.

On this foggy 27 February 1945, the staggering weight of these burdened refugees and their need to trudge on, emerged into a dirty, showered dawn of snow mixed with dust to the west. She was eager to coax one of the refugee families in the park to post a letter to her husband, Rudi. His only address was Obergefreiter Hans-Rudolf Meissner, L 12158, LGP Wiesbaden, Germany. Quickly, she sat at her small writing desk to pen the short note. Ruth's hopes ran high that the letter informing Rudi about her plans to flee with the children would still reach him. Her fingers trembled as she handed the message to a lovely young woman with one child bundled onto her skinny frame. The woman's cold, grimy hands reached out to Ruth to take the note. Ruth waited long enough for the woman to tuck the note and a bit of cash hastily in her rucksack. They smiled at one another with understanding.

Her vitality and grace were still intact in the dim candle-lit hall of the manor house. In a blind rush down the dark hallway, she nearly collided with Anneliese and her five-year-old son, Klaus-Dieter. As a result of the mele earlier that day, their clothing was dishevelled, and Klaus's copper-coloured hair resembled a rooster's comb.

Ruth immediately noticed a change in Anneliese's demeanour, but she knew not what was plaguing her. Was it her weary state? Anneliese leaned against the massive thirteenth-century barrel-topped hand-carved cherry trunk for support.

She appeared pale and weak. In her haste to hang on, she nearly knocked over the vase of yellow hothouse roses resting there that Ruth had arranged the day before.

Her face stark and bewildered, Ruth asked, "Why on earth did you travel from Kolberg on the night train?" Anneliese and Klaus-Dieter were away for a time in Kolberg to allow Anneliese to recover from her minor surgery in the Baltic Sea's invigorating air. They were not meant to return until later that week.

Taken aback by Ruth's early hour walk in the dark hallway, Anneliese answered quickly. "What we have seen in the city over the past few days is terrifying. I felt it was best for Klaus-Dieter and me to find our way back home before the trains no longer run. Most are jam-packed with the Nazi SS, German army or refugees."

"The sight must have been horrendous for you both." Ruth shuddered at the thought. "Have you recovered from your surgery? You still appear rather frail and ashen to me."

Anneliese's eyes brimmed with tearful terror, and then she shook her head. "It is not my illness troubling me. It is the devastation my son and I have been veiled from out here in the backcountry of Pommern. I was panic-stricken by my short trip to the city, which has now opened my eyes. Can you imagine that the pharmacies in Kolberg are distributing free poison so the ill-fated can take their own lives before the Russian army attacks? While transferring trains in Gross Jestin, I spoke to some of our neighbours. Our friends could only speak of the carnage they saw during their travels to the city. I trembled when Pinnow picked us up with his horse and buckboard, and we made our way through Moltow to deliver us home."

For an anguished second, Ruth closed her brown eyes and flinched from her deep sorrow at needing to escape. She regarded the 250 residents of Klein Pobloth as part of her extended family. When possible, Ruth indulged in helping care for their children or assisting a family if an illness occurred.

Fingering her face's slender natural beauty, Ruth regretted she had not yet escaped and was unsuccessful before in escaping with her three small children. Ruth's right hand brushed back strands of her mahogany-colored hair that were beginning to surrender from the combed folds at the nape of her neck.

Feeling anxiety build in her, Ruth brushed at the tears threatening to drop. "Anneliese, this is dreadful news," she said tenderly. "You must realise that I have been considering escaping whenever the opportunity presented itself. However, someone or something always stood in my way!" Ruth tried to keep the accusatory tone out of her voice.

Anneliese winced. "Yes, I understand how difficult we have made it for you and your children. My mother has been unreasonably stubborn. Sadly, she will not discuss the situation any further." Anneliese's embarrassment peeked through her lightly freckled complexion. "You know how clever my son is in getting secrets from little Hans-Georg. Before I left for Kolberg, Klaus-Dieter and your

Ruth's Resolve to Escape Heightened

son argued about who was going on a longer trip. Little defenceless Hans-Georg flushed excitedly when he crowed about your plans to take an extended journey."

Ruth's reservations sprung from when she suspected Anneliese was perhaps the cause of her latest failure to leave with the royal equestrian school travelling through Klein-Pobloth. Anneliese had informed her mother and Herr Risch of her plans more than once. But she could not dwell on that now. "Over the past five years since I moved to Klein Pobloth, I have seen the beautiful hills flourish with golden ripe wheat strewn with bright blue cornflowers and red poppies. The Baltic Sea breezes made their way inland. They entwined themselves through the fields, giving way to our woodlands and causing their canopies to dance. I loved the sight." Ruth sighed heavily, for she and Rudi were in close partnership with nature. Rudi, who graduated with a degree in agriculture from the college in Stettin, had assured her that every square inch of usable soil was cultivated.

Ruth paused for a moment. "These days, however, it has been gravely frustrating for me to hear the steady breeze flow over the fields with the explosions of voices from the terrified refugees outside my window. I fear finding a poacher in our dense woodland beyond the house who then encroaches onto the fields until it becomes too dangerous to hunt for the many bounties the woods hold."

Ruth gazed out the nearest window toward the fields dotted with white snow melting into the rich brown earth she loved so well. The supreme irony was that the more drastic and determined her demands were, the more sarcastic Herr Risch became. He painted a detailed picture for Dolores in order to secure his position at the estate. Foolishly, Dolores found his charms irresistible.

Grimacing to Anneliese, Ruth said, "By the thunderous bellows soon to roll over the land, there is no more time to dilly-dally."

The orange sun was high enough now to send its warmth through the elongated windows on the first floor of the Klein Pobloth manor house, casting its way into the ancient culture within.

Anneliese clutched Ruth by the shoulders. "I must flee with Klaus-Dieter. You have thought of escaping several times. Are you now going to actually flee?"

Ruth held her perfect rigid posture in place. "Anneliese, I remember before my engagement to your brother when you and your mother abruptly announced yourselves at the front door of my parents' Kempen Estate. You and your mother felt that I was not suitable because my heritage was not as noble as yours. Both of you were disagreeable women who insisted on speaking to my parents. Once I was summoned to join my parents in the salon, you stood by while your mother hurled outrageous accusations at her future daughter-in-law. When you and your mother were sent on your way, my parents encouraged me to call off the marriage, insisting that Hans-Rudolf's family was of the knighthood nobility and could claim that their legacy dated to Martin Luther's best friend, a distant relative. The ancient European families, the von Kaphengst line, could be traced back to 1166 Ludolf von

Dassell, the brother of Rainald v. Dassel, Archbishop of Cologne, and Chancellor of Emperor Frederick Barbarossa. It is impossible to think your family can be traced back to 866, about the time of Charlemagne. My ancestors were not of the nobility but highly educated and as impressive as yours."

However, Ruth was proud of her family and needed to remind Anneliese. "The Schlägers are highly educated and cultured, as the distinguished branch of the family has been for decades. Excelling in publishing, banking, and music, among other lucrative businesses, they were wealthy, but many times, I questioned if the sacrifice of losing my identity in Rudi's world was worth it. Eventually, Rudi's charming ways won my family over."

Could she trust Anneliese now? Now was not the time to question Anneliese. She needed to be prudent and move swiftly. Wakening her children or being heard by nosy Emma would be too risky in Ruth's living quarters. Anneliese determined that the second floor, the Lady's salon near the dining room, would be more discreet. It would be away from the prying eyes of Herr Risch and Dolores, who would be overseeing the farm workers by now.

Motivated to rush out of earshot, Ruth wondered where to turn next and then agreed with Anneliese that the second floor would be their secure haven. Still furious at the thought of being detained, Ruth led the way up the waterfall stairway leading to the smaller ladies' salon. She took Anneliese's elbow, with her son trailing behind and scurried the two through the grand hallways. With twelve-foot ceilings, the main dining room floor was covered in light-coloured parquet flooring. The birch table and chairs splendidly conveyed the distinctive features of the Empire style. A substantial white tile oven stood beside a built-in buffet on the house's north side. Hanging shelves displaying Dolores' painted plate collection circled the room's perimeter. The meals were prepared in the kitchen and lifted to the dining room by a dumbwaiter, where the maids served the guests.

Anneliese's whisper was more intense now. "Ruth… Ruth, when you go, we must flee with you!"

Again, Ruth was startled at her request. "Anneliese, send your son to your bedchamber while you and I sit in the salon."

Before Anneliese answered, with her right hand, she patted Klaus-Dieter's backside three times to scurry him to the children's playroom and then to the southeast side to their bedroom.

After the war had become uncomfortably threatening, Anneliese and her son took residence in Rudi's chambers down the hall from his mother's bed chambers.

Dolores occupied the second floor with its large veranda overlooking the park, the community and the woodlands. Her bed chamber, sitting room, writing desk, and modern facilities were on the west side of the home. If fires broke out or invaders attacked, a tiny, concealed door in Dolores's dressing room could be opened to the spiral stairway leading to the basement or the red-tiled roof.

Ruth's Resolve to Escape Heightened

Impatiently, Anneliese nudged Ruth to get her attention. "Ruth, follow me. The salon will be chilly. This is where I hid from my mother as a child when I did not wish to be found out so she will not find us now."

Ruth determined it was to her advantage to consider Anneliese's plea. Being by herself out there in the crowds of humanity was terrifying. Being with Anneliese and Klaus-Dieter would be in her best interest for the safety of her children. For a moment, Ruth felt faint. *Keep calm.* The whole confrontation with her mother-in-law would not be fruitless. She had already stepped over enough obstacles. Today would be different, and she would face it with brave confidence.

Ruth fingered the light switch on one of the antique crystal candelabras resting on the baroque table. The two lamps and the grand crystal chandelier were converted to electricity at the turn of the century. As she and Anneliese entered the great baroque salon that doubled as the ballroom, Ruth took in every detail as she had many times before.

Even though her parents, Georg and Luise Schläger, felt it was a fool's game, Ruth's interest in design had not faltered. In addition to the residence, after the fire in 1909, the famous German designer Arnold Kramer had designed the room accenting the light parquet floor with a red Persian carpet and warm yellow silk fabric wallcovering with a soft, bold yellow motif. French Louis XVI ebony furnishings inlaid with silver drew attention to the well-appointed room. The bay windows housed von Zieten silver, a service for sixty, and elegant royal blue and gold hand-painted china dishes enhanced by the von Kaphengst Crest. An eighteenth-century square grand piano was placed near one of the Erkers on either side of the stylish space. Beside the elaborate limestone fireplace at one end of the room, Dolores and her maids used the spinning wheel to turn the Angora from her rabbits combed into a fibre. After dyeing the yarn, Dolores knit jackets with matching caps for her four grandchildren.

Quickly, Ruth turned to walk by the lunar grandfather clock and the dumb waiter to make certain the lift was securely closed to the cooks' and maids' quarters. The eggshell-coloured red oven and five other chimneys stoked from the manor house's basement served the Lady's salon. The chilly salon was heated only for special occasions. A small cabinet housed the ivory, hand-painted, oval miniature likenesses of the von Kaphengst and von Zieten family back to the 1300s. They were displayed like a family scrapbook to honour their long-standing ancestry.

The manor house contained a kaleidoscope of history. As Ruth hurried to be at her sister-in-law's side, she took in every detail, for this would be the last time she would view the life-size portrait of Prince Heinrich of Prussia. It was one of the many gifts given to Christian Ludwig von Kaphengst, her husband's great-great-great grandfather, five times removed. Ruth's exquisitely groomed, petite fingers drew over one of the countless pieces of antique silver also passed down by a relative. The gifts were awarded to General Hans Joachim von Zieten,

Escaping the Russian Onslaught

Prussian Hussar, Frederick the Great's favourite general, and then to his son Count Friedrick Email von Zieten. These men of prestige and position were honoured by portraits taking centre stage on the elegant Rittergut knighthood estate.

Nonetheless, life was reduced to a single imperative of survival. Ruth knew they could not remain at her husband's ancestral home. Life hung onto their traditions of the past by a gossamer thread.

The room's ambiance did nothing to lighten the mood. Ruth could see Anneliese's nervous eyes as she sat and turned to face her with an anguished expression. Hysterical, she begged. "Ruth, now I am the one to plead with you. Please! Please, can you see it in your heart to sneak us out of here when you go? This week, firsthand, I have seen the poison infesting our country. I beg of you! You have always been so much stronger in your persistence than I have. You must see I cannot break away from my stalwart mother by myself. The only way I can drag my son and me from the clutches of her hold on us is to slip away with you."

Ruth was not certain she was ready to forgive Anneliese's earlier indiscretions and her cold, aggressive treatment of her. In a stern, quiet voice, she commanded. "Shhh. Anneliese, you need to keep your voice down, or none of us will have the opportunity to leave. Your mother is already fuming at the thought of us leaving. I cannot imagine what she will do if she finds out you have the same idea. I would not put it past her to lock us both in our living quarters."

"With my time of recuperation in Kolberg, I assure you, I feel well enough to travel. I promise you, Klaus-Dieter and I will not be any trouble to you in your quest."

Again, Ruth pondered the idea. Would this notion be wise? Anneliese did not distract herself from everyday pleasures like working in the garden as Ruth did with her father at the Kempen Estate. Besides, Ruth was cultured in French, the arts, theatre and the opera with her intellectual and high educational achievements, living in a refined household. She had an extraordinary aptitude for cuisine and formal entertaining, a trait well-known to the people close to her. Ruth also took pleasure in aiding the labourers by calling Kempen their home and delivering a baby when needed. Her extraordinary capacity for love and vitality ruled her life. Ruth did not know Anneliese well despite living under the same roof. Still, she knew Anneliese typically busied herself with trifling pleasures such as reading, archery, playing tennis on their grounds, and swimming in the nearby Baltic Sea.

Ruth could not abandon her sister-in-law when she came to her for help. Rubbing her petite, chilled hands, Ruth said, "Perhaps it is foolhardy to attempt such an arduous journey. Then again, two women and four children will give us an advantage over my leaving with three small children by myself. If this is what you wish to do?" Ruth spoke as if to read Anneliese's thoughts. "Months ago, I arranged with a friend to stay at Irene Zimmer's and invited my family to use her Schloss Prüzen as a haven if the time arose. The type of castle that will suit you. It

Ruth's Resolve to Escape Heightened

is located near Güstrow in Mecklenburg-Schwerin. Irene is a kind soul and would welcome all of us into her castle."

Ruth studied Anneliese's expression to see if she was serious about joining her.

"Your foresight will save my family. I beg you again, please take Klaus-Dieter and me with you. Achim and Rudi will find us there if we do not come home in a week. The chaos will surely be over by then."

"Then you need to decide within the hour. Who knows if Pinnow will have time to ring his alarm bell to warn the community? The only radio station still reporting announced that the Russian army are on a three-day march from our front lane. Who knows if we can hold them off? As women, who knows? I can only imagine what horrific torment lies in front of us when the Red Army sees vulnerable females. Without question, we would be obliged to do their bidding."

Next to Klein Pobloth was the Lübchow Estate. The estate's mistress, Klara Schumann, must be warned before the Russians attack. Would Ruth be able to contact her before she escaped? Since Ruth's arrival at Klein Pobloth, Klara had become a dear friend of her little family. When the fire in 1909 destroyed the roof and backside of Klein Pobloth, Klara and her husband Fredrich Schumann had invited Hans von Kaphengst and his newly widowed daughter Dolores under their roof. Like Dolores, Klara was also widowed in the Great War. Thus, Klara and her two sons, Horst and Frederich-Wilhelm, were Hans-Rudolf and Anneliese's lifelong friends. The four young people attended the same boarding school in the Thüringen Mountains. Then, the boys participated in the agricultural department at the college in Stettin together. After graduation, the three boys enlisted in boot camp simultaneously and were soon off to war.

Much to her chagrin, Ruth concluded their only alternative was to flee like thieves on the early morning train from Gross Jestin. "We must leave now," Ruth declared, "before all the train services suddenly halt. Or, even the unthinkable, take us in the direction of who knows where. As Rudi has informed me, the Russians do not take prisoners. Instead, they choose to kill anyone in their path."

Unbeknownst to the two women, Baroness Dolores von Kapengst Krause Meissner had slipped next to the door, left ajar ever so slightly by Klaus-Dieter. With his noisy entrance to his bedchamber directly next to hers, she knew her daughter had returned. Thus, she had gone searching for Anneliese.

Dolores stood silently, eavesdropping on the two women. Dolores burst through the massive antique walnut door when she discovered their plan. Her copper-coloured hair accentuated the raging blaze building in her crimson cheeks. Her eyes were icy and full of judgement. Dolores bellowed loudly at the two women. In surprised shock, Ruth and Anneliese jumped to their feet and stood up.

With a bitterness not able to be squelched, Dolores placed her hands on her hips and bellowed dramatically in her low-pitched voice. "You have been discovered!" Dolores stamped her right foot on the walnut parquet flooring like

Escaping the Russian Onslaught

an irritated child. "Ruth, you are deserting the estate that will someday belong to you and your husband. In my eyes, you are a coward! You are shirking your duties as my son's wife."

Ruth's heart hammered in her chest as Dolores's bitter words burned like flames exuding from her lips. Nevertheless, Ruth would not back down. Giving up her firstborn to adoption in her youth and then the seven years of her marriage with Rudi, years of living at Klein Pobloth without him when he was called to active service, had etched her into the person she was today, a woman of steel reserve.

Surprised to be challenged again, Dolores shook her head vehemently. With her cavernous mouth, she yelled, "Ruth, keep your wits about you. You know those are just rumours. They say this is nothing but propaganda. I will not listen to it nor your appeal. You and your children must stay to protect Klein Pobloth. You must set an example for the others from the estate. Ruth, you and Hans-Rudolf must not forget your legacy by standing your ground!"

Anneliese took a deep breath. Awash with tears, she said, "I was about ready to tell Ruth of the horrific acts against Germany before you burst through the door. True and accurate reports of what is happening in our country have been suppressed for years from us out here in the hinterland.

"Mother, events in our country are more than the catastrophe of the Titanic in 1912." Tears of anguish rushed down Anneliese's face. "While in the overcrowded hospital, I needed to room with several women who were severely burned by the Russian torpedoes sent into civilian ships carrying an overload of children and women refugees. Thousands of women and children travelling to Kolberg were killed when their ships were mercilessly torpedoed. Therefore, most did not get out. Reports of these impoverished refugees will most likely be reported in later years when this area along the Baltic Sea is in neutral hands once again."

A fire built up in Ruth: she must come to terms with what had occurred at Klein Pobloth, Kolberg, and along the Baltic Sea. As she listened, tears of grief filled her eyes.

When Ruth spoke to Anneliese, her voice cracked out of empathy. "I cannot grasp the enormity of what you are telling me about the thousands of refugees. Just think about the many children and women who must have succumbed to the ocean and the freezing waters."

Dolores puckered her brow and turned her furious gaze to her daughter. "Anneliese, what do you have to say for yourself? I am most disappointed in you, my only daughter. How can you possibly think of fleeing?"

"You do not understand, Mother. Sadly, in this war, the Russian U-boats surrounded the Kolberg waters. The German people used this as their last means of escape into ships on the Baltic Sea. Thousands of people died by taking this route."

Dolores's tremendous uproar reverberated quickly throughout the house, frightening the four children out of their beds and awakening everyone else. Soon,

Ruth's Resolve to Escape Heightened

four sleepy, bewildered youngsters surrounded the three women. Ruth caught sight of three domestics peering between a door with their heads slanted, one stacked on top of the other.

Everyone stood in utter silence as they tingled with sadness. Ruth's children, Susanne and Hans-Georg shook in fear of their grandmother's anger and the accusations hurled at their mother. Ruth swept the toddling Dorlies into her arms and held her fast against her breast as if her twenty-one-month-old baby girl could protect her from the Baroness. Out of angst, five-year-old Klaus-Dieter hid behind his mother's skirt.

When Anneliese did not respond, Ruth boldly broke the silence, trying not to frighten the children with her words. "My intuitive sense of what is happening around us is that the Russian army will be at our doorstep within three days, if not sooner." Catching her breath, Ruth continued her argument. "Time and again, our flight has been postponed by the efforts of Herr Risch or you. Dolores, you must understand! We must escape from Klein Pobloth. My determination will not give way to your demands. My three children and I are fleeing in a few moments. We must have a head start on the people fleeing before the Russians infiltrate Pommern like a firestorm. Out of desperation, Anneliese and Klaus-Dieter have decided to join us on this fateful morning."

"With any luck, the train we hope to take will carry us to Mecklenburg-Schwerin, Germany. Away from Kolberg and further westward until we are entirely out of Pommern. It will not be a comfortable journey. We will leave without any provisions and must blend in with the crowds of other refugees. Both our husbands are fighting in the war, and Anneliese and I see the need to flee. We will be away from Klein Pobloth for only a week or two weeks if the fighting does not die down as soon as the German army foretells. I thought a great deal about this decision. I must take these drastic measures to do the right thing."

Ruth and Rudi had spoken months ago about the possibility of fleeing when he returned from Operation Barbarossa. While there, he became friends with Ivan, a knowledgeable Russian man who had his family live in a cave to escape the Red Army. Ivan informed Rudi that his wife was a Jew, so surely Stalin would kill them all. Ruth was determined to listen to Rudi's advice.

Now, Rudi had been sent to the Western Front. Ruth did not know when she would see him again, but she would do as Rudi asked.

Immaculately dressed in her daytime clothes, Ruth knew her boldness could not be squelched. "For your information, Dolores, Rudi gave me full leave to do what I think is best for our children."

"No! No – Ruth, you are wrong!" Dolores's pleas fell on deaf ears. She turned her back on her daughter-in-law but soon turned to face her again. She huffed like a baby, and tears welled in her blue eyes. "You will see. The settlements along Hinter-Pommern will hold off the enemy. If they enter our country, Herr Risch has promised the Russians will treat us respectfully. He also assures me that he has spoken to the highest authorities and officers in the area. They have guaranteed him the war is going as planned. You need to stay. You must stay, then you will see."

Anger welled inside Ruth as she called out in a trembling voice. "My children's lives are at stake, yet you demand I listen to a *Dummkopf,* a man I have never been able to trust?" Ruth took a breath. She felt betrayed by Dolores and so many of the people in her life. Words of rage erupted once more. "I have always loathed Herr Risch and his haughty wife. Extremely pompous Risch, with his ever-lustful eyes. What a joke he is. He does not realise most of the community laughs behind his arrogant donkey's backside."

Feeling undone by another confrontation with Dolores, Ruth suddenly excused herself. She gathered her children and quickly marched to her first floor dwelling. She needed some respite from the tense arguments that plagued her relationship with her husband's mother and sister. But Ruth had no one in which to confide. Once in her lodging, Ruth collapsed onto her multicoloured sofa and gathered her children in her arms to calm herself. Thoughts reeled through her mind as if there was no stopping them.

Ruth was unwilling to play the part of a dutiful wife who ignored the world around her, the Lady of the legendary Klein Pobloth Estate. She would gladly give up four million gold bonds, a palatial manor house with outbuildings, a community, private ancient woodlands and six hundred and forty hectares of prime farmland to protect her family.

At times, life at Klein Pobloth during the war was at least tolerable. The three women in the house interacted infrequently and held only short conversations. Ruth grimaced when she was obliged to submit to her mother-in-law's many requests; after all, Baroness Dolores von Kaphengst Krause Meissner was still the Klein Pobloth Estate's rightful owner.

Chapter 4

THE EVENING BEFORE RUTH ESCAPED

On the evening before Ruth's attempt to leave, she asked Emma to look after the children while she located Pinnow to help them escape the clutches of their would-be assailants. Ruth noticed Pinnow lighting the lampposts as he made his rounds throughout the village lane at dusk. Shaking away her fears, Ruth realised that she must act now. "I wish to bargain with you, Pinnow. When can we talk?"

"My Lady, before it gets dark, I must unhitch the plough horses and secure them in the barn. You and I can talk there where it is not so cold."

Ruth followed Pinnow down the lane to the horse barn, gazing about, realising that the village had avoided the dreadful hand of the developers. The village stood intact as it had hundreds of years ago when the archbishops in the 1300s set up monasteries throughout the Baltic region, adding cottages as the village grew. One by one, Ruth took in the small houses of the 250 farmworkers' dwellings and the Beulke's cottage dating back 600 years. She appreciated there had been little intrusion, that the community had changed little since its ancient beginning. The residents were proud people keeping the Fachwerk homes in top condition, adding the necessary amenities when needed. It resembled a picture postcard German village. Like the monks, the women of the manor house took the hamlet and sheltered them as angels when they were ill. Little had changed between the commoners and the aristocrats.

"Yes, my Lady, how can I assist you?" Once among the animals, Ruth and Pinnow blew into their palms to keep away the cold. They stood close to the beasts to feel their warmth.

Drawing nearer to Pinnow, Ruth said softly, "I must leave this place. I must escape with my three children. As you might guess, Dolores has attempted and succeeded in stopping me on several occasions. From all that Rudi has told me after returning from Russia about the Red Army's ruthlessness, they are savages. Rudi told me he saw these soldiers shoot down their companions in front of the lines to build a wall for protection or climb over the frozen corpses to gain access to their enemy." Ruth's breathing became more laborious. "They prefer to rape children because the tissue is much more tender. I must flee with my three little ones." Reluctantly, she looked straight into his brown eyes. "Pinnow, I have some Marks set aside for such an urgent occasion." Ruth pushed her hand firmly into her brown coat pocket, drew out several bills, and demurely pulled his hand to hers. "Dear Pinnow, you have been a friend of Rudi's for life and have become extremely dear to me. Will you take these few Marks and drive us to the train station in Gross Jestin in the morning?"

With a sincere gesture, Pinnow folded her petite hand. Smiling, he said, "I feel as you do, my dear Lady. I admit that you must flee with your children as quickly as possible. When Rudi returned from Russia, he visited with me for old time's sake." Beaming from ear to ear, he said, "I believe in comforting his spirit because Rudi has always looked at me as a mentor. While visiting with me, he shared some of his blood-curling excruciating experiences, most of which I am convinced he kept hidden from you. I would be honoured to assist you and your children in any way I can." Pinnow added, "However, I want no part in your proposal if you insist on paying me." Pinnow smiled thoughtfully. "I will meet you on the circular drive tomorrow morning at six o'clock sharp. This will give me enough time to feed the livestock. I assure you that the farm wagon will be hitched up to be ready with the only two workhorses left."

After many years at Klein Pobloth, Pinnow had become too old to work in the blacksmith shop. His family had worked on the estate for generations. His only responsibility was getting food for the red ox or the old horses when they returned from the fields. To make him feel he was still wanted, out of kindness, Dolores had assigned Pinnow, as his father before him, to be the night watchman to make his workload lighter. At night, with his bright golden lantern in hand, he walked the entire length of the village to ensure everything was locked up tightly.

The responsibility of the watchmen had not changed for the past 600 years. Pinnow's grandfathers before him strolled about the village, watching for fires or anything befalling the hamlet. In earlier years, the Vikings terrorised the seas and the lands beyond, causing the greatest threat. These days, if Pinnow detected danger in the community, he rushed to the entry of the lane near his home. With much vigour, he would forcefully ring the village bell. The nightwatchman was also charged with ringing the gong at four in the morning so the workers would know it was time to rise for their daily labours. Pinnow was proud of his duties, though much to his chagrin, in his heart, he knew if trouble were to occur, he undoubtedly would not have the strength to ward off a mouse. Nevertheless, Pinnow's nearness to the family and his kind nature cloaked the village with a warm feeling of comfort.

Chapter 5

THE DAY RUTH ESCAPED

The morning of Ruth's family fleeing, she steadied herself with a deep breath. She hoped to say goodbye to Dolores, so she again ascended the stairs, her children trailing silently behind her. They reached the sitting room door to hear Anneliese say, "Mother, do you comprehend the horrors I saw in Kolberg?" Ashen with resentment at her mother, Anneliese looked more determined than ever. "I must make a complete break from you. Achim and I were pleased with our lives in Breslau. You invited me back home when Achim was called to duty and there were doubts Germany would not retain its position in the war. In a few moments, Ruth has plans for Klaus-Dieter and me to begin the journey with her family this morning."

Callously arguing, Dolores continued, "That is outrageous, Anneliese. You must not listen to Ruth. I have never cared about her. She has always felt as though she is more knowledgeable about everything than you and I are. Besides, you and Ruth must remain and protect the estate from the Russians. That is if they dare to cross our borders."

"Mother, you must come to grips with the terrifying news that the Red Army is within three days of Klein Pobloth!"

Pretending to weep bitterly, Dolores held her head between her forefingers. "I do not believe anything that has been placed in your mind by Ruth. The mere thought of you, my beloved daughter, leaving is daunting."

Anger struck Anneliese harder than ever at her mother's ploy. "Come, Mother, weeping is not your style." She drew back lightly. "Mother, you have always believed the worst of Ruth. Herr Risch has tainted your mind against her because he cannot have her as he has so many others in the surrounding community. Suppose you would only listen, Mother. I have seen the atrocities for myself. Please, you must flee with us."

"I have heard enough! I will not be spoken to in this manner." Dolores turned on her heels and opened the massive door, slamming the door shut behind her with the force of a herd of elephants.

As Ruth's family entered the salon, the electric lights flickered above them. Anneliese turned to her, new determination in her eyes. "Ruth, give me fifteen minutes to throw on a few more warm clothes and as many supplies as I can gather. I will meet you down in the hall."

Ruth nodded. "I am pleased to have you come with us, Anneliese. Remember, dress Klaus-Dieter and yourself in as many layers of woollen clothing as possible."

"*Ja*, yes, I understand," Anneliese yelled over her shoulder as she passed through the same door Dolores used. Klaus-Dieter scampered after his mother.

Tears streaming down their faces, and not understanding, Ruth's three children looked up at her.

"Shhh, children, all will be better in a few days." Ruth's desperate attempt at convincing her children fell short in her mind. Ruth placed her arms around them as she once saw a mother hen protect her chicks from the violent thunderstorms engulfing them.

Descending the massive, lengthy stairway to their quarters on the first level, Ruth and her children scurried through the dark, double French doors. Ruth felt a wave of warning arising as she recalled her days at Lyzeum Queen Louise Schule boarding school. Ruth had realised Ingrid, one of the girls, was extremely indifferent and cunning in gathering paperwork. Ingrid had bullied the other young ladies in the boarding house to help her keep her poor grades up and had schmooze the professors to keep her in excellent standing. Yet, Ingrid did nothing to aid her classmates in excelling in their classes. Ingrid took it upon herself to think of herself as the hive's queen bee while the other ladies were to do her bidding.

As an underclassman, Ingrid had slithered up to Ruth, begging her to do her French homework. To add to Ruth's fury, Ingrid had asked Ruth to help her climb through the bedroom window, claiming that she had met a young man and meant to sneak out to meet him at a nearby Ratskeller. When Ruth refused her request, Ingrid concocted a story about Ruth earlier in the week to leave the house in the same manner. From that point on, Ruth was on semi-suspension for two weeks. She swore that she would never again allow anyone to bamboozle her in that manner.

The children were confused as they watched their mother rush to and fro to rummage through the antique cherry wood wardrobe her parents had given her as a wedding gift. Ruth gathered her woollen clothing, including a striped, brown, orange and teal-blue wool skirt. She also packed the beautiful lambskin leather, fawn-coloured suit, the one that her dear departed father had given her. Reaching deeper into the wardrobe, Ruth fingered her heavy brown woollen coat, ripped the fur collar, and placed it to the side. She hoped Emma would enjoy cuddling into the warm fox fur collar during the cold Baltic weather.

Ruth fumbled about in the wicker sewing basket lined with soft, rosy, pleated silk her mother gave her while at boarding school. She grabbed a needle and sturdy black thread, a noticeable colour that did not match the coat. Swiftly, Ruth stitched several odd-shaped wool patches on the elbows to blend in with the poor people on the journey. The last thing she wanted was to stand out from the crowd and acknowledge that her family was of nobility.

The Day Ruth Escaped

Staring into the rumpus room where the children played boisterously on the floor, she thought *they were happy and cheerful now. Life as a refugee will be so difficult for them. How long will their happiness last? How can I go on?* Ruth realised that her only defence against Dolores was to persevere in her plan before losing momentum. Suddenly, lowering her head in deep thought, Ruth remembered the scented powder she kept in her highboy. Turning on her heels, Ruth reached for the drawer handle. The highboy was too tall for Ruth to see the items inside the drawer, so she stood on her tiptoes. Once it was securely in her grasp, she pulled at the heavy bronze handles. Her hands shuffled through the wooden shelf. There, she found the sweet scent and several bars of soap, already a prized commodity.

A quick recollection of the day she made the soap came rushing into her thoughts. She made them several summers before using old bars and boiling them in water until they formed a solid, creamy jelly-like, vanilla-scented substance. Ruth cut them into individual bars after they congealed onto a hard, flat surface on the cookie sheets. That was the day her mother had telephoned in absolute hysteria, informing Ruth that a letter had arrived telling her that her dear brother Joachim had been killed. A piece of shrapnel had lodged in his brain, killing him instantly. At the time, Joachim's unit was camped near Leningrad, once the famous metropolitan city of St Petersburg, located on the Baltic Sea. From that day on, her hatred for Hitler grew. The Nazi army was responsible for bringing chaos to Germany and generating that madness until the German people accepted war. The Nazis' murderous atrocities and their greediness were unprecedented, save for the Red Russians.

Panting for air, Ruth wiped a tear from her flushed cheeks. She could not allow any more to spill. Her new plan must work.

There was no time to think clearly. Trying to reason, Ruth closed her eyes. What pictures should she take on her journey? She stopped to study each one, coming across Rudi's small photo and a small, silver-framed image of her best friend, Eve von Zitzewitz-Peterson. No. She decided there was no more room for anything sentimental.

Even now, Ruth was overwhelmed with grief. To her, the world had evolved into an abomination. Yet she needed to carry on, if for no other reason than her three children. She decided on a cream-coloured blouse under a green wool sweater that would be a must-have. She suddenly remembered the multicoloured floral headscarf she had forgotten to pack in her haste. Walking shoes. How many items could she carry if she needed to hold little Dorlies? So many considerations.

The backs of her knees felt the tufted green velvet armchair beside the wardrobe. Her weak frame was willing to take a seat for a moment of comfort, but resting was not in Ruth's nature. She leaped to her feet and searched through the wardrobe again. One pair of brown walking shoes she had scuffed earlier to match her coat and her other outfits would be the ticket. Ruth felt she must pack her favourite cutting knives with their hand-forged elk horn handles, four silver spoons, forks and soup spoons with *RS* representing Ruth Schläger, her initials as a maiden, on them. Since men were the ones killed in fierce battles, for centuries, the monograms of an unmarried woman were the custom on silver and other household items.

Hastily, Ruth stepped out of her garment and then redressed in her chosen outfit. She placed a flesh-coloured, tightly fitting rayon and cotton longline girdle next to her petite frame. It contained a small amount of elastic to stabilise the tight-fitting garment. She stretched to attach the four metal clips to the heavy brown nylon stockings she had hoarded for such an occasion.

Weeks earlier in her apartment's privacy, Ruth had used a sewing machine to create several small pockets in the girdle of her undergarments to conceal her only assets, precious family jewels. Her goal was to hide these family heirlooms from the prying eyes of anyone who would dare frisk her. The antique jewellery belonged to the von Kaphengst family. Ruth hid several gem-studded gold pieces given to Christian Ludwig von Kaphengst by Prince Heinrich of Prussia. She also stashed her engagement ring with one amethyst in the centre, surrounded by eight opals. Since Rudi would become the rightful owner of the estate, he had given his wife the jewels as part of her inheritance.

Once the girdle was tied onto her slender body, Ruth fingered the warm clothing she placed in the front of her wardrobe for easy access. She dressed in multiple layers. Ruth had gathered the rest weeks ago: a small silver folding cup and a folding umbrella rolled up tightly into a ball one garment at a time. She stuffed them into a small suitcase and the remainder into a knapsack she could wear over her shoulder or in front if she became too weary.

Turning to where her children were huddled, she dressed each in as many layers of wool clothing as she thought they could manage. Their wool caps were pulled snuggly around their ears. Weeks ago, she prepared knapsacks for them with as many outfits as possible, making the young ones extremely uncomfortable. They were heavy for the youngsters to tote, but there was no other choice than to plead with the children to do her bidding. Each child complained in their own way. They did not understand or like the game that she had promised them.

"The key." Ruth turned to look about, "Where did I put the key to my hutch?" As she moved through her dwelling to recall every detail of her home, Ruth studied her well-appointed, luxurious residence to drink in as many details as possible. "Heavens, I am only going to be gone for a week, but locking the hutch is a must. I cannot forget to lock the breakfront." Ruth fumbled in one drawer and then another. "Oh, thank heaven, here it is." Almost unconscious of what she was doing in her frazzled state, Ruth locked the massive, antique glass front cabinet door and pushed the key into her coat pocket. At the entry of Ruth's dwelling, she stopped to pull down a heavy golden fleece blanket hanging on the French doors to keep her dwelling warmer. She guided her children through the door and closed it softly behind her.

The Day Ruth Escaped

Once out the door and with the blanket slung over her shoulders, Ruth scurried down the long, dark hallway. Susanne's blue eyes glistened with the excitement of the upcoming adventure. In contrast, Hans-Georg's hazel eyes were stern with doubt as brother and sister clung tightly to one another's hands while Ruth cradled Dorlies to her tightly as lightheartedness glimmered in Dorlies' striking blue eyes. "Walk swiftly yet not too swiftly. We do not wish to take a tumble."

To her relief, when she glanced ahead, Ruth spotted her sister-in-law and nephew standing beside a small suitcase at the bottom of the stairs. As promised, Anneliese was back in fifteen minutes. Ruth mused, *Hmmm, this is a first for someone I deemed a snail. I saw my sister-in-law like a sloth lying around with her nose in a book. Our fleeing together will be for the best. How can I put these hard feelings behind me to deal with Anneliese and her son?*

"No dilly-dallying this time, Anneliese." Ruth hesitated and then said in a hushed voice, "Oh, how life has changed in the blink of an eye. Hopefully, there will not be too much damage to Klein Pobloth after the Russians ransack the place. Anneliese, what will happen to your brother and all our dreams?"

With a vacant gaze of sorrow, Ruth watched the sunlight straining to break through the heavy golden damask drapes of the Gutshaus. Gently clapping her hands, she said, "Children, Anneliese, it is time to finish bundling up."

At the bottom of the stairway, Ruth assured Anneliese, "Even though the government confiscated many of the Klein Pobloth goods for the war effort, they left us with enough animals and equipment to work in the fields. So, there are two horses and a wagon for Pinnow to use. Most of all, Pinnow will not turn us over to Herr Risch or your mother. I made certain Pinnow would stand by me. I am pleased with how easily he agreed."

Although the two women could not agree on how to conduct their daily lives and had not previously spoken a civil word to one another in years, now they would need each other throughout this journey into the unknown.

Anneliese placed her hand on Ruth's shoulder. "Great job, Ruth, for pre-arranging your plan with Pinnow."

Ruth squared her shoulders. "Now, we must be on our way!" Ruth gripped her sister-in-law's hand to reassure her that all would be well. Few people from Pommern would be as lucky as they would be. Many had already been driven to other places. She knew not where.

Gripping a candle holder in her left hand and her right clutching onto Dorlies, Ruth led the group towards the entrance of the manor house. The parquet floor creaked under the frantic footsteps, silence otherwise broken only by the ever-faithful lunar grandfather clock. The timepiece held vigil over the numerous red deer antlers displayed down the white walls of the hallway of the Meissner family home, once a thirteenth-century monastery.

Escaping the Russian Onslaught

The fireplace flame flickered from the breeze, causing an updraft to shift through the enormous white porcelain-tiled chimney stretching from the first floor to the third level. The glow cast shadows off the children, causing Ruth's heart to thump. Her own silhouette caught her off guard. Out of angst, she stood momentarily motionless, ashamed of her doubts. Ruth imagined she could hear the monks who built the monastery. The former owners' centuries-old rhythmic religious chants rang through the Roman stone arches that held her home's entry. Intuition told her the monks must have been as aware as she was of the terror lying beyond these walls. They held their duty to adhere to the characteristics of their brave traditions in protecting their flock.

Her resolve grew as she perceived that no aspect of the past 600 years had altered her surroundings. From their vast woodlands, the eeriness of the haunting sounds from the ancient walls lined with antlers from the Reh and Hirsch informed her that their ghosts would remain even after she was gone.

On February 27, 1945, Ruth, her three children, Anneliese, and her son left the manor house. Pinnow's offer to drive the two mothers with their children to the small train station in Gross Jestin was a blessing. The railroad company built the pathway in 1868 and then revamped the line in 1915 by adding an extension for the Great War effort. Moltow, the hamlet adjacent to Klein Pobloth, was too unimportant for a stop. Thus, the train company built its small station in Gross Jestin and then the road onward towards the Baltic, north to Kolberg – the only reasonable choice of departure – and then further west to Lübeck. The train commute to the larger city of Kolberg would be a restful ride, particularly for Anneliese and Klaus-Dieter since they had returned from the municipality only a few hours earlier.

On this brutally cold February morning, Pinnow arrived on the circular drive. He greeted the two women and children with a warm smile and a tip of his grey workman's hat. Stretching his grey-gloved hand, he asked, "May I help you up to the wagon bed?" Pinnow assisted the children onto the wagon with a kind, steady hand.

Standing shivering beside the heavy farm wagon, Ruth and Pinnow gave Anneliese a helping hand up into the bed of the big farm wagon. Anneliese smiled wanly at Pinnow. After colliding with his blacksmith shop with her new bicycle on several occasions, the older man had tended her scrapes. From then on, she had understood Pinnow was someone she and her younger brother could rely on.

Ruth boarded and tucked each child into the few blankets Pinnow had provided. As Ruth slipped the gold fleece blanket over them, she assured the children that it would be warm. "You need to be a big girl now, Susanne. Hold Dorlies tightly on your lap."

Glancing back at the magnificent old building, Ruth and Anneliese could see Dolores on the manor's second floor, peering through her bedroom window behind the heavy damask drapery. Heartbreak clinched both women. Thus, Baroness

The Day Ruth Escaped

Dolores von Kaphengst Krause Meissner did not say goodbye to her family. Instead, she concealed herself out of fuming anger toward the two women who no longer considered her warning.

As with Anneliese, Ruth had expected to say goodbye to Dolores. Despite their disagreements, Ruth admired Dolores, the twice-widowed, unfaltering woman who was the Klein Pobloth Estate's adhesive for her community of 250 families. Dolores's family was deserting Klein Pobloth, abandoning her to protect the property alone. Ruth felt a twinge of regret. She had become accustomed to Dolores's gruff ways, a woman on her own since her husband, Rudolf, was killed in 1915 during the Great War. Utterly lonely and on her own without anyone to guide her, Dolores dealt with the numerous problems occurring on an everyday basis in the normality of living. Dolores had borne the weight of the welfare of the estate and vast woodlands, including the hamlet, for many years. Dolores's German bullheadedness would take this same attitude to her grave.

In Ruth's opinion, it was unforgivable for Dolores not to embrace her grandchildren in farewell. She did not even acknowledge her own daughter. Dolores felt Ruth was giving up her position as the next mistress of the estate and taking Hans-Georg, the grandson who would inherit Klein Pobloth. As an adult, Hans-Georg would buy Klaus-Dieter out of his share of the estate and the fortune. Then, Hans-Georg would lead the legacy of the new generations into the Klein Pobloth Estate. Like all young men of status, Hans-Georg would receive a commission as an officer in the German military. But now, being an officer in the German army was a dreadful mistake.

From the front circler drive to her right, they passed by the parched trampled park, to her left, the horse stables. Then, Pinnow turned onto the black-uneven cobblestone lane, and the farm wagon creaked under them as they passed the home where the Beulke family had lived for the past 600 years. Then, past the school building where the Fengler's resided, and Herr Fengler taught school.

The worn cobblestone road brought Ruth back to the duties at hand. She shifted her weight so Pinnow could hear better. "Since we are not permitted to flee as landowners, I told the two older children to act like we are peasants." Pinnow looked ahead as he clicked the reins to take them along the lane to the far end. Blowing on her ungloved hands, she hoped anything she would say to Pinnow would return to Dolores to drive her point home. "The most trying was when I tried to convince the children their grandmother loved them and that we would return home to greet her in a few days. Another issue was that we were playing a game. Pinnow, you will keep our secret?"

Focusing on the rear of the wagon bed, Ruth discovered that Dorlies was fussing and could not hold still. "I know it is difficult, Susanne, but can you cuddle Dorlies so she will be happy?"

Out of concern, Susanne huffed, "Mutti, Dorlies has decided to throw a tantrum."

Susanne then said, "*Ja* Mutti, but she will not hold still." She pulled the gold fleece blanket about her and Dorlies. Susanne tugged on her short blonde pigtails, concealed by her wool brown hand-knitted cap earlier. Ruth had traded with one of the village children for scuffed leather black laced-up high boots. Susanne's grimy, long white stockings under her tattered blue skirt clung to her body. She had grown out of them, for they were impossible to replace during the last few months.

"*Nein... nein...* Mutti! Sit with you, Mutti?" Dorlies whimpered.

Ruth shook her head. "It is time for you to cuddle your big sister." Ruth eased herself back to the wagon's front, next to where Pinnow was seated. With tears in her eyes, Ruth turned away quickly and pulled her brown coat under her. "Burr, the wooden planks still have the morning frost on them. The winter has been colder than most. Today, it looks like it might snow again. Danke schön, Pinnow, for the extra blanket you flung onto the bench. I appreciate your kindness."

Pinnow's whip popped twice. The team understood his command. The old farm wagon lumbered on its way. Next to them, the manor house dripped with long icicles. The icehouse resembled a storybook cottage. The sunlight cast its rays onto the pine trees, heavily laden with a thick layer of sparkling white snow. The many trees throughout the village resembled a delegation of cathedrals bidding them farewell.

Preferring not to look back at their home again, Ruth glanced with great apprehension down at Anneliese's red-rimmed eyes. Tears streamed down her red cheeks. Ruth understood the stabbing heartache of leaving her breathtaking, beautiful heritage behind, where she and her brother Hans-Rudolf found happiness in nurturing their souls in the nature around them. Ruth's husband had a lighthearted youthful affection for his family, keen eyesight and a shrewd mind. His creative ability to repair any item with what was at hand was still spoken of in the village. Even with his love for mankind, this man with deep integrity might not return from the most relentless war humanity had ever seen.

Ruth had layered old warm clothes on the children, as much as their little bodies could handle. Hopefully, they were bundled up enough against the damp, frigid cold. The children's layered clothing also served a second purpose: Ruth had stitched name tags into each piece. That, plus the identification name tags they wore around their neck, would help them if her family group were to get separated. Then, she had tugged on each child's feet two pairs of woollen socks she had knitted.

Ruth turned to face the huddle in the wagon's rear. "Are your ankles itching?"

"Home... please, Mutti," Dorlies whimpered once again.

Ruth's heart was broken. "Yes, my little baby doll, I realise you do not understand what is happening. Like you, I would also like to go home. Remember

Susanne, Hans-Georg, Tante Anneliese, your cousin Klaus-Dieter, and your Mutti are all going on a fascinating outing."

Brushing his mahogany hair back under the ear flaps of his green woollen cap, Hans-Georg whimpered, "Mutti, I do not like the dirt you put on our faces. Worst of all, I hate the grime under my fingernails." His hazel eyes were wet with tears as he sobbed to get his mother's attention. "Ja, Mutti, I am cold and want to go home also."

"Mutti did this to help you, my son. I hope to give the impression that we have been on the road for some time. I promise you, right now is not the best time to be clean. I do understand you would rather go home. If I were to take your blue mittens off and massage your little hands, do you think this would make you warmer?"

"Ja, Mutti, please... please, I would like that."

"Then scooch closer so I can do so." She leaned over the bench and kissed her son's hands one at a time. The children were old enough to be uncomfortable being unclean. She and their nurse always took pride in helping them remain as clean as possible. Ruth recalled her mother's words, "Always wear clean underwear because you never know if there might be an accident."

As the voice reverberated in her mind, she wondered where her mother was now. The plan was for Ruth's mother, Frau Luise Schläger to stay safely with Tante Louise Schläger, their relatives in Peine, Lower Saxony. With all the uncertainty in the world, who could say? Fearful of the future, Ruth pushed her arm under her old friend Pinnow's elbow. The kindly older man smiled at her and drove on in comfortable silence.

Once on the main street leading through Moltow, the night watchman finally spoke. His voice was heavy, with wheezing he had developed from smoking tobacco that he grew on his plot of land and then hand-rolled into cigarettes himself. "Have no worries, gnädige Frau Meissner. My Lady, you and your children have always had a special place in my heart. The same as your dear husband Rudi has held since he was a small lad."

Relief flooded Ruth's heart. "You do understand, dear Pinnow." Ruth shifted her thin frame on the uncomfortable wooden bench. "I do not know how to thank you, my dear friend. Without your help, we would not have been able to accomplish our quest."

Ruth and Anneliese had taken this opportunity to save their children and their own lives. Ruth felt they had made the right decision despite the physical and mental hardships lying ahead of them. Ruth realised Rudi's prophecy of the destruction of their beloved Germany would soon be fulfilled. The decision to wait several more days might have killed them all. Both she and Anneliese had pleaded with her mother-in-law to come with them. The years were not kind to Dolores, making her a cynical person. The woman was too proud, too stubborn after many years of independence to listen to Anneliese or Ruth. She could only hope Dolores would be spared too much tragedy.

Dolores showed a surprising softening at the end. When Ruth realised that her fortune from the bank in Kempen would never arrive, she stooped so low to ask Dolores for assistance. Although the woman insisted that whatever happened, their place was with her at Klein Pobloth, eventually, and with great reluctance, Dolores pushed several jewellery pieces at her daughter-in-law. These pieces had been in the family for several generations. Without hesitation, embarrassment, or, for that matter, any guilt, Ruth grabbed the jewels. She felt it was a cheap way to make amends and abolish their unstable relationship. Her absolution of guilt was complete.

Nonetheless, it was a bittersweet victory. *But I cannot blame myself now! Too little too late!*

A fretful wind blew the newly fallen snow away from the hardened white surface where it had rested for days. The new snowflakes seemed to be held in suspension before they whirled about the wagon and made their way into the area where the new refugees were huddled. Moving closer to the children, Anneliese adjusted their coats, mittens and hats. Soon, she tugged at the corners of her dark green headscarf to shelter her ears from the bitter cold.

Ruth caught a glimpse of Anneliese and followed suit. Dirty, cold, hungry, frightened and empty-hearted, with the enemy at their back door, they strengthen their resolve. Suddenly, their familiar world was ending. Ruth could not contain her emotion and burst out, "Oh, Pinnow, have I done the right thing?"

"Ja, gnädige Frau, to my way of thinking, you are doing right by your family." Pinnow's face resembled a dried-up potato wearing a bristly white walrus moustache as he glanced down at Ruth. He appeared to be fighting tears.

Ruth was pleased with the older man's tenderness towards them. "At this time, Pinnow, your assurance means the world to me." Lovingly, Ruth placed her hand on the older man's arm, giving it an enormous squeeze. Her mind whirled as the many thoughts of the past few years wrenched her soul. How were they going to manage? She and Anneliese had barely spoken two civil words for over seven years. Now, they were going to travel together with their children to flee from the adversary. Ruth felt that Dolores, Anneliese, Herr and Frau Risch had been her adversaries for many years, but now the world had changed. Necessity called for Ruth to pull in her horns. She hoped Anneliese would do the same, or they would fail in accomplishing this risky undertaking. How could two women who had been feuding most of their adult lives think they could flee their home together with four small children at their side?

Chapter 6

MELDING IN WITH THE REFUGEES

Resourcefulness would be Ruth's guiding light, her boundless courage leading the way. Only her determination would help overcome the repugnance of what lay before her. She had been driven into a political kettle her family group could not avoid.

As far as she could see, Ruth took in the dull grey landscape, wishing that the low hanging clouds would release their stronghold and let the sun's warmth brighten their day. As Pinnow navigated the wagon through the Baltic's damp, freezing cold, the damage to Ruth's nose, cheeks, and chin felt warm and numb, a sure sign that frostbite could set in. Her numb skin brought back the ultimate memories of Rudi's ability to help her through the most significant crisis of her life. Rudi's ability to rejuvenate Ruth had fuelled her with the resolve to rebound from her first relationship. She had stepped into the new role and had a bright future with Rudi and a well-positioned family. Then, becoming his wife had helped significantly to stabilise his love for her. Over the years, Ruth failed to grasp how deeply Rudi's feelings were under the swaying trees in the hushed wilderness of Klein Pobloth. He understood the gentle wisdom of the forest, the knowledge of Ruth's bravery, and her prudence in navigating a crisis. Once more, she yearned to have him caress her nakedness, to warm her while riding in the freezing wagon.

Staring into the iridescent sky caused her thoughts to turn inward. On their honeymoon, Rudi was the man she had always hoped for. After crossing the threshold of the hotel room in Stargard, Rudi's hardness was apparent. He had yearned for her ever since he had first seen her when he was only eighteen and she was twenty. Ruth had begun to undo her suit jacket. He was on fire. "Now it is my turn to undress you." Rudi had nibbled on her neck, sliding his hand to touch the fullness of her breasts. "Let me do that for you." He had reached around to kiss them. "I want to touch you in your most intimate places." Ruth had turned around to meet his manly organ.

Sitting beside Pinnow, she breathed heavily.

"Are you all right, my Lady? Is there anything I can do for you?"

"Everything is fine, Pinnow. I just recalled days gone by and how much my husband and I have missed one another since he was called to action in 1941. We saw each other intermittently, long enough for me to welcome Hans-Georg and Dorlies into the fold of our family. That seems like such a long time ago."

A slight smile played at her mouth as she remembered when Rudi had teased her that she had had too many pear schnapps to drink. Their entire married life, the tip of her nose was continually red, contrasting with her flawless, creamy complexion.

Rudi's tender letters to her while stationed in Russia had again bound them in a crisis. Then, again, he had enlightened Ruth at home before returning to the Western Front. Even though Rudi's eyes were perpetually reddened from fatigue, the deep sincerity of his devotion and safety for her and their family were always paramount for him. The complications subsided when Ruth became entranced with Rudi's charm, to have her longings thirst and burn in her. But then, when did it not? She hardly dared to think for fear of how close they came to breaking their uncompromising stand against his advances on her when they first met. Against her soon-to-be mother-in-law and Annelise's objections, Rudi was determined to have it his way. Yet, when Ruth was with him, the tranquillity she found was boundless.

Known in their household not to wear gloves, Ruth breathed deep for a moment and blew on her hands, cupping them over her nose until they were warm. Then, she waved her arms together to keep them active. The heavy wagon's rhythmic movement lulled Anneliese and the children to doze in the wagon's bed under the warm blankets.

From time to time, Pinnow handed Ruth the reins so he could rub his nose and ears to prevent frostbite. It was common knowledge that if one were not careful, these body parts could snap off in the Baltic cold. After removing his woollen mittens, he blew on his hands and then briskly rubbed them together. Before retrieving the leather from Ruth, he licked his lips and made a clicking sound with his tongue. Soon, the heavy leather reins were snapped to hurry the horse team securely as far as Gross Jestin. On either side of the tree-lined road, the fields beyond were void of activity. The wild boar and red deer that usually scampered about freely had been bagged, baked and eaten by whoever saw them first.

From time to time, Pinnow halted the team to give them a chance to breathe deeply without labouring from pulling the heavy wagon in the freezing cold. The wet Baltic air was known to freeze a creature's lungs when it laboured too hard. Suddenly, they heard a commotion in one of the dried bushes among the birch trees. The commotion startled the team of horses. They had caught the scent of something out of the ordinary.

Listening intently, Pinnow and Ruth froze in their seats. Gripping her cold perch, Ruth went pale. In silence, Pinnow placed his hand close to his eyes to get a better view to search the surroundings for any would-be attackers. There were sounds in the shrubbery that they could not make out. The silence between them

Melding in With the Refugees

became frozen. There was another flurry of commotion. The enemy. Would the attackers make themselves noticeable to so few people? Could the Russian snipers have advanced into the countryside without their knowledge? Yes, the idea was a grave realisation. The two people on the wooden bench studied each other without wanting to alarm Anneliese and the children. Terrified, Ruth lifted her shoulders in a questioning fashion.

Pinnow reached for a whip under his wooden seat, the only weapon available, and gripped it securely over his head prepared to attempt to take down the intruder. Ruth looked for anything she could throw at the trespasser, but not even a stone was available. Someone was still moving under the space between the undergrowth about twelve feet away. Now, the rustling was even louder. What to do? The team was not fast enough to carry them to safety.

Pinnow's snickering took Ruth by surprise. She studied her companion with a worried frown. "Pinnow," she whispered, straining to understand his reaction. Instinctively, she analysed the horses again to see if their demeanour had changed. Their flaring nostrils had eased, their ears stopped twitching, and their jerking heads were calm. They had given up their vigilant posture. Hastily, Ruth glanced beyond to see towards the shrubbery and the stand of trees from which the menacing quivering branches were coming.

Pointing toward the rattling, Pinnow grinned through his peppered walrus moustache. "My Lady, do you see the two squirrels chasing each other? They need to find some of their buried nuts under the bushes."

A gust of the restless Baltic wind sent a new dusting of snow into the wagon's bed. Ruth twisted about and glanced at Anneliese and the children to ensure they were well. She was assured the disturbance had not been detected by them. Holding her cold, red hands to her mouth, Ruth chuckled in relief. "Pinnow, I thought there must be something frighteningly dangerous hiding in the bushes and trees."

Pinnow's voice still shook. "As did I, my Lady," he said reassuringly, then clicked the worn leather reins twice. "Now, it is time we were on our way."

Soon, they were in Gross Jestin, the doubly sorrowful small town, having lost numerous young men during both the world's great wars. It would not take over two or three moments to ride down Village Street 95, where the annual fireman's parade occurred. They headed towards the railroad station. To their dismay the trains were not running on a regularly scheduled timetable.

The family's friend Pinnow helped them bear their burden. He kindly offered to take them 82 kilometres farther, the rest of the way to Kolberg.

A scruffy child hustled toward the station, shouting, "Mutti, the train is coming! Come, Mutti, Loti, we must get on, or we will not get out in time!"

Recognising the young lad of about nine years old, usually kept neat and tidy, Ruth caught sight of his mother, also looking unusually dishevelled and worried, with terror written about her slender face. With a bundle over her shoulder and her daughter under her arm, she rushed towards her blond-headed son. Ruth recognised Frau Mann from speaking to her at the doctor's office. The Talk's Clinic, where she took the children, was at Erich Langer's pharmacy. Ruth recalled that the woman was attractive, reputable and kind.

The weary woman was so focused on her children that she did not notice the wagon until it was almost too late. Her lined face washed with terror for a moment right before she sidestepped the team of horses. As the woman grabbed her screaming child's hand, her headscarf flapped in the wind. It was a narrow escape. Ruth heard her shout to her son, "That is the train to Kolberg. Save us a seat!"

Sending a frenzied excitement through the narrow street, the horses reared, and the wagon skidded in the snow as a sudden explosion steamed from their soft nostrils. Pinnow clamped both hands on the leather and then jerked on the reins.

Before the warning, the urgency of boarding this train strained Ruth's frame. The jolt of the wagon painfully twisted her wrists and spine. She was almost knocked off her wooden perch as a result of losing her hold on the wagon. Off-balance, she recovered gracefully, as always.

Anneliese peered out of the back and then pushed four curious heads with terrifying doubt on their faces out of the wagon's bed back under the blankets. Tante Anneliese ordered them to tuck themselves back under the golden blanket.

The boy's yelling was well-intended but might be ineffective. At best, during the last few weeks, the trains were known to have standing room only.

The very low rumbling sounds did not die along the long distance of the iron train tracks. The snow muffled the rumbling and scratching tone carried for yards across the frozen ground. There was no telling if the team of horses could bring the Meissner family fast enough to find a passage. Under these stressful circumstances, who knew when this train would arrive at the station? In ordinary circumstances, the trains were on time throughout Germany. Schedules you could not count on were just another casualty of war.

Prepared for this type of catastrophe, Pinnow hurried his team forward with the reins still firmly twisted between his fingers. Ruth turned to the older man perched beside her and watched Pinnow's expression fall. His face jerked as his shoulders slumped. "I know you to be a man of honour, Pinnow. Please understand that I must take on this impossible task. Do not fail me now." Tears of regret drew her closer to him. Ruth placed her hands on his arm, but Pinnow's attempt at a faint smile was lost in his peppered moustache. Ruth detected that Pinnow had become emotional. However, she did not see the tears in his bloodshot eyes.

Seeing her distress, Pinnow bent his head and did the unthinkable, touching the Lady of the house by taking her chin with his rough, gloved free hand. He smiled into her weary, soft brown eyes. "My Lady, you are doing the right thing." However, as Pinnow pressed on, she did not detect that he was about to weep openly for this

Melding in With the Refugees

foul fate that he must stay behind and fade away into the deadly mist the war would leave behind, striking like a venomous viper at every corner of their country.

They watched the terrified mobs. Ruth heard the rumbling grow louder, and the wheels roared with the odour of hot oil mixed with coal that arrived long before the train's whistle bellowed next to them – they must reach the train in time. Luckily, the train was slow in pulling into the small station.

With the help of Pinnow and Ruth, Anneliese stepped out of the wagon bed. Ruth, Anneliese, and Pinnow motioned with their fingers as they extended their arms to the alarmed youngsters, who had to be cheered on to fly into their grasp.

As they studied the frenzy, they saw the station filled with pandemonium as numerous people rushed and shoved their way to meet the train that was only a short distance away. Invariably, pushing and shoving broke out. There was no avoiding the consequences, and the family would have to avoid the others in the crowd. Hopefully, there would be no injuries leaving this place, which would likely become a death trap.

When Ruth, Anneliese and the children waved goodbye to the faithful night watchman, sniffles of regret resounded through the group. Turning as if to say goodbye to Pinnow, Ruth saw the long tears the older man had held back fall and make their way down his drawn skin. He took out his sizeable, blue-coloured handkerchief, blowing into it as if he were the north gale itself.

A sudden giggle of delight erupted from the children, followed by cries of misgiving. In this fragile moment, no words were spoken. Ruth and Anneliese took turns to embrace their dear old saviour. Once again, Pinnow sniffed loudly, producing his handkerchief, puffing louder than before, causing happy chuckles to erupt from the children once more. Pinnow rubbed his bristly white walrus moustache, quickly tucked the blue cloth back into his pocket, and then bent to squeeze each child's wind-bitten, pink cheeks. Not to get thrust into the hordes by the mob and with no time to study the passersby, the family stuck together in a tight huddle next to their farm wagon for protection. The children's tiny hands clasped together, their woollen mittens going up and down as they waved Pinnow farewell.

Exhausted and shivering from the frigid air, Ruth, the children and Anneliese backed away from Pinnow and the farm wagon. Ruth grabbed her suitcase and then raised little Dorlies into her tight clasp. The group hustled toward the train with their backpacks slung over their shoulders and Ruth and Anneliese toting two small suitcases. Pinnow and the wagon were quickly lost from view as he departed with a click of his reins.

To adjust to their new, distressing location, Ruth and Anneliese gathered their brood. They walked silently until the children saw the big, imposing, black engine's wheels pushing the black and white ice out of its way as it crept into the station.

A shrill of delight suddenly filled the cold air when little Hans-Georg yelled, "Mutti, look, the train looks just like the one I play with at home." As they continued to watch, Ruth noticed Hans-Georg, even though he was a timid child, stood watching in wonder.

One of Hans-Georg's favourite toys was a train set given to him by his father on one of the last times Rudi was home on furlough. After Rudi's tour of duty in Russia, he had a layover in Kolberg. While there, he had walked the welcoming, familiar streets to revisit his old stomping grounds. Across the cobblestone streets, to the left, stood the toy shop Rudi and his mother had visited over the years. To his astonishment, he had seen a Märklin toy train displayed in the window. Elated, Rudi had sauntered into the shop, hoping the government had allotted him enough money to buy the toy train set for his son.

The black iron beast held a particular place in Hans-Georg's heart. Hearing her son's gasp at the enormous size of the engine, she said, "Yes, my sweet, this is the engine that will take us on our new adventure."

The family watched the steam engine huffing its way laboriously down the tracks, sending out white-grey steam as it screeched to a halt. The children were terrified and frozen in their tracks. Once the big giant came into view, a bitter wind blew into the only train car still available.

Susanne overheard Ruth's comment and said, "Mutti, I want to go too. It has been a long time since you took me on a train, but do we have to take this train with all these dirty people beside us?"

Struggling to rush forward with her knapsack on her back and lugging her suitcase, Ruth snatched Dorlies and her bag into her grasp while Susanne and Hans-Georg, also with their backpacks on their tiny frames, grabbed onto her tattered brown coat.

Anneliese clutched her son and her small suitcase. She asked Klaus-Dieter to adjust her rucksack, sliding sideways off her threadbare grey coat. "Now, son, we must hurry to catch a ride on this train. Be careful of the steps, for there seems to be no one to help us."

Luckily, decorum took over as dirty hands shot out to everyone wishing to enter the train from the passengers already within. A woman in the front cried, "Come take my hand so I can pull you in. Hurry in so we can be on our way again."

The overhead compartments throughout the coach were taken long ago, at the train's origination. The first to find a vacant seat was Anneliese and her son, who had to sit on her lap – followed by Ruth's family, dumped into the next two empty seats. Dorlies pulled her way onto Ruth's lap. Then Susanne helped her brother into her chair, coaxing him to sit beside her and the suitcases crammed in the small area.

Shivering, the woman she recognised earlier with her two children was too weak to move further. She also plummeted into the once luxurious, now tattered, tan-blue cushioned chairs behind Ruth and her family. To make certain all was in order, Ruth studied her surroundings. She silently counted her children, her luggage, and Anneliese and Klaus-Dieter. All was in order. Now, there was nothing

Melding in With the Refugees

more that she could do. She yanked on her eldest daughter's coat. "Susanne and Hans-Georg try to sit still and not fidget so much." Ruth distracted her frightened children. "Hans-Georg, tell your sister what you can see out of the window."

Outside the train, the conductor shouted. "Standing room only!" He waved to the car's back. "Push to the rear so more folks can escape to the west."

The wagon coach was filled to the brim. Bedraggled folks who were standing stepped aside. Unexpectedly, a Nazi SS man emerged from the car in front. His pristine spit-shined black boots lengthened his trim black-white-red-collar uniform. He silently reached for the essential papers.

Ruth's facial muscles tightened in what was indeed a scream. However, it was mute to everyone but to her. She told herself not to be a coward because their papers were all in order.

With a crash of iron beginning to screech on the rusty tracks, the large wheels under their upholstered seats rumbled, and on either side, white steam escaped. Now, they were on their way. They watched as the stern SS man passed by without an incident. The relief of his passing through the car could be felt throughout. Ruth and the others took these short moments to relax as much as possible.

Chapter 7

KOLBERG

Ruth could see that in front of the family lay Kolberg, a Hanseatic League city first mentioned as a municipality in the seventh century as an essential commodity for producing salt, dating back to the Vikings. It was known as Salt City because of its bountiful salt from the Baltic Ocean, which was collected into the mouth of the Persante River. Over the centuries, the harbour became known for its ideal spas, long beaches and tall dunes. For decades, the Meissner family had spent many delightful hours relaxing on the white beach and dining in famous restaurants.

On this bitterly cold morning, a depressing atmosphere hung under the low clouds, with occasional patches of blue skies reflecting on the snow, which had turned a muddy grey from the black soot the slow-moving trains left behind. In 1940, the census had recorded Kolberg's port city by the Baltic Sea as 36,000 residents. Many of these folks had fled before Ruth's family arrived.

Ruth lifted herself on the armrests, squirming in her tattered, upholstered train seat to get a clear view through the frost-covered window. She breathed deeply. She was puzzled by the many empty streets. At the turn of the train car, she saw that thousands of others were pouring into Kolberg, jampacking the side streets with swarming hordes of people charging to and fro as they attempted to escape by ships, trains, horses, carts, wagons or any other means possible. From the ghastly cries and clattering disturbances of the chaos occurring on the streets, the silence within the train car melted into the passengers shivering from terror.

She ran the tips of her fingers against her temple. Her all-consuming passion for fleeing drifted into one heap of confusion. Doubt flickered in her heart during this time of great upheaval. Did she do the right thing? The winds of politics could change at a moment's notice. For the sake of her family, she must be prepared to change with them.

It was mid-morning. The nimbostratus clouds hung low, shrouding the historic city of Kolberg and suggesting more snow. Once the train pulled into the town, the haziness drifted toward the Baltic Sea, allowing Ruth to recognise the iconic lighthouse on the mouth of the Persante River. The February waters beyond them dripped with icicles, yielding a hostile environment. The river was divided by an island that led to Pommern's rural areas and one of Europe's important ports, the

Kolberg

Port of Kolberg. The famous spa town, with its Strand Schloss, exquisite hotels along the beach, the Theatre Park and Adolf Hitler Square, was deserted. Ruth recognised one of the oldest symbols of the city, the iconic green-oxidised, copper roof of the St Mary Evangelical Lutheran Cathedral by the sea. Her husband had been baptised there, and Hans von Kaphengst, Dolores's father, was buried in the churchyard.

The train carrying the fleeing families pulled through the city's gothic walls and then passed beside the moat bound in a blanket of heavy snow. Ruth recognised the Kur Hospital only too well. Susanne had been sent there a few months earlier after her pony kicked her in the chin.

In 1944, Hitler had announced the city was to be a stronghold to give the military a strong presence in Kolberg, therefore, making travelling through Kolberg unbearable.

German soldiers were called in to renovate the Pommern Wall in 1944 to keep the Red Army and Polish Army from overthrowing a chunk of their world. Thus, the terrain was carpeted with a strong presence of German soldiers and the Nazi SS. The town's many factories, where once the smokestacks turned the air into a musty-white cloud, were void of steam. The new fishing port on Memeler Street was also closed, and the Holzgraben area was empty.

The sweetness of bygone days would soon be fused with the clash of three armies: the German Army, the Red Army and the Polish Army. Germany attempted to hold on to tradition, but the other two countries were hungrily pushing to stamp the landscape and its people into the ground while forcing the remainder into the icy Baltic Sea. It was known that both Russia and Poland coveted the port city. If, by chance, Germany lost the battle, what country would first stake its claim?

When Ruth saw the gloomy carnage on the streets, her body jerked, and her stomach lurched inwardly. Hitler and his henchmen were such beasts. The German people were like children believing in anything to escape the terrible dilemma after the Great War. Following the Great Depression, and in conjunction with Hitler, other worldwide leaders screamed their way to power. Sadly, Germany's forlorn, hungry people were fooled into believing Hitler.

Ruth and Anneliese were the spectators to the multitudes of casualties roaming the streets. The thoroughfares appeared more like scenes from a horror film than life through her window at close range. Ruth quickly signalled her sister-in-law to make the children gaze down. Ruth fingered the patch on her tattered brown coat and noticed the thread had come loose. Thankfully, she had remembered to pack a few needles and thread in a small blue envelope along with one of Rudi's letters. If the family should get separated or one lost or injured, the address on the envelope around their necks could be used to contact Hans-Rudolf Meissner, their father. Since Dorlies was too young to speak clearly, the coin-sized birthmark on her sternum would be the best way to find her.

Escaping the Russian Onslaught

While the train made its way through the city, a light dusting of snow swirled about the blood-stained streets filled with throngs of people, cars, wagons, trucks and German officers on their mounts.

The family must stay on its toes. From the extremely bombed-out areas, particularly the large cities, Kolberg had once been a refuge for young children and those who required higher education. Now, the sidewalks and streets were streaming with children screaming because they had no mothers at their sides to protect them from the evil surrounding them.

Older adults threaded their way from here to there, seeking a welcoming handout to satiate their hunger as the gaunt appearance of despair set in. Elderly arrivals pushed baby buggies, some filled with children and others with household possessions. The youngsters shoved carts of all sizes.

The loathing for Hitler and his henchmen once again built in Ruth. She loathed their poisoning audacity, deceit, mendacity and distorted fabrications toward the Jews. From the beginning, Hitler had deceived his armies and misled the German people. This 28 February 1945, with not enough manpower, the stronghold appeared weak. On 22 June 1933 the people had given in to Hitler's tight control when the Nazis banned the Social Democratic Party, thereby breaking the threaded stability of Germany as now they saw it come to its knees.

Being aware and alert at all times of her surroundings, Ruth did not doze off like many of the early risers on the train. The nearer the train got to the throngs of people outside her window, the clearer Ruth heard a muffled voice crying in the distance. "Run for your lives! The Russians and the Poles will slaughter the people and bomb our city!"

Everyone was fleeing, and Kolberg was in chaos. The young and old were rushing towards the famous Baltic port or the train station, the only escape routes.

The children and Anneliese were terrified by the constant click-clacking of the wheels traversing the iron tracks. Since the fog lifted and a semi-blue sky made the inside of the train brighter, a sunbeam caught Hans-Georg on his dozing face. Rubbing his eyes to remove the film of sleep on them, Hans-Georg longed to watch what was occurring on the black cobblestone street. Out of curiosity, he knelt on the seat to peer out the window and stuck his hazel eyes and nose onto the compartment window. Sniffling, Hans-Georg turned to his mother in the next seat. With anxiousness on his delicate expression, he asked, "Mutti, is my Vati among the many soldiers I see on the streets? So many people seem to be hurt. Did we come to help them?"

The many soldiers had made Ruth think of Rudi and Achim Hertel, Anneliese's husband, among the many men sent to war. At Hans-Georg's question, the children's eyes raised again, staring aimlessly into the enormous racket of the crowd.

Feeling gutted, Ruth surveyed the crowd turned asunder by her own people. Was she lucid in her quest to escape? Dolores and Herr Risch called her crazy

Kolberg

for undertaking such an excruciating excursion with her children. Indeed, had it been madness that drove her? Perhaps her loathing for these two people was so intense that she was blinded against good sense. How could she leave the security of their home? Had it been Ruth's ego that drove her out of their home? Would these gruelling questions burden her for the remainder of her life? Then again, she followed her husband's instructions.

Her son had asked a question, and she must answer him. She smiled deeply into his questioning hazel eyes, and after organising her thoughts, she finally spoke. "Son, the year and month you were born, remember that is in March 1941, your father needed to support our people in the middle of our country. These men in the military came into the city to help. So no, liebchen, Vati is not here."

After another atrocious five minutes on the sluggish train to the red brick Kolberg station among humanity's wretched and helpless mass, the train once more hooted to move the people away from the tracks as it pulled into the building with a tall half-moon window. The mob was so enormous that people covered the tracks carrying their meagre, tightly packed belongings. The train creaked as it halted from time to time to move people out of its way, inching them to the side as it moved the people to a secure location. With four long, extended, hearty whistles, it took longer than expected to halt as close to the train station as possible.

The long-extended shrieks caught Dorlies' attention. Giggling, she asked, "Oh, Mutti, Mutti," her eyes as broad as the moon's smile, "what is that tooting?"

Ruth's attempt at shutting out the shrilling sound from her mind failed. It reminded her of the death that would occur throughout her country within the next few days. She gulped as she studied her daughter's astonished expression. "My love," she cuddled her closer, "don't be frightened. That is the wonderful train we have been travelling on." Holding on to Dorlies with her left hand and her right hand shaking from the cold, Ruth knelt in the next seat to adjust the other children's clothing. She glanced up to see Anneliese scanning the hordes irritably waiting by the station. It was still early, and there seemed to be little hope of them securing passage today. What would happen to them? With the wet, icy winds gusting from the Baltic Sea in broad bands onto the dry land where Ruth's cluster must find standing room only, who could survive through the night? Indeed, not the four small children?

Jets of grey steam were released from either side of the engine. The whistle blared once more to move the people off the rails, squeezing them onto the tiled walls that were once kept brilliantly white. Today, with standing room only, the walls appeared as though they had black rocks stacked as high with people and their possessions as a tall man's shoulders, leaving only the upper white portion to creep its way to the soaring ceiling. Slowly the train thrust the heavy snow out of the way, and then, the black beast was inside the Kolberg station, filling it with white steam escaping from its giant iron wheels. Ruth and Anneliese knew well the large building with its towering ceiling boasting a half-moon window. In earlier times, the building had been a high society location, a place to be seen and dine in an elegant restaurant.

As they descended from the train car, it became evident that switching trains might be unachievable, a sharp contrast to what Ruth witnessed less than a year ago. The situation fed her hatred for Hitler and his SS: the wealthy and the poor confronted with death knocking at their back door, people with greasy hair, dried grey skin, bloodshot eyes, runny noses, tattered clothing, many sobbing children rooted among the masses, hiding their faces from the SS, and clinging on to the hope of surviving.

She was deeply saddened by the exasperating indication that getting a train might be impossible. Ruth let her gaze travel over the crowded space. Where once joyful laughter and friendship could be found, now there were only hostile machine-gun-toting Nazi SS troops. The soldiers scrutinised everyone as they circled through the crowd. Individuals grew silent when the SS passed. The loudest sounds were the shallow breaths of the alarmed masses in the building. It was as though the Black Death from the Middle Ages hung like a cloud over the multitude. No movement from the crowd could be detected, and the fear of being noticed sent them into statue-like concealment. With nowhere to stand, the countless refugees disembarking from every compartment were fearful of being singled out by the ruthless, deadly disease that was the SS.

The area was insufficiently built to hold the hordes packed into the space. The fire hazard was enormous. Ruth gazed down at her children, who had difficulty breathing in the foul air. Another ripple of angst rushed through Ruth. As she gasped for breath, a ghastly woman threw herself toward Ruth. When the middle-aged woman was upon her, Ruth noticed that the woman's eyes were filled with bitterness. As she tried to jerk Dorlies out of Ruth's arms, Dorlies' scream of terror mixed with pain echoed from wall to wall.

The woman's actions were so rapid that the rest of the family did not detect her approach until she was upon them. When Ruth heard her daughter's shrill scream, her stomach lurched. Luckily, Ruth moved swiftly. Without conscious thought, her grasp was so firm about her child's abdomen that she thwarted the woman's attempt to snatch Dorlies. Ruth shoved the forlorn young woman out of her way.

Uttering a harsh curse, the woman fell to her knees. Hitting the cold tile floor, she grunted, and her painful, blood-curding scream echoed throughout the building. She suddenly became silent and stood up, grappling at the wall to stand upright. The only thing the woman could do was race away eerily, wailing on her own, disappearing among the masses, never to be seen by Ruth's family again. Ruth could not utter a word. She closed her tear-rimmed eyes and cuddled her children like a mother hen.

Her older children stared up at their mother, their eyes filled with fear. They were so small and innocent. Trembling from the incident, Anneliese stood to take Ruth's shoulders and glanced down at Ruth. "Are you and Dorlies all right?"

Kolberg

Indeed, the incident was scary. Kidnapping by mothers who had lost their babies was common. When the woman realised her misdeed, she twisted around and shrieked as she disappeared amidst the crowd. The grief was too great for her to bear, and she thought another child would fill the void.

There was something about the moment that changed to an instant kind of grief for the woman who must have been desperate to recover any child in her arms. Turning in the woman's direction, Ruth and Anneliese studied each other. Sniffling a bit, "Anneliese, I was so terrified!"

Reassuringly, Anneliese placed her hand on Ruth's shoulder again and said solemnly, "Ruth, that woman must have been insane."

No one else in the large hall noticed the madwoman. Everyone tended to their own worries to stay clear of the SS. Ruth's family cowered from the fearful confrontation. Thus, they tightened their group, inching to find a tiny space along the ice-cold, white tiled wall, one of the only spots still available. Both women eased their way to the cold tile floor, patting it to guide the three children to sit at their feet. The snatching attempt had frightened Ruth and Dorlies out of their wits. Tears streamed down her daughter's tiny, trembling face. Ruth secured Dorlies around her body with one of her cuddly baby blankets.

The two women and three other children in the station wished to let out a blood-curdling scream, but they dared not. Trembling, Dorlies sobbed into her mother's embrace. In contrast, the other children quietly wept into their woollen mittens from the frightening feelings they had had since leaving the security of their home.

Hinter-Pommern, behind them, the refugees flowed like a rushing river, hoping to flee into vorPommern, then onto Mecklenburg, the same area where the two women were hoping to find their way to the castle. From what Ruth gathered, most refugees who took refuge in the station came from the border closest to the Eastern Front. The only news Ruth could hear from the mixture of voices was intensely bleak.

Tears were forgotten in the wake of the disastrous conditions. Hans-Georg became oblivious to the morass of dangers about him. He glanced at the tall ceiling, smiled, and then erupted in giggles. He pointed upward. "Mutti, look at all the sparrows fluttering around the ceiling."

Following Hans-Georg's pointing right blue mitten, Dorlies chuckled happily into the warm wool blanket while Susanne and their cousin glanced up and giggled into their mittens.

As the hordes of people were waiting in the station house to vacate Pommern, Ruth was faced with the grim realisation that they could be recognised. Ruth made a tight fist to contain her fear as she pushed the children gently forward. Gazing into the crowd to shroud herself from the approaching deadly mist, Ruth shifted Dorlies and her frame to the left to ease her weary body. When Ruth drew her form upright, she discovered a pair of shiny black boots marching toward them. A Nazi

SS man was moving in their direction. Enraged, she rolled her frame away from the SS man towards the wall. Adjusting her headscarf closer to her face, Ruth nudged her sister-in-law, leaning close to Anneliese to alert her of the impending danger. She grabbed Anneliese's hand tightly and whispered, "I can feel the tension of the multitude as they slowly turned their shoulders to the wall. I can also sense the SS soldiers are annoyed at the disturbance generated by the people endeavouring to flee." Then she melted back into the wall.

Her sister-in-law glanced at the children and added, "I hope the children understand their silence is of the utmost importance."

Her expression was daunting. Ruth warned, "Above all, we must stick tightly in our cluster so we do not lose each other. Understood?"

Anneliese chimed in, "Klaus-Dieter, did you hear Tante Ruth?"

"Ja, Mutti," the three little ones echoed back, with Dorlies playing copycat in her fragmented words. "Ja, Mutti." After her accomplishment, she beamed at her mother.

Her tender smile and brilliant, happy blue eyes reminded Ruth of her husband's. She tenderly touched her daughter's face as she gazed into the crowd, her lips tightly shut out of concern.

The children cowered back to the wall, as did everyone else in their vicinity. Mercifully, the SS marched past, and the echo of the high black boots resounded off the grimy tile floor throughout the tightly jammed building like hundreds of shotguns.

Ruth was glad she had insisted everyone in her small cluster be genuinely grimy now. Thus, they would appear as not belonging to the nobility and that the family had been escaping for a lengthy period. Ruth stared into the masses. Her mind panicked as she recognised a face in the distance. A former gardener from Klein Pobloth, who had joined the SS, happened to be on duty.

While the family was hunkered down against the wall, Ruth sat straighter against the cold wall with her shoulders slumped and nudged her sister-in-law. She clutched Dorlies, who was still resting on her lap, tighter and reached for the other two. She moved closer to put her arms about them. Shaking her head in dismay, she shut her eyes. The warmth of the winter sun streaming through the half-mooned window of the station was welcoming. She opened her eyes again, and the light streamed through the window directly onto her family. She could see the SS soldier more clearly. He was a few yards to her side with his right hand fingering his Lugar. Striving not to watch him, she whispered to Anneliese, "Do you see him?" Ruth found that the SS man was watching the family. She was terrified and wished that she could scream but dared not.

Detecting her anxiety, Anneliese asked, "What is it, Ruth?"

Ruth's eyes were affixed on the SS soldier as she gestured in his direction, trying to alert Anneliese to his presence.

Barely able to catch her breath, Anneliese whispered back, "Ja, does he see us?" Out of panic, she turned her face away from the direction of the SS man.

The three older children sensed their mother's nervousness and became extremely fidgety. Ruth pressed a finger to her lips to quiet them.

Would the SS man prove to be dangerous?

Feeling her face burn out of fear, Ruth silently mouthed, "Don't look at him." She cuddled into Dorlies to comfort her as her mind raced for ways to distract the soldier from her family.

Without warning, six-year-old Susanne called out, "Guten Tag, Herr Bukowski." In a split second, Ruth clasped her hand over her elder daughter's mouth.

At Klein Pobloth, Ruth and Susanne had assisted Herr Bukowski in planting the park and rose garden. He had always been kind to the child who learned to love gardening from her mother and Herr Bukowski. Would that kindness cost them their lives now?

Wearing his black boots with pride, Herr Bukowski marched, then sauntered, stopping mid-stride. He played a fool's game by passing Ruth's family. The guard twisted his heels unexpectedly and then turned sharply, clicking together the heels of his shiny black boots. Ruth knew something had changed from the look on the SS man's face. When the SS man heard his name, he laughed sarcastically when he spotted Susanne and recognised her, and his stern expression softened slightly. He shrugged and kept his gaze downward.

Breathing the foul air deeply out of relief, Ruth realised what had happened. The SS soldier was not going to betray them. Instead, he made his way to the opposite side of the large auditorium. Indeed, instead of confronting them, he pretended not to know them. Ruth was certain that the man noticed that Susanne recognised him.

Thankfully, Ruth used good judgement in clamping her hand over her daughter's mouth so that he could ignore the outburst. He let the family slip through along with the other refugees without giving them any direct eye contact.

Ruth experienced euphoric joy. Her thin lips relaxed, and her fear receded. His act of compassion touched her. She studied Anneliese's pale, pessimistic face and said, "This is truly a cruel twist of fate."

Anneliese could not look away from the guard and studied him while she spoke softly. "Surely, he only wanted everyone else to see his outward masculinity where two women were a concern."

Nonetheless, Ruth chose to take a more optimistic view. Her family would forever be grateful for the gardener's momentary compassion. Ruth could see him deliberately not interacting with them. Considering his position as a guard, he must have understood that the noble family fleeing would be shot if they fell into the SS's or the Russians' hands.

Ruth's palms grew clammy with sweat from the fear pulsating through her entire being. At this moment, how could she not admire a man who put his own life on the line for them? He could have easily felt he needed to fulfil his obligation and deviously turned them into his superiors with the thought of being rewarded afterward.

Ruth struggled not to shudder from the turmoil as the tense moments passed. She did not wish to cast her confused trauma onto the older children. They could not understand what was about to afflict their young lives. Dorlies was too young to comprehend their dire situation when she only wanted her mother to snuggle her. Ruth and Anneliese had to pretend every action was a game during this horrific day, but everything was far from that. Ruth was about to stand up to suggest purchasing the tickets now available at a window across the wide hall, but suddenly she had another thought.

As Ruth reached for the Marks in a brown wallet around her abdomen, Anneliese watched her struggle to find a safe spot for Dorlies to rest. "With the three little ones, standing in line to obtain our tickets is difficult, Anneliese, it will be better if you push your way through the mob." Ruth spoke her mind. "If there are any issues with receiving our passage, you are so much better at convincing people to see it your way than I am." With a smile of reassurance, Ruth realised that taking Anneliese along was a good turn of events. Not to lose her rhythm of thought, she added, "Be sure to get the return tickets for a week or two back to Kolberg." She smiled warmly at her sister-in-law, "I will see after the children's safety."

In agreement, Anneliese shrugged, realising she was keener on dealing with adults than children. She inched her way up the cold white tiled wall to survey the crowd. Spotting a narrow opening, she leaned down so Ruth could hear her over the commotion. "If I hurry, I am confident I can take on the task of forcing my way through the droves." With her head held high, Anneliese's defence was to tediously elbow her way to the overcrowded ticket stand.

Soon, the building was flooded with pandemonium. Waiting in long lines, Anneliese heard the confused folks' chatter reverberating throughout the hall. From time to time, Ruth could see Anneliese's slim figure across the building, and her sister-in-law shifted her weight from here to there as she stood in one of the three exceedingly long lines. Ruth saw her sister-in-law slapping her hands around her body to keep herself warm.

Hearing several cries of hostilities from within the crowded chaos from a distance, Ruth continually watched as Anneliese shifted from leg to leg to give her the strength to stand in the excruciatingly slow-moving line to secure their ticket. Ruth momentarily closed her eyes to the ever-present fears, quickly opening them to the booming chaos within the walls.

Once Anneliese received the lightweight, brown cardboard tickets, she pushed back through the angry crowd toward Ruth and the children. As she came closer, Ruth noticed Anneliese's excited look as she pushed through, trying to return to her cluster. Ruth looked up at Anneliese and cast a questioning, worried glance. Ruth stared across the masses at Anneliese and felt the minutes run together. She saw a woman beside Anneliese collapse. Other than Anneliese, no one came to the woman's aid. Someone shoved Anneliese to the side. An SS man spared her from being trampled by the crowd. He pulled the unconscious woman across the room. He ended up sitting the woman upright, against the wall, on the far side of the room, away from the overflowing footsteps that could crush her.

Once beside Ruth, Anneliese beamed like a cat who had tasted a scrumptious mouse. Ruth was overcome with euphoria and wanted to leap up and down in joy, but she thought it was better not to attract further attention to her group. She had many questions, and Anneliese was eager to answer them about purchasing the tickets. With a nod of yes from Anneliese, Ruth exclaimed, "You got them!"

She listened to Anneliese relate what had happened. "Many poor people standing in line are being turned away because they do not have enough money to get transportation. Some are being detained because of questionable paperwork." Anneliese gulped. "Thank heaven, the documents I have from travelling to Kolberg a few days ago are still valid." Hearing the horror of what was happening behind them at the ticket stand, Anneliese shuddered. She pushed her headscarf closer to her ears to block out the noise.

To Ruth, her words were a Godsend.

"We were luckier than most. Because of you, we had the Marks ready to pay for the migration." When Anneliese grew silent momentarily, she caught her breath and raised her eyebrow. "To purchase the tickets for our train journey to Schloss Prützen was impossible. I did the next best thing. I got tickets to carry us to Rostock and hopefully further."

Expecting the worst, Ruth felt her stomach lurch. She was already apprehensive that she might lose her children. Once again, Ruth studied Anneliese, who did not consider Ruth's misunderstanding. By smiling calmly at Ruth and the children, Anneliese went out of her way to set things right. Soon, Ruth's heart leaped unexpectedly when she heard her sister-in-law's voice again with the surprising news.

"Ruth, I do not know how you pulled it off. Your records are in superb order. Also, the money we had between us paid for the tickets. The woman at the ticket counter could not assure me when our train might arrive or, for that matter, assure me that it would travel through Mecklenburg, and she did not know how much farther. She did, however, convey that our best chance to escape Pommern was to take these tickets. After this, there was no assurance that there would be any other trains today." She became grim once more, "As of yet, the office was not selling tickets for our return tickets. If ever!"

Escaping the Russian Onslaught

Exhausted from battling with the mob, Anneliese took the cuff of her grey coat and pulled the wool across her forehead. She fought back raging tears and said, "Now, I know how difficult it will be to continue this journey." She learned something important today: not all people were as kind as they had been in earlier years. "The people in line were dreadful, trying to ram their way forward." She waved the tickets. "Ja, I could hardly believe it myself." Anneliese carefully held tight to the prized tickets in her hand for fear of another refugee grabbing them from her clutch. I cannot believe our good luck. The timing could not have been better for us. We will be able to leave this brutal place behind us."

Looking forward to staying with her friend, Ruth studied their voucher to lift her spirits. Their epic escape became a reality as Ruth whispered, "I have ticket number 9878 for my family. It will be my family's Godsend." Frowning a bit, she reminded Anneliese, "We must remember to be extremely frugal with our funds to have enough left over for next week's return trip."

The impact of obtaining tickets would significantly prepare them to navigate this terrible crisis and step into their new role in life. At the west wall of the building, with a few moments of a new spark of energy filled with optimism, Ruth's family cluster sat side by side.

As usual, the trains were running behind schedule. For hours on end, their little group sat in the corner of the building while they waited impatiently for their turn to grab a train to escape from their beautiful Pommern.

Another wave of terror exploded from the crowd, triggering Dorlies to challenge her surroundings by becoming conspicuously irritated because Ruth would not let her run loose. Instead, she pressed her daughter back into the safety of their little corner. She cradled Dorlies with her little head against her mother's soft breast, hoping the little one would nap. As Ruth had become accustomed, restless Dorlies did not obey her mother. Without warning, she let out a blood-curdling scream. Ruth clamped her hand over Dorlies' mouth, gazed tenderly into the child's blue eyes, and kissed her silk-covered forehead. Swiftly, she looked around to see how much of a disturbance the outburst had caused. All heads were turned in their direction, but no one moved toward them, for the people were occupied with their own terror and the safety of their loved ones.

Ruth felt the need to explain her daughter's actions to Anneliese in order not to arouse suspicion in the group and because the rift between the families had been a part of her household. In a low voice, "I will never make this mistake again. Her piercing scream brought attention to all of us. I know her problem. She needs to relieve herself and does not understand how or where it can occur." Dorlies, like all her children, were trained to be clean just after they began walking. "Dorlies was so proud of herself. Now, I must smash all my rules since I do not have a place for her to go," Ruth lamented. "I must learn to always have a little tin can available for my children's use. I should have thought of this before, but I do not know where to get my hands on one at this juncture in our journey. She will have to stay dirty."

Unfolding the heavy fleece blanket she had retrieved from her bedroom door, Ruth whispered comforting words to her daughter and then wrapped the gold fleece blanket around her shivering children. Dorlies eventually dozed off, though she fidgeted uncomfortably. Ruth wondered how many layers of her clothing would be soiled. Dozing off occasionally, she awakened and stroked Susanne and Hans-Georg, who had settled against their mother's tattered warm brown coat.

Chapter 8

THE ARRIVAL OF THEIR TRAIN

As one-and-a-half endless days passed, several trains screeched away to who knew where. Nervously, Ruth could see the moon cresting from the eyebrow of the train station's half-moon windows. Steadying her nerves, Ruth kept her eyes glued to the platform display. Ruth heard one of the SS soldier's heavy boots stamping the tile floor under her. Quickly, the man brushed her shoulder, startling her at first. She wanted to swing about but remained motionless. Before she could move, Ruth recognised Herr Bukowski's deep hoarse whisper was upon her. With his warning words, his breath reeked of tobacco. Ruth could see that the SS soldier's mouth jerked nervously as he spoke. Ruth was desperately trying to hear him. She dropped her guard. The SS man's hard-shaven face brushed next to hers. "I implore you. Take the train appearing in the distance: this train might be the last." Instantly, the gardener was off as rapidly as he appeared.

She felt honoured that the SS guard had chosen them out of all the others in the hall. Her kindness over the years had paid off. She would remember to be extremely kind in the future. Ruth felt her body become hot from the flicker of hope within her. From the unexpected good fortune, Ruth barely had time to whisper to a dozing Anneliese. "Hurry – hurry, pick up your things. I believe this must be our train about to come to a stop. We must take this train. There might not be another!"

At Ruth's command, Anneliese sprang to her feet. Containing her anxiousness, Ruth was ready to charge for freedom. The women snatched up their children and bags, allowing their momentum to carry them forward. The six escapees dashed through the crowd, pushing as they clambered along the tracks and barely holding onto their backpacks and suitcases tucked securely about them. Their momentary element of racing was of no advantage. As the train inched closer, a foul stink filled the air, gagging all in the vicinity. Ruth saw the conductor hang his head from the black iron door frame to her right, brushing the sweat from his worried forehead and turning onto the steerage with the other, with the large black engine lurching to a stop to avoid crushing people covering the tracks. A sudden screech: Ruth felt a sharp sting brushing against her leg, escaping grey steam mixed with hot flaming sparks, flooding the air around them. Foolishly, anxious travellers stood too near the tracks as many folks as possible bolted out of the way from the massive black

The Arrival of Their Train

iron wheels, and others were yanked out of the way and then helped to their feet, and their belongings were crushed under the weight of the iron beast.

From under the mist came a voice, "Oh! No... not this train. We cannot take this train. It is filthy with cattle dung." Ruth heard a woman beside her group complain, thinking grimly how soon all her family members would match Dorlies' dirty state.

Hastily, Ruth and Anneliese tucked their children firmly under their arms like mother dogs gathering their litter. The train was upon them. The woman was correct. To their dismay, it was a livestock freight train. Once the engine screeched past them, they could see numbers of young soldiers clumped together in the cattle cars. The elderly, too old to fight in a war, were merged with the young soldiers. The soldiers wore tattered, green-grey German uniforms, all blood-stained, with scraggly beards, and empty stares of hunger and anxiety mixed with terror.

They stared through the wooden slats to get a better view of the people on the platform, but their hopes failed when no family member was there to greet them, further drawing them into their darkness, squeezed together shoulder to shoulder. Those soldiers in the back shoved their way through the crowded openings to grasp a breath of biting frigid air.

Ruth could see their breath steaming out of their mouths. A cold shiver ran down her body when she saw their teeth were yellow and black, with drops of dried blood oozing down the side of their mouths. The terrifying image reeled through Ruth: getting the children accustomed to blood and this filth, even for a few days, and surviving in the muck, plus the roar of the crowd, would be an extreme challenge for the children, herself, Anneliese and the other families to endure. The children never knew a filthy place like this: Klein Pobloth horse stalls, cows and pigs in the barns on their estate were much cleaner than the ones they were about to enter.

Susanne said, "Mutti, see the cattle cars. Those are the same types of wagons that pick up our dead animals ready for the glue factory. We are not going to go on that train."

"Susanne, keep your head down so you do not see the foulness going on about you." Susanne was old enough to follow her mother's instructions without question.

"Hans-Georg, you do the same," Ruth told her son soothingly.

"Mutti, it is dirty in there. The nasty smell hurts my nose, and besides, the yelling is making my tummy hurt," Hans-Georg grumbled. Still glancing at her, he gagged from the stench.

His mother swiftly cupped his filthy face and kissed his tear-stained cheeks.

Anneliese was quieting her own child's distress. "Shhh, Klaus-Dieter. Act as Tante Ruth told your cousins. And yes, Ruth..." Anneliese gazed in despair at the soldiers, "I see... It terrifies me how many young soldiers have bandages over their heads and limbs. Can you see there is blood oozing out from underneath?"

A sudden hush fell over the cluster as a gust of wind blew the foul smell of dried blood mixed with human dung outside the cars. The people backed away from the cars as much as space would allow. Plus, infected limbs pointed in their direction and the ugliness of the war interacting with these blood-stained soldiers revolted them. Even though the soldiers were kinsmen, they disdained the diseased soldiers.

Out of terror, the flock standing next to the car shrank back when one of the panicked young soldiers lunged forward and shrieked out a pitiful war cry, clasping the wooden railings, jerking them fervently as he could. "Let me out of here!" he cried, rattling the wooden slats bitterly. He spat, "All I want to do is to go home to my new wife." He yelled louder, tears of panic streaming down his unshaven face. "All I want is to see my new baby!" He released another piercing wail, "I don't even know if it was a strong boy or a beautiful baby girl." The others in the car were oblivious to his plea for help, and the crowd turned away sadly. They could do nothing to help this God-forsaken fellow, locked between them and the world outside.

The crowd immediately exchanged anxious glances with the injured soldiers, who had not recovered and required aid beyond their abilities. Several women in the group fell onto the wet, cold tile floor, struggling to rise. In contrast, others hastily snatched their children, facing the injured soldiers. The soldiers had insufficient aid from the defunct government that Hitler promised would last a thousand years.

The wooden doors swung open when the train lurched next to the platform, providing the soldiers with uncertain freedom. They appeared eager to hobble out onto familiar soil. Once off the train, the soldiers did not know where to go. Their homeland was already lost. Some had arms in slings, and most did not have weapons to use as crutches to carry them to hopeful loved ones waiting for them. They looked determined not to show any fear.

One young soldier caught Ruth's eye: He could only be fourteen, with injuries severe as if the boy had been blown apart and could not survive. The child wore an expression of longing as though homesick for his mother. The saddest part about these soldiers was that they fought to defend a country already lost.

Susanne clung to her mother's legs, and promptly Ruth felt her daughter's weight tugging at her brown coat. Clutching Susanne's tiny hand, she felt her eldest child's hand tremble and then considered her face, understanding that Susanne could grasp the enormity of the situation.

With fear, Susanne said, "Mutti, with all these people and so much noise, I cannot hear what you and Tante Anneliese are whispering about." She gazed deeper into her mother's vivid brown eyes. "Mutti, I am afraid of getting separated from you because I cannot find my way home from the station to Klein Pobloth." Susanne began to sob bitterly, with Hans-Georg following her lead. Suddenly, Ruth had three wailing children in her arms.

Ruth had no time to react to them or to reassure her daughter. The river of refugees rushing toward the train nearly knocked her over. They must act fast if

The Arrival of Their Train

they were going to board. "Anneliese – Anneliese!" Ruth nudged her sister-in-law's shoulder, "There is no other choice since this might be the last train coming our way!" Her wits about her, Ruth scanned about in terror. "You stay in front of me, clutch onto Klaus-Dieter, put yourselves in the front, and we must hang onto each other's clothing."

The women allowed the crowd to push them toward one of the open train's filthy wooden doors. Her thin lips tightened when she barely kept hold of Anneliese and her three children as her cluster pressed through the mass of people toward their salvation.

To find a safe corner of the cattle car turned into a stampede. Ruth let out a breath she did not realise she had been holding when all their feet were firmly on the filthy cargo car floor. Anneliese led the group to a corner of the car, where they leaned against the wall as more people crowded around them.

Ruth's family members were required to be more alert than ever. Fear propelled the passengers into shoving elbows, shoulders and knees, which became intolerable. Clutching onto Dorlies, Ruth swung into position with her right foot touching the filthy straw first, curled her toes into her shoes, and stepped in to get a firmer footage. Holding onto the edge of the doorframe, her right hand held on for dear life. The two youngsters bravely followed her aboard, their mouths quivering as they grasped their mother's tattered brown coat. Ruth saw Susanne hide her nose in her coat to shut off the rank whiff of human waste mixed with foul-smelling straw hitting her nostrils.

Dorlies' eyes and mouth were clamped shut, attempting to push her nose between her mother's lovely, warm breasts, hoping to enjoy the fragrance of her mother's powder. Regarding her older two, it appeared they would be sick at any moment. She saw her youngest close her eyes to make the world around her evaporate.

Ruth could only lift her head to see the filthy dust filtering through the air. She wrenched her back and saw there was nowhere to go. The family must adapt to survive these wagons and fulfil their mission. Inside the car, the two women crouched while pushing their children closer to the door if escape became a must, yet far enough away to keep track of the children next to their knees and keep them away from the ice cold.

Ruth saw a woman with her child pressed into the wooden slats attempting to wedge themselves free. As the woman came closer, Ruth moved over and reached out to touch her. The woman jerked sharply and then saw Ruth's gentle, kind expression. Desperately wishing to help, Ruth moved over as much as possible and said softly, "Sit beside us." It was not easy to see the woman in the shadows of the train car, yet Ruth heard her moan in gratitude, and the only thing she noticed was no expression on the thin woman's face. Ruth shivered at the thought that the young woman must have travelled for some time, but Ruth had no words of comfort. However, she could feel the woman's body relax beside her.

Escaping the Russian Onslaught

Outside their freight car, women and children were stumbling over each other to leap on the train. The creaking of the wooden slats under them caused Ruth to become aware of her surroundings again when she saw the hysteria of the people attempting to occupy the wagon and was frightened out of her skin when the mad mob attempted to pull others out of their car to get a place on the train westward, out of the way of the charging Russian onslaught. The clusters surged forward, undeterred that the freight car floors were not covered with new straw.

The cars jerked sharply, indicating an unsteady journey to come. Through one of the planks, Ruth could see the grey-blue trousers of an SS soldier in his heavy black boots marching more briskly towards the train. Herr Bukowski reappeared, hurriedly helping women and children onto the train. The SS guard firmly grasped the heavy iron bolts, unbolted the rusty iron latch with an awkward grunt, and threw open several other cattle-car doors. As in one giant swarm, the mob clambered onto the cars to crawl their way up to the filthy wooden planks.

Through a crack in the boards, Ruth could see the situation on the platform. Though the containers were already full to bursting, a soldier appearing too old to fight and ready for a rocking chair, motioned for more folks to climb into the small areas. When the freight cars were packed to his satisfaction, his shaking arm slammed the door shut and rammed the bulky iron door jamb over the sunlight. The dismal space would be their home for who knows how many days. Soon, the air in the cars was thick with distrust.

Ruth noticed one of the men shuffling nervously as he motioned more people into another car, sweat beading down the man's forehead. He took his dirty left cuff, wiped his weathered brow, glanced at his jacket and then sniffed the cuff. A sudden frown appeared on his beet-red, unhappy face as he realised his blunder and tried again to wipe the sweat off, but his sleeve was so dirty that his face became even more filthy. Ruth could not help but feel for the forlorn fellow. She knew this frustrated old soldier would be called to defend the town after his duties were finished at the station, which meant that his chances of escaping Kolberg were slim to none.

A shrill whistle echoed down the tracks, followed by a fierce, resounding voice. Ruth recognised it as Herr Bukowski as he suddenly ordered, "Get this train on its way toward Güstrow!"

Startled by his miraculous orders, Ruth stared down at her brown walking shoes, her heart pounding in her chest, and she felt cold and sick. His announcement shook Ruth raw. How did the easy-spoken, quiet, shy gardener know where she wished to travel with her family? Was the SS man observing her family the whole while without her knowledge? Ruth never considered that the SS soldier sought her out. Earlier, Ruth did not give it much thought that, after Hitler and the Nazi Party came into power, the gardener and Herr and Frau Risch became great friends. Over the years, the Rischs' continually requested that Dolores invite their friend

The Arrival of Their Train

Hermann Göring to go hunting at Klein Pobloth. Thank heaven that Dolores would not give in to the couple's request.

Göring and Hans-Rudolf were both nobility and became acquainted in the air force before Göring became a member of Hitler's henchmen and the dreaded military officer known today. While Rudi was at Stettin College, he met with the young Göring in his military office to help save the estate. Dolores requested Rudi take a week's hiatus from his education to find aid for the farm. The two men did not agree politically and did not maintain their relationship. After the First World War and the Great Depression, all landowners were hit hard by not receiving the right prices for their goods. Because there was a misunderstanding about the interest owed to the bank, Dolores could not pay the back taxes. Like many other large landowners throughout Pommern who had to borrow money against their property, Klein Pobloth had been about to be seized by the bank.

Everything fell into place when Ruth became aware that the gardener knew where Ruth wished to escape. She and Rudi suspected the Rischs to be members of the Nazi Party, yet proof was never found. To spy on the many unsuspecting members of society, in many cases, the Nazi Party members kept their affiliations hidden. Her naivety took Ruth off guard, but she vowed not to make such a grave error in judgement again.

In the upheaval of the unscheduled trains the refugees boarded, Ruth's cluster could only hope they were travelling in the right direction. This train had been travelling previously for untold hours, if not days, and now the six travellers squeezed as close to the wooden planks as possible to breathe the frigid yet fresh air into their lungs. They had only a small space for squatting room once secured in their spot by the wide planks. In other freight cars, droves of women and children were standing or sitting on sheets of filthy straw, which reeked of manure and urine and dried blood ground into the floor beneath. The refugees moaned in despair waiting for their next stop.

A gruff voice called, "Get these folks on their way!" The cattle car gates closed, and the soldier slammed the padlock shut. The steam engine hissed and sputtered coal-black smoke as it finally pulled out of the Kolberg train station.

Ruth looked through the planks at the Persante River and heard the clashing clang of iron against iron resounding down the tracks moving over a low bridge barely above the river. Ruth watched in terror as the train barrelled over the icy river, almost sloshing the freezing water into the cars. "We are all going to drown!" A woman screamed as the train rushed down the black iron tracks. Ruth's heart beat wildly in fear at the thought of plunging into the icy depths below, but as the train rolled on, the steady rumbling of the wheels calmed her.

Within moments, the train crossed the narrow stretch of Salzberg Island over a small tributary of the main river and then westward, leaving the smell of the Baltic

Sea and memories of their home behind. Blinded by tears that Ruth could not let fall, she frantically struggled to hold on to her courage.

Their train was stopped occasionally to allow military transport trains to pass by them. Peering through one of the cracks of wood to drink in the shafts of light, she saw the sun disappear behind a dark, ugly grey cloud. With a heavy heart, her disappointment began to overwhelm her. The train had not moved for some time, or was she so impacted that she had not noticed the passage of time and movement?

A few of the refugees somehow recognised that Ruth's family group had an undeniable quality of wealth about them, and it became obvious that they were new to the idea of fleeing. These frayed, hungry souls cried out to her group, gawking at them as if they could assist them in some manner. Ruth recognised their despair, and all she could do was lift her hands and shrug her shoulders in a desperate plea, indicating there was nothing she could do.

Ruth shivered as she whispered to Annelise, "From the back where we are, the light casts shadows over them, making their bloodshot eyes underlined with sunken-in purple seem ghastly. Is this how we will end up, wedged in a cattle car and shipped away like animals to slaughter?"

Sounds of iron clanging rang out once more as other cars were hitched onto the back of the one in which the family was travelling. Ruth fearfully turned her head as she heard the cattle cars bolting together with a hard thud of finality. She made no sound and knew not to call attention to herself and her family. She believed, however, that God was with them on their flight. He was giving the two women and their children the precious gift of freedom by allowing Ruth to trust her instincts.

Chapter 9

THE FREIGHT TRAIN IN WINTER

The trepidation Ruth felt from the thought of escaping overwhelmed her as she stared out between the filthy, wooden slats of the freight car. Her heart burst into anguish after countless excruciating hours of delay from the powers at hand on the transport train. The train slowly clattered by houses laden with icicles nearly extending to the ground this late February afternoon. With every motion from the iron engine pushing forward, the odour of danger hung about them. A firestorm could consume them at any moment, and Ruth would be helpless to stop it with the overcrowding of the cars and the many violent people escaping alongside her family in the overloaded freight cars. Could she protect her children on this dangerous journey?

Word passed quickly through the car that this was one of the coldest winters on record. With their bodies half frozen, Ruth's cluster trembled from apprehension about their future. Were it not for the many souls packed into one car, all would be frozen. Hunger, thirst and terror crept into their being. The family was packed in like sardines on a filthy train car to escape with the confused multitudes into the centre of their country. Keeping the children fully bundled, Ruth clung to her ultimate goal to get out of the train trip alive. Attempting not to doze off, Ruth kept her eyes fixed on the children with their knapsacks on their backs. As passengers aboard the long, unsafe train, they were ready to take flight at a moment's notice.

A German army blockade was set up at a junction before the Oder River. Authorised by the SS, their orders were to grab any men hiding as imposters on the train. Everyone was forced from the cars. The children hung on to the adult women, and young teen girls shivered out of humiliation when frisked for any sign of manhood. Ruth was the next woman to be frisked, screeching angrily as the soldier's hand moved toward her feminine parts, and wished for it to be over quickly but dared not utter a word though his infringement against her was demeaning and cruel. Ruth's cheeks burned with fury as she began to jerk her right hand upward toward the violent SS man's face, but she thought the better of it.

Confused, Ruth, Anneliese, the children and the other refugees were even now trembling at seeing the grisly sight of Stettin. In the wee hours of the morning, as they looked about, a hush fell over the line of refugee travellers when the people gazed across the annihilated city. Where the Vikings had settled in the ninth century, it was the largest Baltic port city and where Rudi had attended boot camp and later trained as a soldier. Ruth tried to breathe normally but could not. She thought about Stettin being where she and Rudi had strolled along the port and chatted about their future together eight years ago.

As day broke, they saw that the third-largest city in Germany had been thrust into the forefront of the fires that had exploded earlier. A military port city, air raids by the British Royal Air Force had flattened much of the town in April 1943, and once again in August 1944, as the British bombed to finalise their terror on the city, and it was a devastating sight to behold.

The state-sanctioned news reports blamed the Allies for endlessly bombing the ancient cities of Würzburg, Dresden, Hamburg, Kassel, and Mainz until they were unrecognisable. It would take ages for these cities to recover.

The United Kingdom, the United States, Russia, and Poland were determined to ensure that the Nazis would never rise again. Ruth wondered why the Allies had taken so long to try and stop Adolf Hitler's colossal war machine. Were the United Kingdom and the United States heads of state unaware of the massive crowds that gathered when Hitler promised the German people victory for a thousand years during his speeches? Were they unable to predict that Hitler's machinations would ultimately lead to war? His cruel ideologies included the mass murder of Jews, Poles, disabled individuals and anyone who did not fit into the Aryan mould.

The German army was so vast that it was rumoured that the soldiers and their equipment stretched from the Baltic Sea to the Adriatic. Indeed, the German army seemed larger, more organised and more destructive than the world had ever seen.

On Stettin's elegant streets, where only one stately ancient building stood, nothing but ravines of grey-white stubble could be seen. Throughout the city, lights could be seen flickering in the distance. Ruth perceived them as people who lived in their grim hovels and had not deserted the town and it took an effort to gaze at the torn landscape. She did, however, spot the Stettin Berliners Tor, one of the town's iconic symbols. Ruth went pale. The sight once again left no doubt in her mind about how much she despised Hitler for his psychopathic and narcissistic ideologies.

Challenged with boarding the car again, obtaining their space proved significantly easier than Ruth thought possible. The impact of goodwill came over Ruth as the folks inside became more stabilised by moving to the areas they had occupied earlier.

The steam billowed from the engine, and soon after the cars jerked onward. There was an unfamiliar jolt as the train travelled on a pontoon bridge over the Oder River. No one on the train, especially the children, had known such complete darkness of night, unnerving the travellers. If the train catapulted into the ice water, they would be trapped like fleeing rabbits. Thus, Ruth hoped the

The Freight Train in Winter

youngsters would not question the unusual swaying and water sloshing against the barrels supporting the rails.

Over the heads of their sleeping children, Anneliese could not help but whisper to her sister-in-law, "We are going over a bridge like a floating raft. If the bridge goes down, the whole train will be forced into these icy currents."

Not asleep, Susanne tugged at her mother's sleeve. Her voice was quiet yet urgent. "Mutti, I hear water all around us! Mutti, are we going to drown? I can see the black water through a peephole next to me and feel it lapping at the train, trying to swallow us."

Ruth peered at her daughter with a soft smile. "Shhh, Susanne. It is going to be all right. The train is safe while we are travelling over the water. Besides, if you squint carefully, you will see clouds covering the moon tonight, so the water will not glitter with little lights. Rest your head on your knees, and you will fall asleep."

Pulling her knees under her, Susanne insisted, "I do not feel well, Mutti. I want to lie down, but there is no room. Hans-Georg told me that he does not feel well either and is struggling to put his head on my lap to get some sleep."

With what she hoped was a smile at her daughter, Ruth urged, "Do the best you can." Susanne nodded and tried to settle into a comfortable position, but her attempt at shielding the other children from the devastation failed and they began to cry like most of the children on the train, and keeping little Dorlies under control turned challenging.

Shivering in their little corner of the hideous, reeking transport car, Susanne stood to stretch and then yawned, resting closer to her mother once more, almost sitting on her sister. Dorlies clenched at her mother's clothes out of distress. Ruth clutched her twenty-one-month-old closer with her right hand, and the toddler began to bellow from terror mixed with anguish. With her left hand, she stroked Hans-Georg's pasty white face so she could study her frail son closer and noticed that he hid his face with the palms of his hands wet from tears as his body shuddered with terror.

Anneliese and Klaus-Dieter knelt, clinging to each other as if this were the last time they would see one another.

Whistling from the train filled the air, and then the winter skies were aglow from shafts of moonlight. There was an awful racket under their seats. From the train wheels, fiery sparks from the tracks edged the refugees, pummelling their spirits even further.

Out of childish curiosity, Hans-Georg stared through the small spaces of the wooden planks. "I spotted much water mixed with dirt and sleet tossed beside the train. Mutti, the bridge did not hurt us. Will we need to go over it again? I am terribly hungry and thirsty."

"As soon as the train stops, I will look into my knapsack and find something for you, and there is some cheese that I brought along from home. Remember the little silver folding cup? When we stop, the soldiers helping us will divide some water." Ruth bent to kiss his brow, "For now, do not watch, son." She smiled into her son's inquisitive hazel eyes. "Squeeze your eyes shut." She kissed the lids. "Remember, your birthday is just around the corner." One by one, Ruth stroked the strands of light brown hair escaping from under his cap. "Pretend that the happy moonbeams around us are firecrackers sending you a wonderful birthday party."

Hans-Georg studied his mother as if she had gone daft. "Mutti, I am old enough to understand. Besides, I know what is happening. I will be grown up soon. Remember, I will have my fifth birthday a few weeks after Susanne. Then, you can see how much I have learned. I will be old enough to take care of the family since my Vati is not with us."

Overcome with motherly love, Ruth held her children tightly, calming them as much as possible. Ruth turned to Anneliese. "I think we can breathe easier now. The trembling of the train sounds different."

The train faltered a bit and then began to sway as the engines whistled three times.

"Hallelujah, what a tremendous relief," Ruth said, louder than she expected, dropping her voice. "This means we made it over the bridge!" Another enormous jolt made the passengers aware they were safely on land again. Ruth rubbed her dripping, cold nose, a habit when stressed, which tended to be red on the tip. As before, the comforting motion held her fear at bay. From the rear of the car, Ruth heard a woman's voice, then another, as they began reciting the Lord's prayer. The other folks joined in. "Our Father…" Some women sang. While others sobbed, one woman's eyes glazed over, and then she hooted hysterically until she almost fainted. Tears of saddened defeat flowed like a river of dreams pouring into the depth of their losses. A flute was drawn out of a backpack by a woman standing nearby, who placed the instrument between her lips and began playing a Mozart concert for them.

Overnight the train filled with refugees from the province of Vorpommern and Mecklenburg, the land well known for its six hundred lakes and a sea of grasses, with magnificent ancient castles standing in clusters.

Susanne peered through one of the wooden slats out of innocent, fearless naivety and piped up, "See, Mutti, now the trees and this town are frosted sugar cream, and from the sun, they are sparkling gold."

Giggles of delight erupted from the older children who understood her meaning.

Her mother reminded her, "Soon, it will be your sixth birthday, Susanne, so we can celebrate when we arrive at the Schloss."

When the opportunity presented itself, Susanne peered between the planks of the freight train and spoke softly with a hint of delight. "Mutti, I love the look of this town we are passing with the weather decorating the city to look like a cake."

"I am so very hungry," Hans-Georg licked his lips, "The church steeple looks yummy."

The Freight Train in Winter

Susanne said, "The tower reminds me of a white buttercream frosted cake sprinkled with powdered sugar." It was a bright, sunny day with a white powder of snow covering the splendid old Güstrow Schloss with spirals inspired by the much-admired Italian architects during the Renaissance.

Anneliese leaned over to look out through the cracks. "It has been rumoured the train tracks are damaged. If I am not mistaken, we are passing by the historic city of Güstrow near Rostock."

"I think you are correct, Anneliese. If so, we are almost to our destination."

The sun streamed through the wooden planks of the cattle car, casting eerie golden bands of defused beams through them. Ruth's hushed voice could not be heard over the yelling of the sounds in the crowd. The light, however, was enough for Ruth to gaze at Dorlies, "Her forehead is warm, and her cheeks are so rosy as if she has a fever."

A teenage girl shouted in the tightly jammed crowd, "We made it to Güstrow. Can you believe it! The little girl over there is right! With the glorious sun glittering on the newly fallen snow, the castle in Güstrow seems frosted in buttercream. I want a bite, and I can taste the delicious cake."

The train screeched to an abrupt stop.

Ruth heard the soldier's loud footsteps announce his presence. He was an insolent, grizzly man, grunting as he shifted his stiff, bulky frame and hastily ordered, "Everyone out! Everyone off the train. Now! Out, now! Take your belongings off the train and step away as far as possible. We can take you no further!" He marched along the wagons, yelling the same orders to be heard down the tracks.

The soldier's voice was close to Ruth now, but she could not see who he was speaking to. "These people call themselves lucky to get out, but they have no idea what they are in for."

The refugees must find an alternate transportation route from here on. If they hoped to go further westward, they were disappointed. Because of the hundreds of war activities that had taken place in the area, the train tracks were torn asunder as far as the eye could see.

Keeping a watchful eye on the railroad tracks, the heavy iron bolts were thrown ajar in one motion from the other soldiers down the tracks. An armed, older man holding a machine gun appeared at the dilapidated cattle car door. Outrage over what had transpired in his country could be heard in the soldier's raw orders to the crowds in the freight car.

The older man poked his head in. "From this point on, you folks must distance yourselves as far away from the train tracks as possible because you must find safety by 5 p.m. There have been so many refugees that they are stealing from one another. Walk into the town, and these people will put you in their homes or barns."

Ruth glanced toward Anneliese long enough to see her dismayed eyes filled with tears. She muttered in great annoyance, her tears inspired by indignation. She spat, "Ridiculous! So, what are we supposed to do now?"

The soldier turned and barked sharply, "Out!" His second effort to remove the refugees from the train was successful and achieved in short order.

After gathering their few belongings, a young, disabled boy whined uncontrollably, causing the group to be silent. The adults in the group understood that their disorderly conduct had triggered the lad's distress. They also understood that, somehow, his mother must have kept him hidden from the view of the Nazis, or he might have been euthanised. The Nazis were notorious for their ruthless cruelty toward the disabled and elderly. The young and beautiful were revered as gods to couple with one another to create the perfect specimen. Their wish was to breed a superior race where no one needed to be cared for by the government.

Everyone on the train grabbed their belongings, disembarking with the group they travelled with. Every person plummeted out of the cars into the mud and then under the rainy skies. The area soon was alive with hustling activity as they tried to find their way to move on to a new destination. Many, unsure what to do next, stood and stared into the distance.

Anneliese glanced at Ruth with wide-eyed fear and gasped, "Thank heaven we know what must be done, Ruth."

Ruth tried reassuring her cluster, speaking softly over the terror from within the enclosed stench. In the depressing atmosphere, she still had hope. "Yes, Anneliese, this is where we must get off and get to Anita Lang's sister."

Once their belongings were gathered, Ruth pushed open her cream-coloured fold-up umbrella. With the gusty winds hitting the canopy, it turned itself inside out. Ruth could not control the wobbly small metal handle, so everyone stood in the wet, cold air and wondered what to do next.

Ruth saw more wrath in the space around them and wished she had time to contact Irene Zimmer about her latest arrangements. Ruth bit her lips to keep from inviting the strangers to join her family in the large castle. If she were at Klein Pobloth, there would be ample room in the thirty-four-room mansion to invite them in. When the farm produced grain for bread, fresh meat hanging in the icehouse and canned fruits, fresh milk and vegetables, everyone could sleep on a full stomach. Then, Ruth would entertain as she enjoyed doing with her talent for fine cuisine and pursue the couture for which she was known. These days were over, at least for the next two weeks.

To her right, several scuffles broke out between the annoyed passengers. Ruth stepped to the side, dragging her group with her. Not feeling safe in the intolerable elements, Ruth hoped they could find a way to reach Anita Lang's sister at her Schloss. Anita had been her boarding school friend at the renowned Lyzeum Queen Louise Schule in Belgard, Germany. After Anita's last visit to Klein Pobloth in 1941, she had met Hans-Rudolf at Hans-Georg's baptism celebration.

When the telephone lines were still working, Anita had told Ruth she had spoken to her sister Irene, who had urged her to telephone her friend Ruth Meissner. Living extremely close to the border of Poland and Russia, Ruth might need shelter if the war turned bad for Germany. The war dismally failed Germany. Before the war erupted, many German people and other nations had deemed that Hitler and the Nazi Party must be stopped. However, the Nazi Party's rise was so rapid, strong and dangerous that it was impossible to suppress.

When Ruth had telephoned Irene, back when fun and giggles were still the norm, Ruth and Irene Zimmer had immediately become fast friends even though they had not met. If the need arose for Ruth and her family to flee, they would be welcome at Irene's home with open arms, and Ruth would call Irene to prepare for her family's arrival in Güstrow. Schloss Prüzen was a short distance away from the city. During their last telephone conversation, Ruth had told Irene that when the Red Army was about to enter Pommern, she would be on her way to stay with her.

With her ear constantly to the radio, Irene had heard the radio reports that the Red Army was about to break through Germany's easternmost borders. Even though gasoline was rationed, she would drive the ten kilometres to Güstrow every day to see if the Meissner family had arrived.

Chapter 10

GÜSTROW

After the foul air on the train, Ruth breathed in the welcoming fresh country air. The grey gravel crunched as Ruth hurriedly gathered her brood while seeking to recall Irene's directions. "From how I understood the instructions, I think this is the way," she told Anneliese.

Ruth wearily brushed her hand over her forehead, leaned next to Anneliese, and said, "If my memory serves me right, Schloss Prüzen is quite a distance from the train station at Güstrow, the nearest town to the castle."

Scanning the horizon, she did not see Irene's black Mercedes-Benz Tournament, no vehicle was in sight. Trying to focus on her new surroundings, Ruth attempted to calm her nerves to no avail.

Feeling the unrest, Hans-Georg tugged at his mother's coat, studying her expression and staring up at her, letting out a great sigh of fearful discomfort. His cold white cheeks were kissed red from the crisp winter air, and he sobbed with his tired, hazel eyes only half-open. "Oh, no... no, Mutti. We are too tired to walk to the castle."

A chorus of displeasure from the children rang out. While weary, Anneliese and Ruth summoned the courage to move on as instructed by the guards watching the train. They pushed their belongings far away from the black iron beast to avoid further confrontation with the soldiers.

"Now, children," Anneliese swiftly spoke her mind, "your mother has found us a lovely place to live for the next few days. We will need this short layover until we can get passage on another train to travel home again."

The women sat on their suitcases out of weariness and allowed the children some freedom. Ruth watched them carefully. She giggled in delight when she saw a small blond curl escape from the nape of Dorlies' woollen cap. The young child flew into her mother's arms and was warmly embraced. "Come here, children. Let me make sure that your clothing is tight around you." She looked at her son, dancing about to indicate his need to relieve himself. "Come to Mutti, and we will find some high bushes so you can go potty again." Studying her daughter, she said, "You should come along since our last break was some time ago."

"I can watch after our belongings," said Anneliese. Ruth took them behind the nearest outcropping, and after a few moments, they were back at Anneliese's side.

On their way back, Susanne said innocently, "Mutti, I needed to go potty so badly, but I didn't want to upset you by asking again."

Güstrow

Smiling slightly, Ruth said, "The journey has been difficult. Remember, we will celebrate your brother's and your birthday at the Schloss." She lovingly patted Susanne on her rump, "Come along. Everything will be all right, and soon we will stay at a wonderful castle and have as much to eat and drink as we want." Lovingly pulling her daughter's pigtail, she said, "I bet we can all take a long, soothing, hot bubble bath."

Anneliese and Klaus-Dieter were back quickly, but Ruth could feel her sister-in-law's trepidation. Her mouth curled out of frustration, and her distressed look was obvious to everyone around her. "Anneliese, we can walk for a little while. The children must manage."

While Ruth's motley family began to pick up their belongings, one of the other passengers, who had been on the train, spoke up. She looked at Ruth and said, "Hello, my name is Ingrid. My sister resides within walking distance of the station, within walking distance for adults. You folks wait here, and I will rush to her place and tell her about your difficulties." She smiled eagerly, "I may be able to assist you. My sister's home is on a farm, and I hope she still has her red ox if her family and neighbours have not butchered the animal to keep food on the table."

Elated, Ruth smiled. "How nice of you to offer us assistance. It would be wonderful if your family could help." Relief washed over Ruth's thin, tight face. "After our terrifying train ride, the thought of walking that distance is overwhelming."

The newcomer to the group kindly addressed Ruth's family: "Ladies, children, study the trees beyond the grove to your right."

As one, the cluster turned to feast on a happy sight.

"Yes, my sister, Helga must have heard the train pulling in. Helga came to rescue us with her lovely red ox Lottie, who is pulling a large wagon all of us can ride in."

Ruth exclaimed, "Lottie, at this moment, is the most beautiful ox I have ever seen!"

Rummaging through her knapsack, Ruth found a pre-stamped, blue envelope that also served as a sheet of paper. Gingerly, she sat on the small suitcase, which almost tipped her to the ground. Ruth caught her balance on the gravel, upright again, and with a pencil in hand, her tears filled her eyes as she scribbled. I have lost track of time. *Is it the end of February or March?*

Feldpost
Obergefreiter Hans-Rudolf Meißner
Wiesbaden
My dear, dear Rudi,
1 March 1945

Dearest Rudi
We are out. It is done by the skin of our teeth and against the grain.
We do not know anything else. We left furiously with the children, Anneliese and Klaus. We also look like it. Crossing my fingers that you will still come. Always your Ruth.

Gathering her saliva, Ruth licked her dry lips to seal the letter as best she could. She turned to Ingrid, "Please, my dear, can you and your sister post this letter for me?" Ruth lifted her letter to the young woman, a sense of urgency in her eyes. Smiling, she said, "My husband Rudi must know my whereabouts. It has been too long since we last heard from each other."

Ingrid was glad she could help with this vital information. Her warm smile held hope for Ruth and her family. "Anything I can do to help you would give me the greatest satisfaction."

When the introductions were clear, Ruth gave Ingrid and her sister Frau Holtz her directions to Schloss Prüzen, a grand castle that stood as a beacon of hope in their journey. Within seconds, everyone clambered onto the wagon with their belongings, their hurried footsteps echoing. With a click of a long leather whip, they were off, the wagon jolting forward. Soothing emotions came over the small group who had thankfully been rescued from beside the train tracks, a sense of relief washing over them. A warm feeling of comfort came from hearing the red ox's hooves on the cobblestones as the group travelled toward their haven, the rhythmic sound lulling them into a sense of security.

A short time later, Ruth pointed at the magnificent castle that looked as if it were guarding the surrounding area. "Oh yes, I see it in the distance. Children look yonder."

Anneliese pointed to a woman making her way toward the cart. "Irene Zimmer must have heard the train whistle also. Can you see her coming in her luxurious automobile? She is waving her white handkerchief in recognition."

Ingrid pulled on the reins, and the ox came to a halt. When Irene opened her car door, Ruth stood to wave in gratitude. Her friend's lean silhouette stood out momentarily against the icy snow. Shouts of joy erupted from everyone in the wagon.

Waiting anxiously at the side of her car, Irene was impeccably dressed in a navy dress, with her white lace collar accentuating her well-formed, petite figure and stretching out her slender arms to receive the family. The two women hopped off the wagon with a relieved laugh. Irene's well-rounded lips kissed Ruth and Anneliese on their cheeks as if they were her sisters.

Enjoying her new friend's impulsiveness, Ruth realised this woman was the full example of propriety and sophistication. A moment later, pools of delight beamed in Irene's green eyes. She reached for Dorlies and took her from Ruth's arms to cuddle the toddler in her grasp.

The young child's tiny fingers became entangled in Irene's brown hair to secure herself in the woman's grip. Dorlies arched her back to study the newcomer to the group. Soon, the other children made their way down with the aid of the adults. There was a moment of silence, allowing the group to breathe deeply and relax.

Splashing through a puddle, Ruth threw her arms around Irene's neck as if she were a child and placed her head on her shoulder, and her body quivered as if she were about to sob.

Happily, the group expressed their gratitude to Frau Holtz and her sister, who were soon on their way back to their farm. Ruth studied her friend for approval. "Frau Irene Zimmer, I would like you to meet my sister-in-law Anneliese and her son Klaus-Dieter, who decided to travel with me at the last moment." Ruth's smile was brighter now, "I hope you will welcome them into your home for the few days we will be here?"

Taking her hands into her own, Irene shook Anneliese's right hand. "Naturally, my dear friend, there is plenty of room for all of you," she smiled at Anneliese. "The more, the merrier. We will throw a party for your visit with me. It has been too long since I had anyone stay in my home."

Irene placed her arm around Ruth's small waist to reassure her friend that all would be well. "I imagine you are starving, weary, and extremely grimy. A good hot bath will get you all well."

"You, dear Irene, are not mistaken there. The children seem a little feverish. They have likely gotten a chill by travelling on the frigid freight cars since this cold, damp air has only added to their discomfort."

Ruth could not believe their good fortune connecting with Irene as planned. Now, they would receive real news about what was happening around them. Surely, by now, Germany had won the war. Ruth hesitated. Would the family be able to go home in the two weeks promised? Would Dolores be safe at Klein Pobloth and still carry her anger with her? Her first desire upon their arrival was to telephone her mother to see about her safety. There would always be time to bake Hans-Georg a birthday cake to surprise him on the seventeenth. Going home would give her time to plant spinach, lettuce and carrot seeds.

Irene moved them swiftly as the auto took the family down the tree-lined, cobblestone lane by the school and two lakes, then to the castle with its red-tiled roof. Even though her family came from a lavish home, Ruth was overcome by the stylish Schloss Prüzen's appearance.

Chapter 11

SCHLOSS PRÜZEN END OF FEBRUARY AND MARCH 1945

The castle Ruth's family was driving towards was luxuriously appointed and infused with historic elegance. Its five fireplace stacks of pointed, stylish gothic pillars reached toward the sky, embellishing the four stone eyebrowed caps on either side of the building, creating a welcoming cover over the four elongated windows on both sections of the ample double circular staircase entrance.

As the family gazed upward to the welcoming double, forest green doorway, the castle's grandeur became apparent. Ruth and Anneliese carried their few belongings up the nearest double waterfall steps. While Irene cuddled sleepy Dorlies, the other weary children laboured to hop their way up.

The weary family stepped into the castle built in the 1300s. Ruth noted the young children's gazes were fixed on the impressive crystal chandelier illuminating their surroundings, with the lighting beams casting a kaleidoscope of soft, welcoming glow over the countless century-old portraits, a tribute to generations past in the airy two-story foyer.

Ruth's attention was drawn to the tastefully decorated powder-blue and crimson Lady's salon on the far side to the right. The white, glossy-painted woodwork reminded her of the welcoming warmth she felt at her parents' home, Kempen Estate.

Graciously, Irene showed each family to their new quarters. Ruth was welcome to reside in one of the large bedroom suites, and arrangements would be made for one room with four beds for the children next to her room. The children were delighted to sleep near one another. Anneliese took up quarters farther down the hall.

Staying in the castle was full of unexpected pleasures. At Schloss Prüzen, Ella, the maid, assisted in giving the children calming, long, hot bubble baths as promised. Once the children were snuggled under their high, lofty white feather beds, a hot, comforting supper of roasted fresh vegetables and baked chicken was served to the two boys on individual bed trays. Susanne jumped into bed with Dorlies to help her with her tray. The children's eyes and smiles widened when the

Schloss Prüzen End of February and March 1945

meal was accompanied by hot chocolate heaped with heavy white velvety whipped cream. The children were delighted about the treat since Ruth did not allow them chocolate this late in the evening. Ruth and Anneliese smiled with delight at seeing them so happy. Ella gave the children hot water bottles to help warm them further.

After their supper and a welcoming bath, several drops of liqueur were added to the hot tea to warm the ladies' shivering bodies.

Ruth's three children had a burning fever on the family's first morning at the castle. Ruth asked Irene for something to relieve them and help with their aches and the appearance of what she thought was the beginning of a sore throat. Ella quickly produced a jar of ointment called VapoRub. Ruth rubbed their tiny chests with petroleum jelly, discovering a telltale rash from a menacing virus across her children's bodies. She knew the rash tended to appear about fourteen days after exposure to the disease. Her mind abruptly travelled to Klein Pobloth, where the children must have been exposed two weeks earlier.

Ruth paused. Embarrassment surged through her body. Knowing that moving westward where it might be safer was impossible for a couple of weeks, Ruth cringed. It was a horrific, long time. The longer they waited, the greater the risk. Ruth took a sip of tea to calm herself before she spoke to the two women at the breakfast table.

Feeling discouraged and humiliated, Ruth informed Anneliese and Irene about the spots on the children. Knowing what the children were about to undergo did nothing to calm her anxiety.

Dismay filled Anneliese's face, then she threw her hands in the air and grabbed the nearest chair to stop trembling. "What more can happen?"

Ruth studied Irene, who took the news more lightly and placed a reassuring hand on Ruth's shoulder with a sympathetic smile. "Oh, Ruth, I am so sorry. You and your family have endured such heartaches. It hardly seems fair."

A frown of displeasure played on Anneliese's beet-red face. Folding her hands about her waist, she huffed, "How did they catch the illness?"

Ruth felt a blush fill her cheeks, hesitant to ask Irene in case she might answer no to the family residing longer. "It must have been the refugees from the equestrian school travelling through Klein Pobloth a few weeks ago. I invited the officer and his family to sleep in my apartment." Her mortification peaked again. "His children had a slight fever but no sign of the rash."

Anneliese surely must have remembered the circumstances. The officer had kindly offered to let Ruth and her children escape when his family accompanied the equestrians, one of her many failed escape attempts. Earlier, she had become aware that both women had followed her every move, but Ruth did not understand how they knew her actions. In the middle of her preparations, Ruth knew someone was eavesdropping. Unannounced, Dolores and Anneliese had burst into her rooms without warning and immediately stopped her plan of escaping with the lieutenant and his family by accusing Ruth of deserting her post in life to protect Klein Pobloth at all costs.

With a stiff upper lip, Anneliese added, "We might as well make the best of it. Ruth, if your three have the measles, Klaus-Dieter will undoubtedly be ill in a day or two." She fled the room, doubtless to find her own son and put him to bed.

Irene raised an eyebrow at Anneliese's departure and stared out the door after her. "Ruth, my sister talked about your zeal and ardour when she met you years ago but that seems to have been stripped from you since you began living at Klein Pobloth." She turned to face her friend, "From what my sister has told me about the actions of your in-laws, there was a lot you had to deal with there. Well, I will do what I can to help you now. Let me fetch Ella, the only one left in my employment in these dark days. She will help you and your sister-in-law care for your children so you can get some much-needed rest."

"Thank you, dear friend." Ruth added with a small quivering smile. "Perhaps when this ordeal is over, I will regain some of the spirit I lost from trying to escape under the clutches of my mother-in-law. Now, I must tend to my little ones." She turned toward their room.

The castle became their haven as the children came down with measles. The children spent their days lounging about, huddled in blankets while seeking to suppress their hacking coughs and sneezes. Ruth, Anneliese, Irene and Ella played nursemaid to their every need: cleaning red, runny noses, soothing sore throats and hacking coughs, keeping their little hands from scratching the sores, and getting them to drink enough liquid to keep them hydrated. The drapes were drawn.

Dusk fell, and the children finally fell asleep. As shafts of light struggled to cast shadows on the horizon, Ruth's arms could sense the spring warmth drifting through the windowpane. She settled at the window with a small piece of paper and wished to post a letter to Rudi. She was unsure if he would receive it, but she must try.

Feldpost
Obergefreiter Hans-Rudolf Meißner
Wiesbaden
My dear, dear Rudi,
2 March 1945

Dearest Rudi,
I already wrote to you yesterday, but I want to write the same today since I do not know if I included all the lines. The children, Anneliese, Klaus-Dieter and I, are in Prüzen by Güstrow Mecklenburg. We spent twenty-four hours in a railroad freight car, bringing us to Rostock without changing trains. We had to stand for seven hours for a place on the train. In the railcar, it was better than we thought.

Schloss Prüzen End of February and March 1945

> *The children could lie down on the hard floor to sleep. I had the old golden-yellow plush curtain as a cover, which is large and warm.*
>
> *The controllers did not stop us on the Hecht, but nothing was cleaned up, so I was frightened. Mentioned in the OKW report today: Glim, Soltau, Rummelsburg and Gen. So, this was the alarm. Hopefully, we will be safe here. But where should one go now? Everything is so groundless. I thought about whether I should contact Frau Hübe in Körlin.*
>
> Ruth

Writing the letter only increased Ruth's burden. By 1942, the OKW (Oberkommando der Wehrmacht), the German High Command, had concerned all the German people because it placed most military decisions in Hitler's hands, making Germany helpless to disobey any order given by the party.

Ruth reviewed the few days when she could have made a greater effort to receive Anneliese into the folds of her young family years ago. When a fire at Klein Pobloth had gutted the rear of the ancient building, Dolores was a young, widowed woman. The servants had dragged the garments from the house into the park, away from the fire. Dolores's second husband, Rudolf Meissner, had added the third floor to the home. Many of Dolores' mother's elaborate gowns, dress parade army officer's uniforms and accessories took up residence there, stored in the massive wardrobes until Dolores had asked the two women to help refresh the incredibly beautiful dresses.

Back in 1940, Ruth and Anneliese had had a delightful afternoon. That morning, Dolores had asked the two women to help freshen the large wardrobes on the house's third floor. They had been stored there since Dolores's mother, Louise Lentz, contracted tuberculosis and died when Dolores was a young child. Her father, Hans von Kaphengst, became extremely overwrought by his wife's death and stored his wife's wardrobe in large armoires lining the walls. When Ruth and Anneliese had seen the silk, satin and velvet garments, they gained Dolores's permission to model the gowns. For those few hours, a friend had taken numerous black-and-white photographs. The sisters-in-law had chuckled at the thought of the small waistlines the women were required to maintain during the early 1800s. The two young women had had a delightful afternoon modelling the frocks. Ruth wished she and Anneliese could have kept the bond created during that time.

Ella took her turn in keeping an ever-watchful eye on the children. Ruth, Anneliese and their hostess Irene sat beside the small green tile oven in the breakfast room, comfortably sipping homegrown rosehip tea, a radio playing in the background. The shades were drawn to prevent the cosy light in the room from spilling into the darkness. This way, they could avoid the chance of Allied bombers passing overhead and bombing the Schloss.

"Irene, this tea is so inviting," Ruth said as she sipped, desperately trying to suppress her negative emotions and enjoy the moment. But her fears spilled over as she reflected on the past. "Do you think –"

Attempting to suppress her fear, Anneliese interrupted, "Shhh! Listen closely. Someone is hammering at the back door."

Ella was at the other side of the manor house, tending to the children.

Extremely curious and laced with trepidation, Irene took off her brown leather shoes and tiptoed through the long white hallway decorated with too many Hirsch and Reh horns for her taste, a style similar to many Rittergut knighthood estates.

The banging knock came again, more softly this time. "Gnädige Frau, I must speak with you," and then another soft tap. "Gnädige Frau. My Lady, I must talk with you." The hunched-over old caretaker had rushed to the back door, banging on the brass lion with the end of his wooden cane.

Recognising Matthias, her loyal night watchman, Irene set the green door ajar enough to acknowledge that he was alone.

Matthias's breathing was strained. Before entering the hall, he rubbed his feet on the bristly brown willow mat. When he saw his Lady, he removed his grey workman's hat and bowed his head. Making eye contact with the mistress of the house still made him uncomfortable. Before the Great War, eye contact between nobles and servants had been strictly frowned upon.

Distressed, Irene saw Matthias's eyes streaming with tears, choking on his words, nose mucus caught between his lips, which he wiped on his grey woollen coat cuff. "My Lady, the Russians are surging stronger and closer to our area. Please, I beg of you, my Lady, can my wife Hildy and I flee?"

Irene took Matthias by his balding white head in her graceful grasp and kissed the shiny bald spot. When he raised his weathered face to her, she studied his wet, brown eyes, "My wonderful lifelong friend and saviour on many occasions, I am surprised you and Hildegard are still trying to watch over a land already lost."

"You must also escape, my Lady!"

"I will see. I will see. After the war, my dear husband will come to me. He promised that he would. And as you know, my dear Matthias, my husband always keeps his word." She saw the concern in his teary, soft brown eyes. "Hurry home now and fetch your wife; you must rush away to the west. To your relatives in Hannover, is it?"

The old watchman bowed and then disappeared into the darkness.

Ruth knew attempting to move the children in their weakened state following the measles would not be prudent.

Chapter 12

TENSION BUILDS FARTHER

Following Matthias's request to flee, uncertain of when the turmoil from the invasion of Germany would swoop over Schloss Prüzen, black shades were tightly stapled about every crevice on the windows, and the use of fire and voices was kept to a minimum. That Germany would lose the war hardly seemed in doubt any longer.

The Pommern border had officially fallen to the Russians besieging the countryside. The indications of what happened to a country in combat lay before them a few days ago: the horror, the destruction, the irrefutable losses of life, limb and body, the thousands of souls lost, never to be seen or heard from again. Germany's breadbasket and the access to the Baltic Sea port that other nations around Europe had coveted for aeons were lost. Germany had held control of this port since the time of the Vikings. Since then, the Bishops of Rome, the Teutonic Knights, and the countries of Denmark, Sweden, Poland, and Russia had been in hot pursuit by getting their stake into Pommern's rich earth, salt, and magnificent seaports along the Baltic.

Stepping into the light of the children's bedroom, Ruth was struck by the calmness surrounding the room with the lit candles revealing Ella, a handsome, tall woman, five feet seven inches, with a plump yet well-proportioned figure, reading bedtime stories to the children safely huddled under their fluffy, white, feather comforters. Ruth noticed that Ella knew of her presence. The maid brushed back her blond hair and halfway turned to Ruth, placed her forefinger over her lips to indicate all was well.

Back with the other two women, Ruth forced a smile. "Hitler promised us victory. Well, I guess that does not make any difference now."

"Follow me," Irene said, soon melting into the shadows, her voice full of sadness. "We will be attacked any moment, so follow me to a secret hiding place." Once at the back of the manor home, they arrived at the kitchen overlooking one of the numerous lakes left behind by the ice age.

Irene's husband's forefathers were exceptionally ingenious because they built a separate building to house the kitchen to prevent fires. Natural gas and electricity were added when the home and the kitchen were attached. Before then, people lived in fear of fire started by a careless kitchen attendant. That threat was now significantly reduced, so the two buildings were connected. In building the attachment, the castle owners determined hiding areas were a must since wars and famine in Pommern and Mecklenburg were the norm for decades. Bays for the family's precious belongings were constructed in several places along the hallway. One of the small coves was a hiding place for a cubby hole leading to a hidden room housing a shortwave radio.

Irene glanced at her two guests. She had been driven to the need for news. "I have a shortwave radio which receives stations forbidden in our country for many years." She beckoned for the others to follow. "Ladies, we must hurry if you wish to listen as badly as I do. You must help me push the left bronze antler off this stag's forehead." Irene pointed to the massive bronze ornament in the hall. "That will release a small opening where I can place my hand and pull the lever to unlatch a slit for us to enter." As Irene gave her instructions, the three women's hands lay on one another. "On the count of three, I would like you to push on my hands with much force."

Groans of hard effort echoed through the wide hallway. Their attempt was rewarded with the sound of bronze grinding on stone. To their astonishment, the locking mechanism sprang. Ruth and Anneliese smiled at Irene, and Ruth whispered, "It opened."

"Yes, we cannot waste a moment." Irene's voice dropped as Ruth and Anneliese inhaled deeply to make themselves thin enough to squeeze through the slight opening. "For the moment, do not step any further." Soon after, the racing of heavy metal chains clanging on metal pierced the darkness. A cold breeze flowed about Ruth's legs, drifting into her teal-orange and brown woollen skirt. Mustiness hung heavy about the area, and the rawness of the moment struck her. Behind her, a soft golden glow flickered from a kerosene lantern in Irene's shivering right hand. Then with the other, she beckoned Ruth and Anneliese to follow. Negotiating the fourteen steel steps was exceedingly awkward with only the dim light. The confinement of the crude metal treads did not suit them. In this uneasy silence, they found their footing, and in a rush, followed in Irene's footsteps. From above, an electric light burst into the darkness. The chamber was surprisingly large. In the dimness, Ruth could barely make out the room's contents containing a sturdy wooden table and four chairs.

No one spoke. Irene carefully made her way to a wooden shelf where a deck of cards and dried food were stored upon a five-foot-high shelf. There was a much-loved and tattered teddy bear with its left ear hanging down the frayed body that even the humblest of people would not recognise or wish to possess. The cards, foodstuffs and the bear remained on the shelf as Irene gazed lovingly at her toy. With a satisfied smile, Irene said, "My husband's grandfather wanted to be cunning in his thinking. To lure the trespasser to that side, a diversion of the playing cards, the bear and the dried food was used."

Tension Builds Farther

As much as Irene liked her guests, the family's classified information must remain concealed. She requested that the two women face the wall and cover their eyes while Irene skillfully moved to the opposite side of the room, giving her the security she needed. Tucking her frock between her knees, she knelt and used her forefingers in a fast-rhythmic combination of motions to press the spring open to reveal her hiding place on three wooden knotholes in the flooring space, pushed the wood aside, and yanked out a four-by-six-inch, chiselled, grey rock. Again, she used her nimble fingers underneath the area to spring open the compartment that housed the wireless.

"The SS rifled through the home on many occasions, but the soldiers did not discover our special place." Placing the black wireless from the concealed area on the small table in the room, Irene located the sought-after radio station, turned on the device, and began to rotate the knobs carefully. The three women leaned closer to hear the voice of an uneasy woman's warning announcing, "The Russians are advancing more rapidly than expected upon our Eastern German Fatherland." Gasps of dismay rang out in the small room. Grumbling reverberated from the cold room's wall when the shortwave transistor crackled with interference – nothing more could be heard. In frustration, Irene spun the black dials once more. Between static electricity intervals, snippets of news and mere phrases filled the air, some quiet, some broken. During these times the women held their breath with the anticipation of what news would come next.

The horrific, heart-wrenching radio news was that the Russian troops had penetrated Pommern and West Prussia, with the port city of Kolberg and the nearby city of Danzig falling at the beginning of March. With Klein Pobloth located between the cities, their beloved homeland was doomed. Ruth's fretful thoughts turned to her dear mother and two sisters, Elizabeth (Lilla) and Margret. Had Rudi and Dolores survived? What had become of their thirteenth-century manor? Had their home been burned to the ground? Would the artifacts of Rudi's ancient bloodline tracing back to 866 be lost? What about their dear night watchman, Pinnow, and his family?

Ruth's thoughts also turned to the many other good people she had known in the village: the Beulke family, members of which resided on the same plot of land for 600 years; the kind teacher Paul Fengler and his family; the numerous maids and household staff and all the proud citizens who called Klein Pobloth their home.

Ruth looked troubled, her mind riddled with questions and reeling in horror, pain and doubt. Ruth still could not digest torrents of thoughts that rapidly exploded about her parent's estate of Kempen and the inheritance of Ruth's dowry that she hoped to bring from the bank in Belgard. Lives mattered a great deal more than money and material goods. Nevertheless, Ruth could not help wondering about the eight million Deutsche Gold Bonds to be divided between Rudi and Anneliese's families that now were no more. The countless valuables:

Escaping the Russian Onslaught

the priceless life-sized portrait of Prince Heinrich, always a novelty in the grand salon, the antique furnishings, the family silver pieces handed down from Count Friedrich Emil von Zieten, son of General Hans von Zieten, who had advanced the Prussian Cavalry to victory time and again on behalf of Frederick the Great. What was to become of Ruth's family?

Anneliese's ear was closest to the receiver – a scream – without warning, her frame went limp and then slithered into a crumbled pile on the wooden floor. Irene and Ruth heard a muffled thump as Anneliese hit her head on the cold rock Irene had removed a few moments earlier.

Stunned by Anneliese's unexpected plunge, Ruth and Irene rushed to kneel at her side, quickly assessing her injuries in the glooming light. From the impact on the hard rock and flooring, Anneliese shivered uncontrollably. Her right cheek was beginning to redden and swell. To help Anneliese regain consciousness, the two other women patted her hands frantically. Several times, Anneliese moaned. Soon, her blue eyes were open, though glassy, and they followed Ruth's index finger as she slowly waved it in front of her sister-in-law's face.

As Anneliese attempted to hold her head upright, her tears flowed like waterspouts. Then she began to wheeze, cough and cry simultaneously, causing hiccups to erupt. No water or handkerchiefs were available to soothe her. Kicking and squirming, she wailed uncontrollably, unable to control herself. Sobbing hysterically, she whispered, "Ruth, can you find me a handkerchief?"

As was her habit, Ruth produced one from the cuff of her green sweater. As she slowly pulled out the white lace cloth caught in its holding, she was trapped in her emotions, unable to react quickly. Once again, she became acutely aware of her sister-in-law's sobbing voice that rose to a frenzy. "My mother? My poor mother? What will they do to her and my beloved Klein Pobloth?" She screamed out even louder. "What is to become of us? Where will we go from here?" Clutching Ruth's arm, she wailed, "What is to become of us, Ruth?"

When Ruth heard her name called out, she shifted her body to keep it from becoming rigid in the freezing cold. She had been distracted by her own grief, with her eyes half-closed and brimming with tears. Still stunned by the horrific news, Ruth wished that she could protest in such a way as Anneliese was allowing herself to do. Over the years, Ruth had moulded herself into a woman of strength, taking ownership of her reputation, and did not rely on anyone or anything but her self-esteem. It was beastly not to have the time Ruth wished to mourn in her own way. Her mouth tightened when she became aware of her surroundings and she turned to Anneliese again.

Momentarily, a frown played on her mouth, annoyed at the thought that she and Anneliese had been at odds with one another so often. Arguing constantly about the minor details while fleeing, they must now make the best of their relationship for much longer than anticipated. She mused grimly. *Calm down, relax.* Her eyes

Tension Builds Farther

half-closed from the sorrow of defeat in her heart, Ruth's mouth tightened. *Where are my husband, my mother, and my two sisters? Is my dear Kempen lost as Klein Pobloth is?* Ruth had been so engrossed in her own sorrows that she did not notice Anneliese could not rise from her frantic state. At first, Ruth felt little energy to aid in her sister-in-law's hysterical state.

Caught up in their own anguish, both women carefully studied and observed Anneliese for any signs of injury after her experience of dropping onto the cold floor. The damage was minor, and everything appeared in order. They looped their arms about Anneliese's waist and assisted her into the nearest walnut chair. A fountain of sorrow took hold again. Trapped in her grief, Anneliese was not prepared to continue such an arduous journey continuing to flee elsewhere. She leaned against Ruth who wished to cry out but could not.

Irene clutched the younger woman like her sister. Cautiously, she spoke, "From my understanding, your freight train was indeed one of the last trains able to travel to the west."

"Oh!" Ruth said, "God must have looked in our direction when our train took us to the west."

The three women slumped over in their chairs, arms holding their broken-down frames while they wailed openly. The darkness of the hidden room was an appropriate atmosphere for their grief. Buried in their concerns over their loved ones, the women could not comfort one another. Their secret places of sorrow were too deep. They were undone.

First, Irene's sobbing became silent. She looked up and met Ruth's eyes as Anneliese continued weeping and muttering uncontrollably.

Endless time passed when Irene suddenly spoke. Her voice was thick with tears. "Take as long as you need," she said. With grief in her eyes, she told them, "I will tend to the children." Nothing could be said to reassure anyone in the household at this moment. Irene slipped out of the room, leaving her dear, broken-hearted companions with their grief.

Ruth studied Anneliese. Despite their previous disagreements, her sister-in-law and the children were the only family she had left. In this horrible situation, they had to rely on each other. She stood from her chair and gathered Anneliese into her arms. The two women wept openly in each other's embrace for some time.

Chapter 13

URGENCY BUILDS

In the days following her first letter to Rudi, Ruth had found it difficult not to slip into apathy or despair as she cared for her sick children. She sat in the same chair she had used earlier in the week and penned another letter.

Feldpost
Für Hans-Rudolf Meißner Wiesbaden
Absender: R Meißner
Schloss Prüzen by Güstrow
7 March 1945

Dearest Hans-Rudolf,
Hopefully, you received my last mail. I am here with Anneliese and all the children. What became of Mother and the Klötziners? I do not know. We only have that which we could carry. The children are sick. Hopefully, they will be better soon. On the train, they became cold through and through. Hopefully, they are not too ill. Anneliese was surprisingly very lovely. We must continue. We want to reach Abensdorf as quickly as we can. In the heat of today, things are not very pleasant for me.
Always your Ruth

In these turbulent times, it seemed miraculous that Ruth and her family had found refuge at Schloss Prüzen, with its vast dining room housing a gigantic table that the family put to good use to entertain the children. Covered in white bed sheets, the table became a secluded cave, which the children could customise to engage their active imaginations. To keep their minds off their country's plight, Ruth, Anneliese, Irene and Ella took turns busying themselves with the children under the large table. The so-called cavern served several purposes: to protect them, keep them in the dark, shield their sensitive eyes and keep them occupied during their bout with measles. The children's tortuous itches were painful to watch. However, the four were not old enough to understand how to keep their tiny fingernails from scratching at the sores the measles triggered. Thus, small craters of infection covered much of their bodies. Soothing warm Epsom salt baths were given to the children several times daily. The four youngsters were eager to slip and slide in the warm waters that, over time, helped to heal their wounds.

The spring winds blew fiercely throughout the day, occasionally dislodging the blackout shades from the ancient frames. Irene asked Ruth and Anneliese to help double-check that all the home windows were darkened securely. The women moved through the long, wide hallway adorned with family portraits and passed several walls lined with family portraits comparable to that of Klein Pobloth. Because the home was also a knighthood estate, red deer and Hirsch antlers adorned the lunar grandfather clock and the hallway.

Irene studied Ruth as she fingered the thick stone walls decorated with heavily cream-coloured wallpaper. "Yes, our home was heavily bombarded during the Thirty-Year War." Irene glanced at Ruth, who was interested in history of all kinds. "The wallpaper, with its oversized motif, reveals seam after seam. You can see where the wallpaper covered the cannonballs. The walls have endured such events over the years. Time and again, the shelled-out area needed to be repaired by the new pieces placed over them. I must note to remove it after the war is over and make other repairs. All the layers of wallpaper on top of each other can cause a fire hazard."

Their footing was unsure as they climbed the steep stairway leading to the gymnasium. When they rose to the third level, the wall straight ahead was devoted to armour, the various daggers, swords and dirks worn by the officers in her family. Ruth was pleased to see the workout equipment the children could explore when they were up and about again. Indeed, several of the elongated casements were undone. Repairs had been made with a long wooden stick with a brass hook on the end of the pole. Anneliese leaned heavily on one of the two pummel wooden horses and began to weep hysterically again. When Ruth saw her despair, she went to lean beside her, taking her hand and talking softly to Anneliese. Ruth was wise enough to understand that nothing could be done for now. Frustrated, Ruth soothed, "My dear sister-in-law, you must calm yourself. It is unhealthy to cry this way – the news has told us nothing – it will be all right."

Confused and troubled, Anneliese said, "I will try to stop. In this cold atmosphere, I was only faint momentarily." She smiled at Ruth. "Thank you for the comfortable haven you found for my family. Where would we be without your steady confidence?"

The caring moment brought Irene to their side. "I checked all the windows and made the necessary repairs."

Anneliese looked at Irene and said, "I will be all right," but as soon as the words left her mouth, Anneliese closed her eyes and began to cry again.

Ruth began to descend the steep staircase. Turning to Anneliese, she realised she would be holding their relationship together. Ruth's gentle voice encouraged her. "We should go back and check on the children."

The women moved swiftly as they entered a dismal, musty atmosphere in the elegantly appointed women's salon where they joined Irene. Occasionally, a hacking cough could be heard echoing down the long corridor. Both mothers worried about their children, although they knew their unrest would quiet in a few days.

Gazing into the bright room, Ruth felt her worries from a moment ago replaced by the memories of happy times she had spent in her parents' Kempen Estate. The glossy white painted woodwork drew her back to the dining room in her childhood home. In her youth, the window boxes surrounding her mother's large, elongated windows were filled with crimson cyclamen every year. The quiet moment passed, only to be replaced by sorrow. Ruth grabbed onto one of the tufted velvet couches the same colour as her mother's delightful plants had been. Cautiously stepping forward, Ruth stopped to dab her wet red nose, drawing a kerchief from the cuff of her green cardigan sweater.

An eerie calm hung in the air as Irene drew the blackout covers more securely over the many rooms' elongated windows. Once back with the two women, Irene rubbed her cold hands together and smiled uncomfortably. "I can still provide heat and keep the early spring breezes out, but who knows how long the fuel will last."

The two tormented women silently slipped into the French-style kitchen. A gentle smile played on Irene's lips as she entered the room. "With Ella sleeping in the same room with the children, they are snuggled fast in their beds. Bless her heart, Ella told me earlier that she was happy to see after the children so we could do whatever we wished." Irene bobbed a deep curtsy. Smiling, "I bring my last bottle of Goldschlager and three shot glasses. Here, Ruth and Anneliese, it is time to get tipsy to rid ourselves of the worries we have no control over. The cinnamon-flavoured schnapps with golden flakes will slide down our throats easily so we can think of the perfect Pommern no longer under Germany's power."

Chapter 14

THE PERFORMANCE

Both mothers marvelled at the children's resilience since they became ill. For days, emotions were tossed hither and thither while the children could not suppress their misery. By 14 March, giggling could be heard from the children's bedroom, a testament to their strength and resilience that inspired hope in the hearts of the two women.

Two birthday parties were in order, one for Susanne and one for Hans-Georg. To add to the celebration of the end of measles, the children were eager to show off their talents. A performance of *Little Red Riding Hood* was in order. The joy and laughter that filled the room as the children brought the story to life with their performance was a balm to the soul, the evening passing in a spirit of merriment which eased the stress.

A stylish fashion show would be presented before the children's evening performance in the theater setting. An unexpected reward was when Irene offered her guests the chance to browse her Hollywood closet to choose one of the many Hunter's Ballgowns draped in her long-unused closets. Ruth decided on an enchanting green chiffon. Anneliese stunned the audience in her dazzling black gown, while Irene's yellow-lime green chiffon pantsuit wowed the audience.

A Victrola played in the background as Ella assisted the children in dressing up for the upcoming event. The boys were dressed in older uniforms fastened in the back with clothespins. Ruth smiled at how ridiculous yet charming the boys looked in their Prussian Blue uniforms while five safety pins tightened Susanne's fine red taffeta and white lace gown in the back, as she pranced about the room, careful not to trip on the skirt of her long dress.

Irene led the two women to her bedchamber and dressing area and asked them to pick out evening wear to delight the children. Anneliese looked divine in a satin floor-length black gown and long white gloves. Ruth chose a chiffon dress with a flowing, cream-coloured, floor-length skirt. Irene was stunning in a yellow-green chiffon dress, short-sleeved top and matching flared britches, and ensembled by crimson, elbow-length leather gloves, a cocktail hat and trendy shoes.

As the women strolled into the dining room, Ella wound the Victrola, bringing the best of Chopin's music to life. The children cheered as they watched the show.

In the makeshift theatre, Ruth noticed that the gold blanket they had taken from Klein Pobloth was used as a curtain to hide the stage.

Joyful Susanne took on the role of the author of her own version of *Little Red Riding Hood*. As the eldest in the group, she cheerfully directed the other children in the little performance. Little Dorlies laughed as she watched the other children perform. Her giggles became infectious, causing the onlookers to giggle despite themselves. They smiled with satisfaction as they watched the show. Happiness filled the house once more.

Days after the successful performance, hide-and-seek became their favourite game. The children did not realise how important the skill of creative hiding would become.

Chapter 15

THE LETTERS

Awakened by a ring at the door, the women sprang to their feet. With Irene leading the way to the door her good farmworker had used weeks earlier, she peered through to see and greet the first teenage postman to arrive after the German army had stopped fighting. Turning to the other women with a confused smile, she said, "The postman handed me two letters for Ruth."

Ruth studied the envelopes Irene held in her hand and recognised her mother's handwriting. Her worries turned into joy, and Ruth rushed to Irene's side with an enormous smile. "For me? For me?" Ruth's girlish giggles turned her eyes into streams of tears. Waxen, quivering, she eagerly snatched the envelopes and clenched them in her trembling fist. She gazed at the dirty yellow paper. Her knees trembled as she found the nearest chair. Tears of joy flowed from her eyes. Anneliese and Irene were caught up in the moment, also happily emotional.

To catch a few moments of solitude, Ruth rushed to her room. When she returned, she waved her hand above her head, and her voice cracked. Her faltering words could hardly be heard through her quivering lips. "On 11 March, my sister Lilla Witte posted this note. She tells me how happy she is to hear that we are out. Lilla had still been working on their estate near Körlin. She and her cook Frau Zander fled together. Unfortunately, when they were by Stettin, they were separated among the masses escaping the heavy bombing the city endured. Lilla's group was able to catch a ride on a farm wagon passing their way. For the moment, she is welcome on the farm of the man who owns the wagon. She is hoping to find her husband, Hermann Witte, soon. Lilla informs me our mother is safe with Tante Louise in Peine."

"Ruth... Anneliese, come into the salon. I will send for Ella, and she can put the kettle on."

Elated by the other letter posted on 16 March, Ruth began to weep openly again. "My darling mother wrote that she received the note I posted the night before we fled, informing her of my plans. With it in mind, in her heart, she knew that my three children and I were safe with you, her beloved friend Irene. Mutti also tells me that Lilla was worried about my whereabouts."

Escaping the Russian Onslaught

Ruth gazed at the other two women, calmly trying to sip their hot water. Her attempt at partaking of the liquid ended up in a coughing fit. Regaining her composure, Ruth continued. "Can you believe the note did not take but a few days to reach the Schloss." Ruth dabbed her red nose. "Mutti tells me that she had been travelling to visit friends living in a Berlin suburb. The friends were not even out of the Berlin train station when they heard the bad news about Germany's border being breached. They rushed back to where Mutti sat on a bench, waiting for her train. The friends were so concerned about Mutti's safety that they turned her around and insisted she take the next train that travelled towards the west to her relatives."

As Ruth's complexion became ashen once more, her spine tingled, sending shivers up her back. She breathed heavily. "I cannot believe Mutti's bravery. While Vati was alive, she could barely manage to fend for herself. Mutti was always so foolishly feminine and selfishly playing the martyr, always having headaches or about to faint. All she wished was for her and Vati to move back to Peine. Even though Vati gave her a beautiful estate near Belgard, she disliked country life."

Ruth turned to Anneliese and said, "Now listen to this. My dear mother's flight took her through the heavy bombing the United States Army was hurling on Berlin. Heavy bombing by the Russian army had already destroyed the bridges over the Speer River. To escape the terrifying bombing, her train was forced to zig-zag to find a bridge that was not bombed. The train trip was long, but she made it to Peine, to her relief. What was always a few hours' journey took her from Friday until Tuesday."

A tear dropped over Ruth's pale cheeks. Quickly, Irene folded Ruth's hand in hers. Ruth became somewhat defensive and looked at her friend and said, "I will be all right. I must be strong. Thank heaven my mother is alive." Distracted by her relief, Ruth found breathing difficult, so she pushed her brown hair away from her eyes and hurried on in a dismayed tone. "No food, water, or toilet paper, even after Mutti arrived at my Tante Louise's house in Peine." Ruth lifted her head to her friends as if the two concerned women could help. Brokenhearted, she said, "On arriving at my auntie's, Mutti must have been exhausted.

"Anneliese and Irene, we are lucky to be from a farming community and not in the city. When Mutti wrote the letter, food shortages were becoming problematic, with the infrastructure already broken, and no deliveries were made to the grocery stores. No flour was in the bakeries, and no food stamps were available. How will she survive? Hitler and his heinous henchmen's demonic determination became nothing more than savage bestiality!"

Suddenly, Ruth felt less in control than ever before and began to tremble heavily. She wondered how she could help her poor mother. "I am ice cold."

Irene embraced Ruth by wrapping her arms tightly around her friend.

The Letters

Choking on her words, Ruth said, "My precious mother is always hungry."

During the family's current confinement at the Schloss, Ruth's resentful feelings toward Anneliese had withered as she learned how to deal with her nemesis of so many years. Their common cause of battling the children's ever-growing fevers helped them learn how to cope.

The four youngsters were still weary from the aftereffects of the measles. When Ruth heard the grandfather clock in the hall chime four and a half times, she realised that the children needed to be sent to bed. Eagerly, each child stepped into the large copper bathtub full of soothing hot Epson salt. Ella suggested they play pirates. The children were happy with a strong yell of ho-ho-ho when she told them to place a washcloth over one of their eyes, so they pretended to travel over the great Baltic Sea. She created waves with the sleeves of her blouse rolled as high on her arms as possible and swished the hot water back and forth until it splashed up and down in the tub, practically spilling over the edge. Waiting for them on electrical warming bars were fluffy white towels hung in three neat rows.

After their bath, with the greatest tenderness, Ella dabbed at their sores ever so slightly until Susanne, Hans-Georg, Dorlies and Klaus-Dieter were as dry and comfortable as possible. Ella asked each child to raise their arms, standing in a row as if at attention. With their tiny bodies wrapped in preheated white terrycloth towels, she gently helped pull their nightgowns over their heads as they dropped the towels. Once in their bed, hot cream of wheat cooked with raisins was served on an antique mahogany bed tray. Ruth and Anneliese kissed their children's foreheads one by one, tucked them snugly under their fluffy white comforters, and then closed the door behind them.

Down the same hallway, the three women tiptoed past Ella's bedchamber. Ruth noticed the maid's kerosene lantern flickering underneath her bedroom door, turned to the other two women, and asked, "Since I received my letters, I wonder if Ella is writing messages to her relatives?"

Ella built a fire in the Calacatta marble walk-in fireplace on the far west side of the grand salon. When Irene entered the room, all she needed to do was put a long-stemmed match to set the flame ablaze. One by one, Anneliese, Irene and Ruth plopped themselves onto the two crimson sofas in the enormous Lady's salon. Feeling constantly growing, gnawing despair, sleep would not come to the three women. With their hands each wrapped around a hot cup of makeshift chamomile tea, they chatted into the wee hours of the night. Many an evening, the three women found their favourite symphony recording and wound the gramophone to distract themselves from grim thoughts about Germany's future.

Exceedingly proud of her heritage, Anneliese stared at them and reminisced. "Did you hear our brave family friend Max Schmeling, the heavyweight champion of 1930 through 1932, served in the German Air Force as a paratrooper

Fallschirmjäger after he disagreed with the Führer? I hope he has come through the war without being harmed. We were immediately impressed with his courage when we heard of his assignment with the paratroop unit."

Irene added softly, "Yes, all of Germany cringed when, in 1938, Joe Louis, the black boxer, won the fight. The two rivals boxed at Yankee Stadium in New York City, with some 70,000 fans watching the talented American win his title. From my recollection, within our social circles, it is said that the two boxers were great pals. Therefore, Hitler sent Max to be a paratrooper. We heard much of the fight on our shortwave. It was a very disappointing evening for the Germans, and Hitler never forgave our brave champion. On another note…"

Since some of what Irene conveyed was news to the two women, they hung onto every word. "Having the radio has been extremely informative. We've enjoyed listening to the premiere of the fabulous American film *Gone with the Wind*. We heard the voices of such motion picture stars as the devilishly handsome Clark Gable and the gorgeous British actress Vivien Leigh.

"We were surprised to listen to the sophisticated film actor Robert Taylor during his interview at the premiere. I do not remember the exact words, but he said something like, 'The film premiere was as exciting as watching the 1938 boxing match between Max Schmeling and Joe Louis.' He termed the boxing match as the sporting event of the twentieth century."

Admiring her access to the outside world of the film industry, a world now out of their grasp, the two women studied Irene. The legalities of being found out by mentioning something fantastic, such as British or American movies and movie idols, were out of the question during the height of the Nazi Regime.

Irene could see their interest in her trivial lecture, so she was happy to continue. "I always enjoyed it when my husband's father could smuggle wonderful American and British films to the Schloss. The family would rejoice in the wonders of the opportunity to view the silver screen presented to us. Sadly, it had to be within our family. If someone had found us out, my father would most definitely have been arrested by the SS and then shot without as much as a trial."

Ruth, who was always interested in the goings-on of books and motion pictures, said, "I do not know if you recall that Max Schmeling and Anny Ondra, the German motion picture actress, were married in 1933. Anny starred in the distinguished British director Alfred Hitchcock's *Blackmail* in 1929. Her first talking picture was unacceptable because of her thick accent so Hitchcock had her voice dubbed, much to Anny's dismay. Sadly, after the talkies came out, Anny was no longer used in the British film industry. However, Anny did have a brilliant marriage and career. Both Max and Anny visited Klein Pobloth on many occasions."

"Yes, Max was one of my mother's favourite hunting buddies," exclaimed Anneliese. "He enjoyed the vast, ancient woodlands at our estate. To my recollection,

The Letters

after Max hunted with Mutter, he affectionately called her Tante Dolores. Max enjoyed his visits at Klein Pobloth so much that I recall my mother telling me that Max purchased his Estate Ponickel on the rim of the Trebliner Forest."

Ruth knew issues of interest must always be about what Anneliese knew. Ruth thought she would have the last word: "I only met Max once. You know, Rudi could tame most animals. I recall how much fun Rudi had telling the story about Max holding his hand in the air when he attempted to feed Rudi's pet wild boar, Wally."

Anneliese interjected, "Yes, Wally was our family pet."

"When Rudi and I moved to Klein Pobloth, Susanne was still in diapers." Ruth giggled. "I had wooden clothespins in my apron. On my way to the clothesline, the clothespins rattled, and without warning, Wally came charging at me because he thought I had walnuts in my apron. Wally scared me to death, although the huge black boar would not hurt a fly."

Both Anneliese and Irene were able to have a much-deserved laugh. Irene chuckled as she pulled her hair through her fingers. "Yes, I remember you telling me about that."

"I also wonder what happened to our national hero, whom the Nazi Party labelled their 'puppet.' I cannot conceive how humiliating this must have been for poor Max," Anneliese said as she choked back tears. "With Max's fighting spirit, I am almost certain he made it safely through the war."

"As you recall from the many letters that I sent out expressing my grief, my dearest brother Joachim gave up his life in Russia," Ruth said, "while my nephew, Walter, Lilla's son, gave up his life for the *Luftwaffe,* in Germany's air defence near Paris. The hollowness I feel in the pit of my stomach is indescribable."

Embracing their enthralling chats, Ruth added, "Your explanation of the American films and actors has been fascinating. Adding your delightful stories placed me in a different frame of mind. It was unexpectedly therapeutic. For now, we must leave this dream world behind us."

Ruth added wistfully, "Many years earlier, I believe there was a motion picture called '*Rosenblüte auf dem Heidegrrab.*' "Roses Bloom on the Heather Grave" was about the family Schläger from around Peine near Hanover. Peine is where my parents had their first home, and a street named Schläger is in the city because the men were known to perform in Chamber Concerts for the United Kingdom's George I and through the later years, George IV. Years ago, a story circulated that a beautiful Schläger girl was the heroine who was shown to die in the film. I have often wondered if the story might be part of our family's history. Unfortunately, I will never know." Ruth sat in deep thought before sitting up straight and added, "I need to see after the children."

The women rose from the luxurious crimson damask divan and returned to where the children played in their make-believe world of *St George and the*

Dragon. One child giggled more intently than the next. Ella soon saw the women's amused expressions and recognised they were also having a much-deserved, relaxing moment. Ella offered to care for them longer. A soaking hot bath would allow the three women to ease their emotionally drained bodies and enjoy another hot cup of tea. Ruth, Anneliese and Irene were more than pleased at her offer to occupy the children longer.

Staying in the countryside at the Schloss was more fortunate than anyone could conceive. Fearing the military forces would attack, the women customarily rose before dawn and spent time beside the shortwave radio. The communication was not clear or coherent, more akin to bumblebee buzzing. Snippets of what came across were that the Russians had marched through the Baltic cities and Rostock and were charging onward to Berlin. The British were in the Hamburg area and the Americans were fanned out in Western Europe.

Hearing the radio reports, Ruth, Anneliese and Irene stood silent. There would be no triumph, no going back to their husbands or homes for a long time. Lost in shame, they understood that in 1945, Germany was swiftly slammed and quickly defeated, being butchered from all sides by every country that Hitler and his Nazi government had invaded, digested and then spat out the other end. After his stint in Russia, Rudi had foretold that the German people would suffer the consequences of originally believing in their Führer. As the cities were flattened in enormous numbers, the German soldiers, seeing no way out, retreated until there was no place to hide.

As uncertainty hung over them, the shelter Irene could give the family became their harbour. Still, they constantly pondered what might befall them if they remained a few days too long or if waiting out the surges would be their best bet. Then, perhaps all would return to normal, and the family would travel back to Klein Pobloth. Surely, being among this current chaos would be hell on earth.

It became a contest between the women to occupy the children during the rainy days of early spring. When the sun appeared, they wished to romp in the colourful green areas about the Schloss Prüzen, hunting for the many snowdrops, crocus, tulips, primroses and white asparagus. No matter the time or the weather, the fear of the waves of black wasps flying overhead, snipers, or heavy enemy equipment was ever-present. Thus, Irene and Ella kept vigil over an area close to the castle and lakes for any signs of unusual movement far and wide. The few times available to them outside, Ruth and Anneliese played outdoor games with the four innocent children. If the youngsters followed the strictest rules by staying in their restricted space, Ruth and Anneliese chased them until all collapsed into giggles.

The Easter holiday was early, on 1 April 1945. Everyone hunkered around the large dining room table at noon for a delightful casual Easter party.

The Letters

Everything was prepared to perfection to present an atmosphere of normality, as had become the custom. Old newspapers made into Easter egg chains were hung about the dining room to ensure a happy holiday. When foodstuffs became scarce, the community ate the estate's chickens. Irene surprised the group with a canned ham on Easter morning. While Irene prepared the ham, Ruth surveyed the landscape and skies before creeping out just after dawn to pick the fresh white asparagus.

The various types of tea the women enjoyed had run out weeks ago, and the farther into April, the more they felt the strength of the war's interference.

Days later in the grand old kitchen, the three women fidgeted at the warm rustic walnut antique table, unable to relish each other's companionship as they had when Ruth and her family first arrived. At the end of April, Irene offered to put on the kettle so the three could drink hot water.

Drawing her fingers across the table's surface, Ruth allowed them to dip into the long indentations where years of action from the wooden rolling pin created gentle slopes, and soon her forefinger sailed to where the sizeable cutting knives had left a splinter, and one snagged her forefinger, causing it to bleed. Wiping the blood off with her handkerchief, Ruth contemplated the welfare of the children and concluded, "The children have outgrown their clothing, and Anneliese, our clothes are almost worn out. The weather is in our favor, so tomorrow we will make our way farther to the west, where hopefully the bombing will decrease."

She rose awkwardly and then lumbered to one of the lead windows overlooking the Schloss' vast, once well-kept grounds. She pulled her finger across the glass restlessly. Her eyes caught a glimpse of the gravel road just beyond the tree-lined lane. The street was packed with a river of refugees who had not been on this road weeks earlier.

Anneliese decided to join her at the window. "I am beginning to doubt whether we should leave our haven or take a chance, to meld into the masses to make our way past the onslaught of humanity I now see coming."

"Yes… tomorrow. From the bombing, the Russians are close to Güstrow. We must leave at daybreak. Anything else would be disastrous," Ruth answered.

Anneliese smiled sheepishly. "However, before we get on our way, Irene, can I beg one more soaking bath before we go?"

"Without question, a well-deserved long hot bath is important for you."

Their new travel plans provoked Ruth's anxiety about going through the massive muddle by daybreak. Immediately, she searched for a small grey piece of paper and a pencil and made herself as comfortable as possible at the small desk she had used earlier. *What if there was no way for Rudi to receive my last note? I am so weary. I can scarcely write anything, but I must write to let Rudi know our whereabouts. I want to tell Rudi I miss him and need him with me, but I cannot allow my guard to slip.* Ruth began to write.

> *Feldpost*
> *Obergefreiter Hans-Rudolf Meißner*
> *Wiesbaden*
> *Absender: R. Meißner Prüzen Mecklenburg*
> *1 May 1945*
>
> *Dear Rudi,*
> *We are out! It is done by the skin of our teeth and against the grain. We do not know anything else. We left with the children, Anneliese and Klaus, and we also looked like we were bedraggled. As always, I am crossing my fingers that you will still come.*
> *Always your Ruth*

Her heart pounded as she held her precious mail tucked securely in her small palm and rushed to find a place to post her letter – it was too late to post the note at the end of the lane. Her first attempt proved successful, as she found a young neighbourhood teen willing to help her, hoping that above all else, her beloved Rudi would somehow receive the gift of this letter.

Chapter 16

BYWAYS

As they left the Schloss, Ruth and Anneliese considered themselves among the lucky refugees. Before the family left, Irene described how pleasant the visit had been for her. Being the only one left in the large home did not suit her. If the Americans or the Russians did not destroy her beloved home, she hoped to take in refugees in the future. Irene drove the family to the road nearby with her last drops of petrol. She waited with Ruth and her family until they could finally hitch a ride with German soldiers heading west towards Pötenitz, where the family hoped to stop and rest.

The group hoisted their few belongings onto the small green army truck passing by. Their feeling of peace disappeared as the signs of danger encompassed them, observing how fast the destruction of their beloved country was occurring

Hopefully, fleeing would give the family the security they longed for. Would they be lost to history? Away from the castle began the next battle for them. They must face heightened danger as they escaped. The roads were filled with thousands of women and children attempting to find a haven anywhere away from the attackers. The family soon discovered no law and order existed after Germany fell, with looters lurking in every corner, and there was no outside communication with the rest of the world other than hearsay from the folks who were also fleeing. No governmental system was in place, nor was a reliable railroad system. There was no way to get food. No crops could be transported around the country, no banks, no businesses and no telephones, and money was worthless even if you had it. People did not trust the people they saw next to them. Would life be worth living after the women and children were savagely raped in the chaos? Their physical and moral ecosystem, artwork, history, and the world of antiquity would be lost. The war was dismantling the universe they knew.

Since the family left Schloss Prüzen, they were in such tight conditions in the back of the truck it did nothing to diminish their anxiety as they entered into an area strewn with dead soldiers and refugees. Ruth knew the chance of coming out of this horrendous war unscathed was unlikely. Further westward, the horrifying carnage led the group into a panic-driven state that turned into hysteria. Thus, as time progressed, the two women became more reliant on one another when decisions needed to be made.

Escaping the Russian Onslaught

The freight truck accepted small pieces of luggage, plus only one backpack per person. Trapped inside the green canvas truck bed, crammed like sardines into the small space, dry with thirst, trying desperately to escape among the dirty smell of unwashed humanity was not as degrading the second time they were underway.

The family was running short of water in their knapsacks, and the dried milk, a small loaf of rye bread, hard salami and hard cheese from Irene's home were beginning to run out. Ruth cringed inwardly as she watched her people struggle. Somehow, she would manage as she always had in coming up with a few food scraps. To convince the children, let alone the young soldiers, could become challenging. Ruth raised her chin slightly to help recall Rudi's warning, "Depending on the food you have left, try not to eat bread. Bread will make you hungrier than you were before." *Oh, how I miss Rudi.*

Ruth's desperation dissipated when she saw Hans-Georg and Dorlies sleeping in a spoon position, covering their ears with their tiny coats. Susanne was curled up next to Klaus-Dieter at her feet, covering their ears with the gold blanket from the breeze the moving truck created. The image tugged at her heart, so Ruth closed her eyes. Suddenly, she was desperate to see Rudi's handsome face peering out from under his brown Fedora hat, to laugh at his silliness, hear his infectious chuckle, and savour his comforting body that filled her with the spirit of his being. When she had seen Rudi the last time, he was on leave. He had gazed into her eyes and said, "Ruth, I hope you know how much I love you." He had suddenly clutched her tightly, caressing her before drawing her close again. "Meine kleine Mutti, I promise I will return to you and my children." Rudi's devotion to her and his family was beyond anything she had ever known, and she knew his words were true. She could see his love for her in his brilliant, azure, blue eyes that caused shivers to run down her. Her emotions were threatening her bravery. She choked back tears, becoming alert again only when she heard her sister-in-law's voice.

Anneliese sniffed. "Say what you will, but I would rather be lying comfortably under my *Federbetten* reading a good romance novel." She smiled as if a fuzzy white kitten was trying to hide under her feather comforter, hoping to have snuggled about her.

Wryly smiling back, Ruth joked, "Ja, in your dreams. Who knows if life will ever be comfortable again? You can put that purring smile under your hat and keep it there until the time comes when you can fulfil your dreams." Ruth smiled and then teasingly said, "Well, at least not all of our humour has gone, but we cannot allow ourselves to dwell on the past."

"What in the world is happening now?" Ruth questioned as the engines made a loud screaming sound.

Shifting its gears, the truck screeched. Hearing the eerie sound of rainwater hissing and the screaming on the wet road caused their chatter to halt. Presently, the freight vehicle came to an abrupt standstill, steam exploded from the engine, and the doors of the freight truck flung open. Within seconds, roaring crowds from the other wagons made their way to where Ruth and her family huddled.

The heavy bombers could be heard before they were seen. One of the soldiers riding in the rear opened the green canvas flap. "I think it is the damn Russians. Maybe these beasts are British! There is no place to hide! We will all be killed!" As the truck wobbled from the blast, all within began to scream. Feeling gutted and helpless, everyone within plunged to the truck's floor. The train tracks were set ablaze a short distance away from the truck. The blasted heat curled them up and twisted them, destroyed by the British bombers. Everyone in the vicinity was suffering from the British war machine.

Horrifying sounds of gunshots could be heard closer to the truck. Tanks in the background rapidly fired machine gunshots, and bazooka firing could be heard. Word passed down the truck quickly as a harsh voice ordered, "Everyone – take your belongings – out!" The soldiers fled like rats to escape their inevitable iron cage from the British army invading the area, shoving away every German citizen to the side as if they were raw meat, ready to be cooked and devoured in the aftermath.

The family group was concerned about their safety, not realising the soldiers were angrily fuming. They listened to one soldier's cry, "You might find shelter here in Pötenitz. Get out! From here on out, you are on your own. British troops are about to pour into the town to pound the German soldiers into the ground."

The trucks were stuffed to the brim, with the soldiers and Ruth's family descending into the rainstorm with their meagre belongings. Death was all around them. From above, shadows covered the ground. Ruth looked up to see thousands of white canopies carrying British paratroopers landing. They were engulfing the area around Pötenitz. How long before these soldiers found Ruth's family? As the Russians were known to do, the Brits would destroy and annihilate everything in their path. However, they were more lenient with people.

Moving briskly, the two women hurried their children away from the deadly, deafening bombing. They must escape the screaming masses and find shelter for the perpetually frightened, hungry children. They must find a place somewhere to build a small fire and then find water to boil for drinking and washing their underclothes. Somewhere out of harm's way, somewhere to lay their weary bodies. Hiding places like these were few and far between, and all around them, flames sprang up from gasoline, and shards of debris falling like snowflakes created heaps of rubbish.

Dusk was already hanging low, with the night skies ready to burst forth with more horrors. Ruth suddenly realised that Anneliese and Klaus-Dieter were not at her side. Ruth's children shook at her side, but the others were nowhere in sight. She scanned the nearest burned shrubs… nothing… panic struck. They must be somewhere. She could not lose them now. Ruth must stay with her children, and attempting to find Anneliese's whereabouts was too dangerous. A wind stirred

Escaping the Russian Onslaught

around her small family, causing cold shivers to run down their soaked bodies. Their clothing and knapsacks were beyond recognition. The family was out of food and drinking water. Now, having Anneliese and Klaus-Dieter gone added to their anxiety.

Distraught, Ruth could hear whispering a few yards behind her. As abruptly as the bombing began, it subsided enough to allow Ruth to turn about to get a better view of her surroundings. "There you are… there you are… are you safe?"

Crawling as if they were animals clinging to the wet earth, Anneliese and Klaus-Dieter made their way to where the others were crouched. Once they arrived, Ruth smiled. "I thought we had lost both of you, which could not have been acceptable in my mind. To lose our homes is one thing – but losing each other is entirely different."

Ruth said in a low voice, "Anneliese, nothing surprises me any longer. We are on our own once again."

Anneliese was so overwrought that she became hysterical. "You must not start screaming now," Ruth pressed her lips together in annoyance and shook Anneliese's shoulders to rid her of her continual explosive anxiety breakouts. Against her better judgement, she added grimly, "I suggest you find us a roof for over our heads, and I will mind the children."

Anneliese, swollen with anger, turned her head away. Her body grew rigid. She was angry at Ruth for speaking to her in such a manner. Anneliese sniffed and began to look for the best place to start her search. She turned her head to either side, and then, she made her way through the unfamiliar town and was back in five minutes. With a proud grin, she beckoned Ruth and the children to follow her.

With a quizzical smile, Ruth indicated the youngsters to follow them. She and Anneliese gathered their few belongings and trudged on. Feeling the sharp pangs of her weariness, Ruth rubbed the small of her back and stroked the tears away from her elder daughter's grimy cheeks. Their mother wished she could hug them, but there was no time for such indulgence. Ruth's right hand cupped her daughter's back to push her in the proper direction. "Remember, Susanne and Hans-Georg, hang on tight to one another. I have Dorlies tucked under my arm." Exhausted, the knapsack slung over her other shoulder, Ruth dragged the small tan suitcase along the ground.

They ducked their heads down as low as possible to avoid the heavy shelling and the heat from the flames springing up all around them. The family zigzagged through scorched bodies of children and women of all ages… locals or refugees… there was no discrimination. By the end of the day, this family could be dead, also. The stink was sickening. Shards of glass, red brick, black slate tiles from dwellings, and flames surrounding them. Beside her, Ruth could hear Hans-Georg gagging. Turning to him, she saw that her son had closed his eyes to block out the terrible scene.

A few steps away from the carnage, Ruth looked up amid the chaos to see a charming Pfafwerk house standing alone as if it were the perfect place for them.

Proud of herself for finding such a treasure, Anneliese bit her lip. "Ruth, this is it! This is where we can rest before moving on. What do you think?"

Ruth studied the three-story home. "These people must have fled when the horrendous bombing happened. It looks empty. You are right, Anneliese. We must seize this opportunity, somewhere to hide from the British attackers. We will be lucky if they are the British soldiers, not the robbing bands of thieves that we were warned about."

Ruth placed her forefinger over her mouth and said, "Shh, everyone." Still shivering and shaking from fear, the group became mute. Timidly, Ruth edged open the hand-carved wooden door of the entrance. Ruth froze. Her heart leaped, and her stomach jolted as grit won over. The planks creaked under her feet as she walked over the living room floor.

Klaus-Dieter giggled, regaining his emotions. Ruth said, "Yes, my dear nephew, I know what that sounds like, and I assure you that I am innocent on all counts."

He replied, "I don't believe you, Tante Ruth." The child erupted into giggles once more.

Smiling at the youngsters, she said, "I am happy I could make you find something to laugh about."

She turned to Anneliese, "Yes, it seems abandoned. You settle the children, and I'll explore the rest of the house." Upstairs, she found a clean kitchen and studied the small area. *Where are these poor people now? They could be among those we passed a moment ago, but now there was no way of telling.*

She found an oil lamp, two bluestone plates, and two small stone bowls on the kitchen table. Ruth placed her small finger into one of the small bowls, picked up a few kernels, and placed them on her tongue. "Hmmm, salt. It will help anything taste decent, that is, if we find something to sprinkle it on." Some type of black spice was still evident in the other bowl on the left of the table lamp. "Nice, pepper will help also. Now let me see what else I can find?" The sharp smell of pepper made Ruth's stomach cramp from hunger. She could not remember when she had eaten last. *Yes, the soldiers passed around their rations, so we had a bite just before we needed to abandon the truck. How can the children survive on this type of diet?* Further searching the kitchen, she knew their nutrition would have to come from rummaging through the barren cupboards.

She studied the garden beyond the kitchen window. Looking closer, Ruth saw a well and a pump house. Hopefully, she could find fresh water there. The children would understand, so she turned to Susanne. "Children, sit on the kitchen floor. Then, Susanne will help you count the black round knot holes on the wood floor." She turned to study them. "I hope the water still runs freely from the outside garden pump. Mutti will be right back. Hans-Georg you help Susanne mind Dorlies."

Escaping the Russian Onslaught

An engraved plaque was at her feet when Ruth approached the old well. *God bless the little children.* Somehow, the small sign gave her a great deal of encouragement. Hearing the children's voices, Ruth rushed back into the house to find the youngsters squabbling over who counted the most boards on the floor. "Now is not the time to be angry with one another. Always remember the way to keep a friend is to keep your angry words in your pocket."

"But, Mutti," Hans-Georg piped up, "my pants pockets have so many holes in them my anger flies right out of them." All his mother could do was lovingly ruffle the top of his dark blond head.

Preparing to open the door of what Ruth felt was the kitchen pantry to search for a bucket, she gagged at the familiar odour. Was it what she thought it might be, or could it be something entirely foreign to her? Studying the children, she thought, *If we remain in this house for an hour or hopefully overnight, I must put my fears back into my pocket and keep them there.* Ruth placed her sweaty palm onto the rod iron handle, her knee ready to force the wooden door closed again and slowly pushed on the lever. The questionable yet recognisable stench only increased, causing Ruth to slam the door closed again. Judging what the odour was, she quickly backed away.

Hearing the soft commotion, the children became alarmed and silent. Wide-eyed, Hans-Georg questioned, "Where is Tante Anneliese?"

The temptation of chiming in became overwhelming for Klaus-Dieter. His blue eyes grew wide, he rubbed his wet nose on his coat sleeve. "Ja, where is my Mutti?"

After hearing her son's sobbing, Anneliese appeared. "Mutti is here, son." She glanced at Ruth. "There are two bedrooms on the upper level, but they will be too dangerous to use. However, a coal cellar in the basement would be safe, away from the terrible bombings. No fires can be built, but there is plenty of warm bedding that we can drag down from the upper bedrooms to keep us comfortable."

Steadying her nerves, Ruth's eyes were set with worry. "I am glad you are safe." She frowned. "Before we shelter here, we must investigate the kitchen pantry, Anneliese." She added solemnly, "I need to show you something. I should say I need to have you smell something." Her shoulders slumped and Ruth motioned to the food cupboard. "Follow me to the pantry over there."

The two women moved toward the closed door. Anneliese was beside Ruth's ear. "I smell something, Ruth." She carried one of the two small wooden kitchen chairs closer to the pantry. "Use this chair if you have to prop it shut again."

"So do I, but I do not know what it is. I will set the door ajar."

Anneliese's blue eyes were large in agreement. "You do it. I will stand back with the chair, and if there is danger, you slam the door shut, and I will force the chair under the handle."

Reaching for an empty iron skillet off the stove, Ruth gingerly inched the door ajar. To their surprise, the stench increased, yet nothing jumped out at them. Still whispering, she said, "Hurry to the hearth and find me a candle, Anneliese."

Anneliese was back in a flash with a slender, lit candle. "Ruth, you are next to the door – you go in first."

"Why me...?" Ruth questioned as she held the light closer to the oozing fleshy blob lying on the floor, took a moment to study the unthreatening object, and then scratched her head to laugh heartily before her words were completely out of her mouth.

Cautiously, Anneliese backed away but remained beside Ruth. "Ruth, this is so frightening. I do not see anything to snicker at."

"Oh, Anneliese, you must look at what I found." She relaxed as she found herself watching Anneliese's reaction.

Placing her hands firmly on her hips, Anneliese shook her head out of pure exhaustion from the fear that had sprung in her from the terrifying experience. "It is dough!" She laughed. "The terrible smell is the rising of several-day-old yeast dough rising too long. At first, I thought it might be a rotting body."

"I feel so very sorry for these people because they must have left in an extreme rush."

"We should close the door and leave the dough there."

"You might be right, Anneliese. I have no idea what we could do with it right now. Sadly, we cannot light a fire in the stove to bake the dough. If we remain here longer, perhaps we can dig a hole in the garden and bury it by the pump house."

Shivering from searching the pantry, Ruth clasped her arms about her. "There are a few packages of stale rye bread in here, and I also found one or two slices of Swiss cheese and some cured ham in the icebox over there. We will eat well for the next few days, children, and you can get a good night's sleep."

The cellar became their sanctuary where they rested and the two women played simple learning games with their children.

After the second day in the dark, damp coal cellar, the gunfire around their safe place became more intense. Then nothing. Moments later, the floorboards creaked, several heavy boots stomped across the old wooden floor, and heavy boots rushed through the house. Ruth turned to her group. Words were not spoken. There was no need to hush the children, for they understood the drill by now. The group stood shivering in the corner with wide eyes as if their execution were about to occur.

Inching her way up the flight of stairs, and before she could think clearly, Ruth stood face to face with a baby-faced British soldier, appearing as unsettled as she. Over his shoulder, he yelled, "Hey, Seargent, people are living down here. Two young women and four small children. What do you want me to do with them?"

A raw, broken voice hollered back, "I don't give a damn, just get them out of the way!" We are taking over this building, so get them out of my sight."

With the butt of his machine gun, the young soldier did as his Seargent ordered.

Chapter 17

THE PARADE

After their eviction by the British army, the family once again fell in line with the never-ending parade of humanity overcrowding the byways, struggling to continue westward following their contagious leap of faith.

Ruth could not utter a word in the depressing surroundings. Too thin for her already petite frame, Ruth was buffeted by the wind when she began to pull her small fold-up umbrella from her backpack. She was shoved to the side by a greedy refugee. Ruth did not yield but stood her ground. The woman's grasp for Ruth's protective covering failed. Ruth's anger ignited, and she spat out her words at the woman. "No! You cannot have my umbrella! My dear mother gave this to me. I have lost so much already. I cannot lose anymore!" The small canopy was saved, but as they stepped onto the muddy road, it would not protect her family cluster falling in line with the rest of the refugees trudging westward.

The arduous journey began at dawn since these were the only safe times the refugees dared to stick out their heads, like turtles, as they headed westward. The later daylight hours were too dangerous because other British soldiers might be upon them. Yet now, more than ever, the need to make their way westward was vital. Hence, time became the enemy. Military or civilian, young or old, healthy or crippled, there was no discrimination from death, now their ever-present nemesis.

The goal of the thunderous beasts driving their way toward them was to kill as many Germans as possible. The refugees feared the Russians attacking the area from the rear and jumped at any unusual motor roar. The British blackening the skies could ambush the refugees behind any shrub. The only alternative to joining the masses on the road was to hide in bushes or among trees. Until they were assured the wasps of aeroplanes would not strike, the weary travellers stayed out of sight as best as they could.

In a broken voice, Anneliese tried to keep the conversation light, "It is bedlam. The area is as if colossal herds of dinosaurs had broken out of their fossils, trampling the cities we loved so well."

Ruth was determined to look on the bright side of life. "Yet, I am surprised by my determination to survive these terrible times."

Ruth looked across the rolling countryside and saw nothing more than parched, trampled brown fields filled with people hiding where they could. Ruth's family

The Parade

could be ambushed at any time. Their only choice was to move forward with the moving masses zigzagging through the countryside looking for food and water at any farmyard still intact. Whatever food they found had to be hidden in their knapsacks and among their clothing for fear of being attacked by a starving refugee.

The further they trudged on the unyielding country roads, the more terrifying life became. A farmyard came into view, and Ruth and Anneliese hurried their family along only to find long lines of refugees already there. Once closer to the farmer, Ruth realised he was carrying a pot of cabbage stew mixed with black potatoes that were last year's rotten crop. Eagerly the refugees filled their tin cups that were dangling from their backpacks. With a turned-up nose, the farmer's wife poured the soup into the tin cups.

Waiting for her family's turn, Ruth gagged when she sniffed the stench of unwashed bodies, sweat-laden clothes and greasy hair. A person with exquisite culture and taste, Ruth studied her fawn-coloured suede leather skirt and cream-coloured blouse, which were mussed beyond recognition, aghast, wishing that she had packed more wisely. The headscarf tied around her greasy hair kept sliding into her eyes, and hers, Anneliese's and the sweet children's clothes were not dissimilar to those of the other folks.

Ruth's body went rigid when she heard a commotion when there was not enough to fill everyone's cup. A tall woman in a grimy, tattered dress and a gaunt frame with fierce blue eyes raged as she struggled violently to make her way through the crowded food line.

Biting her lip, Ruth's eyes were drawn to the handsome, aristocratic woman, her mahogany hair draped with a similar cloth as hers. The imposing woman yelled to drive her point home. She tore the ladle from a young, blond refugee about to have the farmer's wife pour her some soup.

Ruth fell silent. Assessing the frenzied situation quickly, she suppressed her hunger as her heart ached with anguish. Ruth grabbed Anneliese's cup and then gently handed the two cups to the starving woman.

The taller woman's eyes glistened with gratitude at the shorter woman. Ruth sensitive with the emaciated older woman who also travelled for safety from elsewhere, away from the Russian border. Ruth lowered her eyes – her mouth twisted – imagining her mother with a distended belly, starving like this woman. She buried her fears, desperately hoping her family was safe and well-fed.

To squash the chaos, the farmer rushed into the crowd with loaves of bakery goods that he had hidden in his barn. Five emaciated women bolted, grabbed him, and threw him into the nearest compost pile. Feverishly, they greedily snatched up as much as was available. Ransacking the barn for more bread, the crowd found what they were after. The resistance from the hordes was driven by the greed of men such as this who hoped to sell their goods on the black market when the war was over.

Her shoulders shook and she attempted to be unobtrusively silent. She was exhausted, so she drew back, rested her head against her cold hand, and sniffled from the wet cold. *Enough of that!* Caught in silence, Ruth bowed in grief, confused about what to do next. Snapping her head away from the grim scene, she turned to see the treasures of her life. Then, Ruth tenderly kissed Susanne, Hans-Georg and Dorlies on their hands.

For the most part they must trust the people in the same situation who were fleeing next to them. Most refugees gave them a mouthful if they had a bite to eat and their neighbour had nothing to eat. Everyone shared what they had. When the family had a blanket, there was always a little corner left for someone else to crawl under. When people go through a disaster like this, they feel like one big unit because everyone is in the same dilemma. No one complains. No one is afraid, or they do not show their fear other than from the thieves roaming free. They are like a herd of wild African elephants on the run to protect their offspring and themselves. During these times, all varieties of people belong together. When one group has something, they divide it with the others without question. If they might not have anything for tomorrow, they shared, for they might all be dead by then. As awful as the whole ordeal was, it was remarkable how some people, especially refugees, helped each other.

Ruth felt Hitler's use of their Fatherland and other nations was quite insane and many people wished him dead. Why could this deranged man not recognise what the world would have to endure after the massive bombings? The horrific destruction continued in every major city where the army had not withdrawn from their massacre. The British attacks were vicious and had already destroyed everything with their endless assaults. Everywhere Ruth looked, abandoned buildings were wedged against one another. Weakened by the rains, inevitably, the buildings would disintegrate, killing more residents. The word on the street was: if there is one German left, that is one German too many. The villages Ruth saw in the distance had been nothing more than 100 mighty furnaces from which no more fire could be squeezed. Germany and its people had given all they had. There was no more to give. When will they understand? The German people were on their knees.

Chapter 18

ON THE JOURNEY

With only a slight breeze rolling off the Baltic Sea and rippling its way inland, the first rays of sunshine broke through the milky dawn, casting glimmering shafts of light to gleam on branches of the few trees still standing beside the road and that had not been destroyed by heavy shelling. In the distance, the horizon glowed with the bombs blasting all around the thousands of escaping refugees. Dust billowed over the road as a small isolated escaping convoy of German military trucks on their last drops of gasoline sputtered by the migration. Moreover, they could not get more gas than they carried with them.

A short distance from Ruth's cluster, one of the trucks came to a sputtering stop and the family watched the wrenching drama unfold when the truck broke away from the convoy. Rushing flocks of children ran in haste to meet the truck in hopes the soldiers had a small morsel for them. Instead, the soldiers, disgusted by the defeat of the German military, bolted out.

Some children were strong enough to beg, while others were too weak and lagged behind. She could hear the voices of the unfamiliar children furiously pleading, "A little bite to eat. Please, soldier, do you have a little food to nibble on?"

There was ample morning sunlight that Ruth noticed a poor woman's plight. Soon, these children could be hers, running up to a stranger begging for food. Tears built up in Ruth's eyes, yet she willed them not to drop and shivered at the sight.

Beside the truck, their mother, a bedraggled woman who appeared to be about Ruth's age, fell to her knees out of desperation. The woman strained to stretch out her arms and clutch onto the driver. From Ruth's vantage point, the soldier driving the truck had his elbow exposed to the elements.

Again, Ruth heard the woman's imploring cry, "Two small children! Nothing to eat or drink… please. Please, soldier!"

Filled with the temptation to follow the woman's lead, Ruth's hopes soon disintegrated when she realised the soldier was too concerned about his sputtering truck. Once more, the woman pleaded for food to feed her children. With his arm he thrust open his cab door and did not see the woman. Instead, he unknowingly hurled her to the side with the door, sending the woman onto the cold, unyielding earth. He dropped his black, mud-stained boots to the ground and brushed away the sweat rolling down his brow, fear mixed with the disgrace of being defeated in war manifested in his sour expression.

As the sun kept rising, his raging temper followed suit. He flung a few swear words at the broken-down vehicle and gave it a swift, angry kick. His two companions sitting in the front jumped down to assist, quickly pushing up their sleeves to inspect the oily engine. The eleven soldiers crunched under the battered green canvas of the truck's bed hastily heaved themselves out to breathe fresh air. Knowing the dangers the bombers could throw at them, they scrambled to the nearest ditch.

Ruth's heart ached as she watched the woman with her children in hand stagger as she hurried ahead along the road. Again, she thought, *I might be this woman in a few days, begging for food for my darling children. I am desperate to find a way out.*

Anneliese muttered, "I believe now the woman is most likely fearful of the soldier." She stopped and added, "I think his troubles will soon be resolved. I see a soft smile playing on his lips."

Calming her nerves and nudging Anneliese as if for approval, Ruth said, "I sometimes had doubted the wisdom of my final act. Unfortunately, I have forgotten what day this might be. Each day, we walked from sunrise to sunset putting in a full day's work searching for food, aiming to make some headway to the west. If there are too many threats of attack, we sit in hiding, waiting until night to walk. To my way of thinking, an opportunity is standing beside us, and we cannot allow it to vanish." Ruth winked at her sister-in-law. "I am ready to do anything. I do not want our children or us to die." Not knowing what the future held, Ruth fell silent.

The threatening spring rain clouds moved in from the sea and the black skies opened with a savage rain that suddenly poured into the truck driver's face. He quickly motioned to his companions to ascend into his cab, so he could head to catch up with his caravan.

In that instant, Ruth recognised that she must be shrewder than the woman who had begged earlier. Ruth caught Anneliese's eye and nodded toward the driver. Anneliese furrowed her brow in confusion. "What are you doing?" she mouthed.

Ruth brazenly pulled up her brown coat to expose her skirt. At first, Anneliese did not get her meaning. Within a matter of seconds, Anneliese caught her intent.

As she flirtatiously attempted to show a hint of ankle, Ruth lost her balance and stumbled forward. Quickly righting herself, she clapped a hand over her mouth to muffle her chuckles.

In a bid for his attention, "Young man… young man," Ruth cooed to the man who appeared the same age as her husband. The young soldier at the truck turned in her direction and studied her.

Ruth saw a flicker of anger cross the driver's face. Out of nervousness, Ruth bit the corner of her lip. When she recognised the soldier's look of desire, Ruth shivered, moved back several paces, and then stood in stunned silence as she noticed the driver watching her too closely, with lust in his eyes apparent. Suddenly, Ruth realised she had gone too far to get his attention. Her fierceness would need to remain intact, or all would be lost. Ruth gulped, clearly ashamed that she could do such a thing. *If only I could turn back the clock.*

Abruptly, the driver took pity on the six pathetic wet travellers. With one wave of his rough hand, the soldier beckoned them on. In no time, the family of six stood beside the truck, hoping to receive a much-desired ride. Ruth knew even soldiers could not resist her baby doll Dorlies' sweet smile. Ruth's heart beat faster as in one swift motion, and without shame, Ruth thrust her youngest daughter into the darkness of the green army canvas at one of the remaining soldiers.

With the aid of the other soldiers sitting near the open canvas flap, "One, two, three, jump," the soldiers took hold of the children's waists, thrusting their hands out to the other children to follow Dorlies into the darkness of the green canvas cover. Anneliese and Ruth pulled up their garments to be yanked up rapidly and hoisted into the back of the moving truck among the soldiers huddled inside the canvassed bed of the vehicle carrying lumber. None of the group relished becoming a captive. As if a cry of victory once inside, one of the young lads let out a piercing whistle of victory in saving this family.

Thinking her shaky voice was steady, Ruth leaned into Anneliese and uttered, "I think receiving this ride was just dumb luck since the poor devil driving the truck is as terrified of being bombarded by bombs falling from the air at any moment as we are."

The men in the rear of the vehicle and the two women hitchhikers exchanged an awkward smile of uncertainty, although the two groups were hesitant to have confidence in each other.

Puffs of white filled the dusty skies as paratroopers dropped from massive, camouflaged aircraft. The refugees were unsure who the paratroopers were: British or Russians attacking the land beneath their feet. To the two women new to the truck, the word passed immediately from the soldiers that it was heard throughout the German ranks that the Americans had conquered the Rhineland and captured German soldiers. To escape, many of these soldiers cloaked themselves in women's clothing to confuse the attacking military. However, fate was on their side, for these German soldiers allowed Ruth's family to ride with them for a few hours. At the least, her cluster could sit on the unstable, irregular clattering boards the vehicle was transporting.

Placing her dirty hand next to her mouth, Ruth spoke softly to Anneliese. "After all the women and children on the road with a multitude of stragglers, I am surprised the driver picked up two women with four children, and I wonder if this was a good idea after all?"

Anneliese was quick to say, "Well, Ruth, you flirted with the driver by showing your ankles."

Ruth waved her sister-in-law's trivial remark away and continued her thought. "The truck may be bombed with the many air raids and then burst into flames at any moment. If this became the case, then the occupants in the truck will become part of a bursting inferno."

Once Ruth's words were spoken, Anneliese suddenly became incredibly quiet. The terror of what might happen drew stern furrows across her forehead. "I think we should close our eyes and not think of such things."

Though there was much tossing about in the back of the truck, darkness made their journey safer until Ruth remembered they were driving on the rickety, worn-out road without headlights. She held a hasty conference with Anneliese. "Despite the tremendous clatter of the wooden timber, I think perhaps the truck's rear remained the safest place for us after all."

The chattering voices of the two women in deep conversation woke Hans-Georg. He rubbed his sleepy hazel eyes. "Mutti. Where are we?" he asked in a hesitant voice. "I think I must have been dreaming. My birthday was a long time ago now. My Vati was not there. Why are we with these other strange men? Why is Vati not beside me instead of these soldiers I don't recognise?" His words rushed sleepily together now. "Mutti, tell me once more about the day I was born?"

With overflowing tenderness for her son, Ruth tucked Hans-Georg under her coat to help keep him warm. His eyes glittered from the bright moonbeams streaming through the tattered covering. His mother began her story, "Now, do you remember the date of your birthday, my sweet?"

"Ja, Mutti." He smiled with pride and then cuddled closer to his mother. "March seventeenth is the day I was born, and now I am..." With much pride, Hans-Georg held up four fingers to show his mother.

"That is right." His mother beamed, pleased with her son, who was always very pleasant and well-mannered, though a bit shy. Her heart was overflowing with tenderness for him. He should have inherited one-half of the Klein Pobloth Estate while sharing the other half with his cousin, Klaus-Dieter. The money had been there for Rudi to buy Anneliese out so the estate would belong to Rudi's side of the family.

"Mutti, what is the matter?" the small boy asked. "I can hear your voice crack."

His mother cleared her throat and then continued. "When you were born, your Vati was home on furlough. He was cleaning up after being outdoors hunting with your grandmother, Dolores Meissner." Ruth sighed deeply. Her mood improved, and she moved impulsively closer to her son. "Today, those days seem aeons ago." Yet another sigh, this time deeper and more sorrowful. "I remember you were ready to come into the world. Darling boy, you did not wait until your Vati was completely shaved. His cheekbone and jaw were half-shaven when he saw his new little baby boy. He took you in his big hands, kissed your forehead, and then placed you against his heart as he clutched you against his hairy chest."

She caressed her son's soft cheeks with the utmost care. "You ended up with soap on your little, rosy nose."

Her son chuckled at her words and placed his hands closer into the soft folds of her body. "I think Vati must have looked silly. If I think hard, I can smell the wonderful fragrance of the soap at the end of my nose. Besides, I can hear his cheery chuckle. Oh, I enjoy my daddy's wonderful chuckle." Hans-Georg sniffed the air. "Mutti, we have not used soap for such a long time. When can we take another long bath and smell the sweet soap? The last time was at the Schloss. I would like to have another warm bath like I had for my birthday."

"Ja, my sweet, I would like that also. I would have placed your sisters into the big bathtub at Klein Pobloth with you." Ruth ran her fingers through her son's silky baby hair. Very soon now, I will try to find a bar of soap and some wonderful warm water, then we can all be clean again." Ruth's heart ached from the humiliation of not providing the simplest things for her children.

"Oh, Mutti," Glee sprung from Hans-Georg's voice. "Warm water would be heavenly. I can hardly remember what warm water or warm food feels like, Mutti."

"Now it is very late. Close your eyes and sleep before morning comes." Ruth slipped her hands onto the small of his back, rubbing it tenderly until she could see her son's eyes becoming heavy as he began breathing calmly. His mother's heart felt like it would break.

Dorlies' head rested on the end of her mother's warm brown coat. Ruth contemplated her lovely, light-blond-haired "baby doll" as everyone visiting Klein Pobloth and the labourers had dubbed her. Her own mother, Luise Schläger, had visited several times and referred to her granddaughter as her "baby doll." While living at Klein Pobloth, on Dorlies' first birthday, Ruth had hired a professional photographer. It was a lovely time when pictures of the entire family were taken. The only absentee member was Rudi, who was already fighting in the war on Germany's Western Front.

Jammed in the dimly lit truck bed, Ruth's mind shut out the curious soldiers studying her bedraggled family. Lovingly, Ruth pulled the corner of one of the grey blankets the soldiers had given her cluster over the toddler's ears, pulling it over Hans-Georg to keep them warm. Susanne clambered up to take her share. Ruth thought back to when Dorlies was born with a coin-sized birthmark on her sternum. The doctor wanted to operate to remove the brown mark after her first birthday, but the war got in the way. As parents, Ruth and Rudi had left it where God placed it. They knew the war could eventually come in the direction of Pommern, quickly engulfing Klein Pobloth. With the birthmark left in place, if their daughter were to be separated from the family, Ruth could more readily claim Dorlies as her daughter.

She regularly reminded Dorlies that God had placed his thumbprint on her chest so the family would not lose her. For months, the family had heard that children

Escaping the Russian Onslaught

were being kidnapped. Untold parents had lost their children in the bombings, and many lost their parents, never to find each other again. Susanne and Hans-Georg were old enough to identify Ruth and speak out to declare her as their mother. The birthmark would be one way their parents could recognise Dorlies, setting her apart from the other children to claim her as their own. For these families, their loss was the end of everything. It was beyond Ruth's comprehension of what their country had become. In a nation where no one had a home or a place to live or food to eat, finding a halfway healthy life was challenging when, at best, there was barely enough food for one day.

Within a few days, the rain ceased. Then, far away, the too-familiar row of enemy aeroplanes again bombarded the escaping convoy from the sky. It was as if enormous, flying grey hornets plummeted their dung onto the earth, exploding and causing vast brownish craters to form.

Coming over the brow of an incline, a sickly stray cat sped across the road, so the truck driver manoeuvred his machine skillfully. Susanne and Hans-Georg giggled when they saw the animal from the back of the green truck. Ruth gazed down at Dorlies, smiling at the cat, but did not know what to think. Ruth felt like a bony plucked chicken with the enemy striking around their vehicle.

Abruptly, their greatest fears were realised. The overloaded green truck with wooden planks, soldiers, four children and two women shivering from fear took a hit when a massive shell struck the vehicle and more artillery whistled too close to them for comfort. The violence against them escalated when the canvas canopy was consumed with flames within seconds.

A shrill voice came thundering through the air. Ducking as he shouted, the soldier called, "Get out! If we stay under this canvas – it will destroy us all!"

Shoving began as a voice barked, "Get out of the truck! Get out!" Another soldier blurted into the glowing flames, "The fire has engulfed the entire surrounding area!" The group inside the truck scattered onto the side of the road, diving into the nearby undergrowth. Screaming, two soldiers' bodies burst into flames. The dreadful smell of burning flesh surrounded the vehicle. Their comrades extinguished the fire the best they could, but nothing could help the two unfortunate soldiers. It was too late to save them. Then, another cry. "Get this damn fire off my back!"

The bombs ravaged the landscape as the soldiers' time in this beautiful... yet ugly world ended.

Ruth clung onto Dorlies when she leaped out first and helped her other two children down from their entrapment. Ducking frantically, Ruth's mind worked overtime, her arm crushing Dorlies' middle and unable to caress her sobs. It was excruciating for the child under her arm, so the toddler let off a shrill scream of protest, partially out of pain and partially from the fear of the raging flames surrounding them. Tightly clinging to her, trembling yet showing their spirit to survive, Hans-Georg and Susanne clung to the hem of their mother's brown coat.

Anneliese and Klaus-Dieter followed their lead. In a flash, they all hid behind a large rock on the side of the road.

Ruth frantically peered over the boulder's edge to find Susanne, her older daughter, nowhere to be seen. Ruth's heart plummeted as she studied the crater and scanned her surroundings again and again as her agony for finding her eldest child intensified. Ruth finally breathed a little easier when she spotted her elder daughter among the debris in a fetal position, whimpering.

From the corner of her eye, Ruth caught sight of a ghastly gigantic splinter of shrapnel thrust into the trampled earth, piercing into the ground which had barely missed Susanne. Ruth and Susanne let out a gut-wrenching scream no one else could hear. The bedlam around them was too intense. Tears built up in Ruth's eyes, but they did not drop. Once the dust settled, the moisture cleared from her eyes. Her heart settled when she realised the hurtling artillery debris had not struck Susanne. Assessing her daughter, Ruth determined her colour was good. What could have happened to the terrified child would have been dreadful. Ruth was close enough to hear her six-year-old daughter shriek in terrified fear. She quickly gave her elder daughter a glance of reassurance to convince her she was safe. Susanne had become efficient at caring for herself, so she scrambled for shelter as best she could and shuddered at the thought of being in danger without her mother's protection.

Ruth ordered the two smaller children to stay where they were, then flung her thin body to the ground, strewn with broken branches and shards of metal and glass. Snaking over the debris, Ruth inched her way over to Susanne, and in one broad swoop, she engulfed the shivering child in a wide embrace, clutching Susanne close to her breast in relief.

Yet, in that instant, Rudi's comment ripped through her brain, "If one must die, the swifter, the better." They had both agreed, very much like her father's death.

Ruth had observed Susanne's bravery a year earlier, when everyone at Klein Pobloth told her how brave Susanne was when her pony kicked her in the chin. Her courage in the hospital was only a year ago and Susanne barely shed tears. Her chin was dislodged, and some of her teeth in the lower part of her jaw shattered. The doctors at the hospital in Kolberg had warned Ruth that Susanne's wound could, at times, expel fragments of bone or splinters of broken teeth for many years to come.

"Oh, Mutti, what happened?" The quivering child sobbed. "I cannot hear what you are trying to tell me."

Ruth cradled her child for what seemed like an eternity and then pushed herself and Susanne back to where her other two children were waiting. No noise or confusion could disturb their momentary solitude, quiet except for the cries of the soldiers hit by the crashing shrapnel.

Anneliese and Klaus-Dieter carefully approached where Ruth and her children huddled. "Are any of you hurt?" Anneliese's hands began to tremble while searching their bodies for any signs of injury.

In a raspy voice, Ruth responded, "We are all right, but we almost lost Susanne this time." Quickly, Ruth disappeared behind a big shrub to be sick.

On Ruth's return, Anneliese glanced around the surrounding area. "What a blessing! I can easily see what you mean. I believe most of the soldiers in the truck escaped safely."

It was a relief to see the soldiers sitting on the side of the road after the danger had momentarily subsided. The soldiers generously passed around insulated tin flasks to share a small swallow of much appreciated water. Ruth and her family were happy to join the group as it took time to pull itself together before re-entering the truck.

Anneliese closed her eyes. Fearful, she turned her head away. Ruth quickly noticed her body language. Both women knew that they must accept these uncomfortable situations. The family group had nothing to lose by waiting one more night with these kind men.

The soldiers were as hungry as Ruth and her family, all trying to flee from war, destruction and those who would harm them. Ruth felt they must put their faith in God and other people's hands, hoping they were good individuals.

While living at Klein Pobloth, Ruth had encountered death, but in this ghastly war, she was faced with the smell of putrefying, burning flesh. To her right, Ruth spotted a bedraggled field doctor rushing toward the ditch where one of the wounded was wailing in the trench.

The doctor dropped his lightweight knapsack on the incapacitated soldier's right side, ripped off the private's green trousers, and quickly assessed the man's thigh. "What's your name, son?" The doctor twisted about and barked, "You Frau. You over there – in the brown coat. Ja, you – find something to make a tourniquet and something to hold his tongue down!"

There was no one else standing close to the doctor but Ruth. Her face drained of blood, her rigid posture adjusted, and a sudden fear wrenched her stomach. The doctor headed toward Ruth. "Are you up to it, woman? Will you assist me?"

The wounded soldier yelled with pain, a raw, gagging sound, "Ja... I am... Luke – like in the Bible." The awkward young blond soldier's screams were muffled as he passed out again.

The doctor thought a woman with three children would have more gumption than the rest of the refugees. To heed his calling, Ruth assigned Anneliese to the children. She wiped the surprise off her soiled face and moved back into the ditch to help the doctor.

Ruth was sick over the carnage she had witnessed a few moments ago and eager to help. Over the past few months, Ruth had become tough as nails and felt that she could handle this, too. In three strides, she knelt beside the dense shrubbery in the ditch, beside the moaning soldier and doctor. Thirst drained the doctor. Over his shoulder, he bellowed at Ruth, "Find a canteen!"

She stumbled through the shredded shrubbery and trees to the doctor's cab. Finding what she was looking for, Ruth scrambled to return to the doctor.

The doctor grabbed the cold container, stepping to the side as he dumped it over the thinning brown hair dripping over his beard, shook his head with water as a dog would, and downed the last sip of much-needed liquid. The doctor studied the wound once more and realised the soldier had been speared with sizeable pieces of burning shrapnel in the front of his thigh just above his knee that then thrust through the back of his leg but hat not broken his femur. The doctor's breathing became intense – his blue eyes, now grey from fatigue, glanced up at Ruth's brown eyes and ordered her to lay over the man's middle to secure him. The doctor began to work on the soldier's leg. Slightly leaping, Ruth draped herself over the howling man's heaving, weighty torso. Two unscathed soldiers noted his body heave up and down. They rushed in to help. Yet the weighty howling soldier could not be contained. The doctor looked for someone else to hold down the injured young man – no one was in sight.

He grabbed Ruth's shoulders. "Do you know how to sew? Well, woman, answer me."

She shrieked back. "Ja, yes, but why?"

The doctor breathed hard. "My equipment is in my rucksack. By now, it is so light you can drag it next to you. What is your name, please? You must do the job – I must help hold this man down."

"I am Ruth – Ruth Meissner." Her heart pounded in her chest as she glanced about. There was no one else in sight to help. She must do the job. Ruth did have the type of spirit needed. Yet again, fear of making an enormous mistake gnawed at her stomach. The soldier was injured severely. His huge, weighty belly would not stop heaving. His body had gone into shock.

Once she was back beside the wounded man, the doctor ordered, "Look in the bag to see what might be left."

Ruth opened the doctor's bag and studied its contents, finding it contained a needle and thread like she used to sew a goose. Spickbrust was one of her favoured cold-cut delicacies served during the holidays.

The doctor stood back. The sudden explosion of his voice caught Ruth off guard. "Can you take over as surgeon and sew the man up?"

This is all so terrifying. Get a hold of yourself, or you will do more harm than good. It is not often I make such a fool of myself. Here is your opportunity to save a man's life. Contemplating the horrendous responsibility, she lost her balance for a moment. This was a man, a young soldier she was to sew up, not a piece of luncheon holiday meat. How to clean out this gashing raw wound? Ruth pulled out the equipment the doctor specified. The only way to sanitise the man's leg was the Irish whiskey Ruth found in the bag and use it as a disinfectant by pouring it onto the vast exposed area in the front and the back of the soldier's thigh. "Step aside, Doctor. I can do this."

She washed her hands in the liquid before pouring the whiskey over the wound. There was no ether, morphine, no way to ease the soldier's pain. Raising her right hand, she poured the alcohol over the raw, exposed flesh in the front. The soldier's agonised scream was so deafening that his mother could have heard him while on her flight to who knows where. The soldier passed out as the men holding the soldier turned him on his side.

Ruth hoped that he would not wake up until she had the soldier stitched up. Before she could stitch him up, she needed to take her fingers and dig around in the raw, meaty part of the wound to see if a piece of metal was left in the opening. *You can do! This fiery piece of shrapnel pieced him. You must help. You have helped with butchering for many years.* The doctor explained that the wound was sterilised by the fiery piece of shrapnel that pierced him.

Ruth wanted to turn around and vomit in the nearby bushes. Her determination took hold, even though the men around her had not bathed or cleaned themselves for days. For that matter, she must reek as strongly as they did. Her throat went dry. A drink of whiskey would be welcome. Think this through before you break down with fear. Remember, you assured the doctor that you could help with the stitching. Ruth's chest heaved as she picked up the needle and thread, remembering not to place the twine between her lips to straighten it. One – two attempts, and the string pushed through the needle's eye. She clenched her teeth. Her hands trembled as perspiration ran down her brow, but she remembered not to brush the salty water from her forehead. Ruth pierced the skin on the front side of the leg, looping thread through the flesh. The men holding the soldier turned the hefty man. Thus, Ruth repeated the process on the back of his thigh. Finished, her right hand went numb, her rump hit the trampled weeds, her body sagged, she wiped the salt from her worn face, and then she was able to rise.

Crouched next to their patient to recoup from the stress, the doctor and Ruth sat for a moment. A look of despair was written on his weathered face. He shared his rage with Ruth. The doctor mentioned that his vehicle was the last in the caravan, and he was riding in his jeep when he saw the bombing in his rear-view mirror, made a U-turn, heading back in the direction he had just travelled. Bitter wrath built up in him, letting his emotions burst forward, burning his path to what he had witnessed during the war.

Although Hitler demanded that all soldiers, as well as women young and old, fight to the death, he and his unit had retreated after they had heard the Russians had smashed through the Pommern fortifications. Hanging his head in grief, he drew his hands through his thinning brown hair. He wished to go home to Stargard, or the "Jewel Box" city of Dresden. "Now I have nothing to go home to. Every part of my world was obliterated into nothing but rubble."

The clock in a distant village church bell rang six times. Momentarily out of danger, the entire group from the truck got some much-needed rest, unlike Ruth,

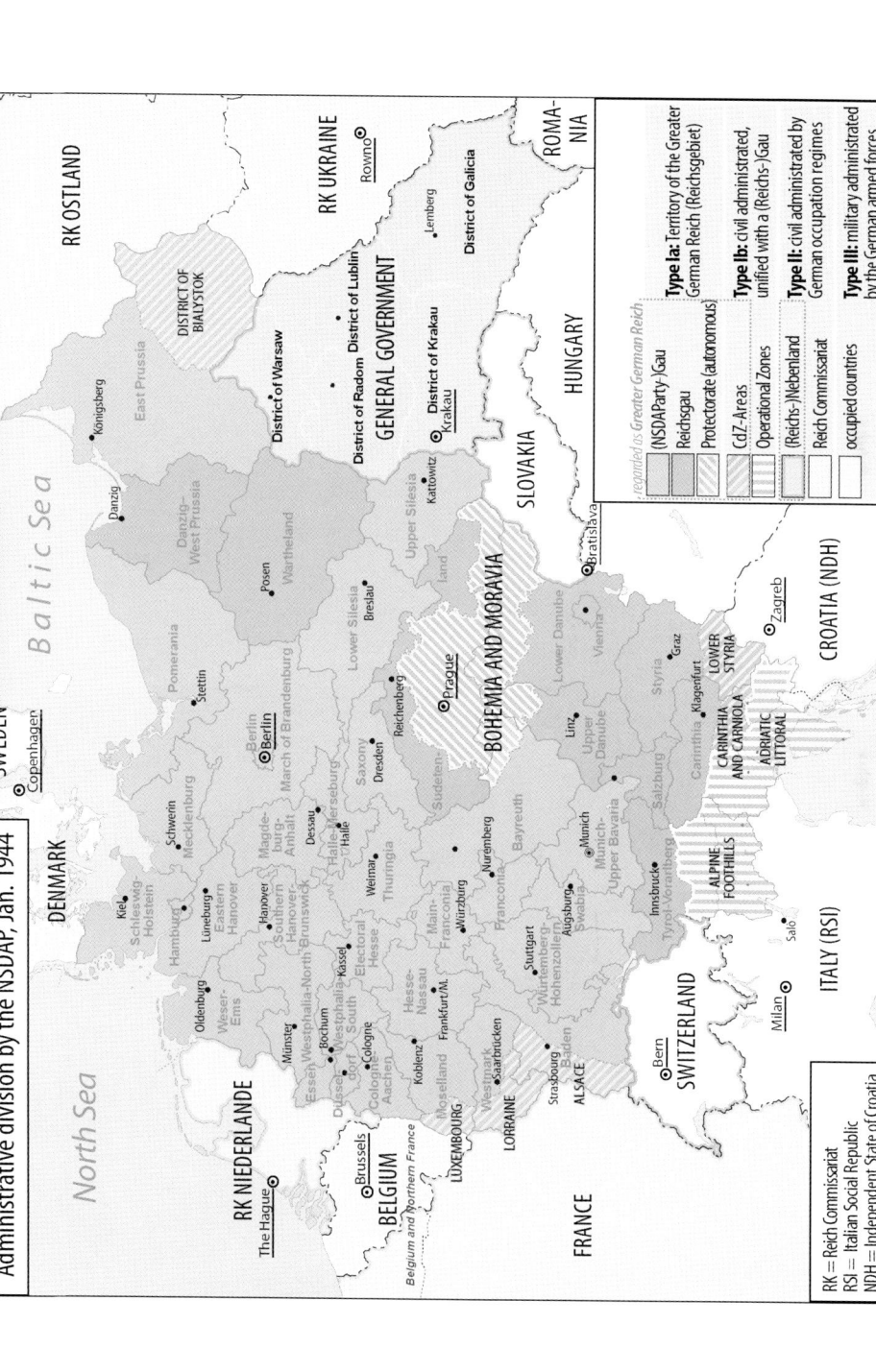

Map of the Third Reich, Germany.

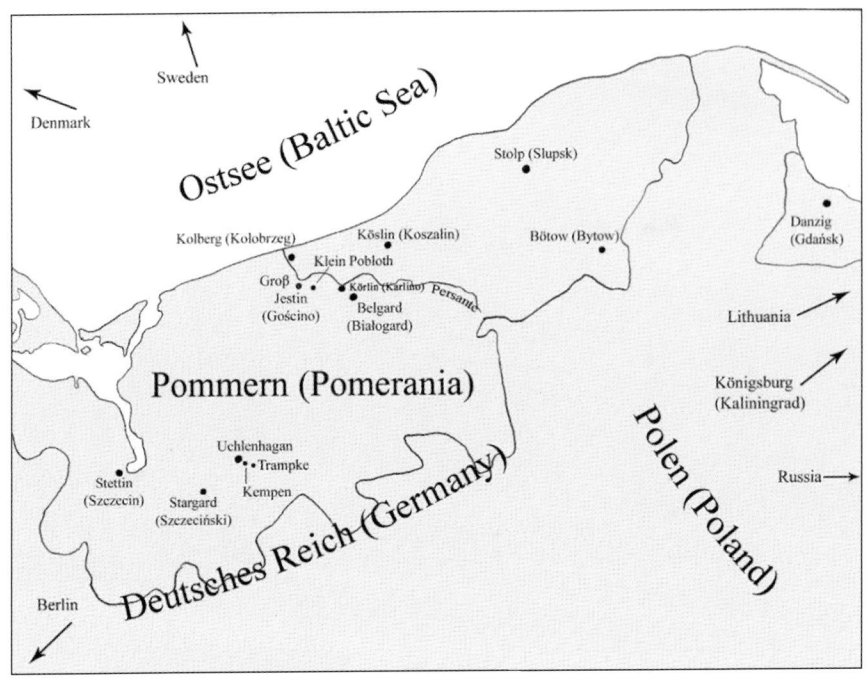

Map of Pommern, before 1945.

Picture of Lübeck Cathedral burning.

Devastated city of Kolberg after the Second World War.

Aerial view of Osnabrück.

Hamburg in ruins, Second World War.

Schloss Prüzen, 1944.

Schloss Güstrow.

Above: Schläger Family Home.

Left: Georg Schläger.

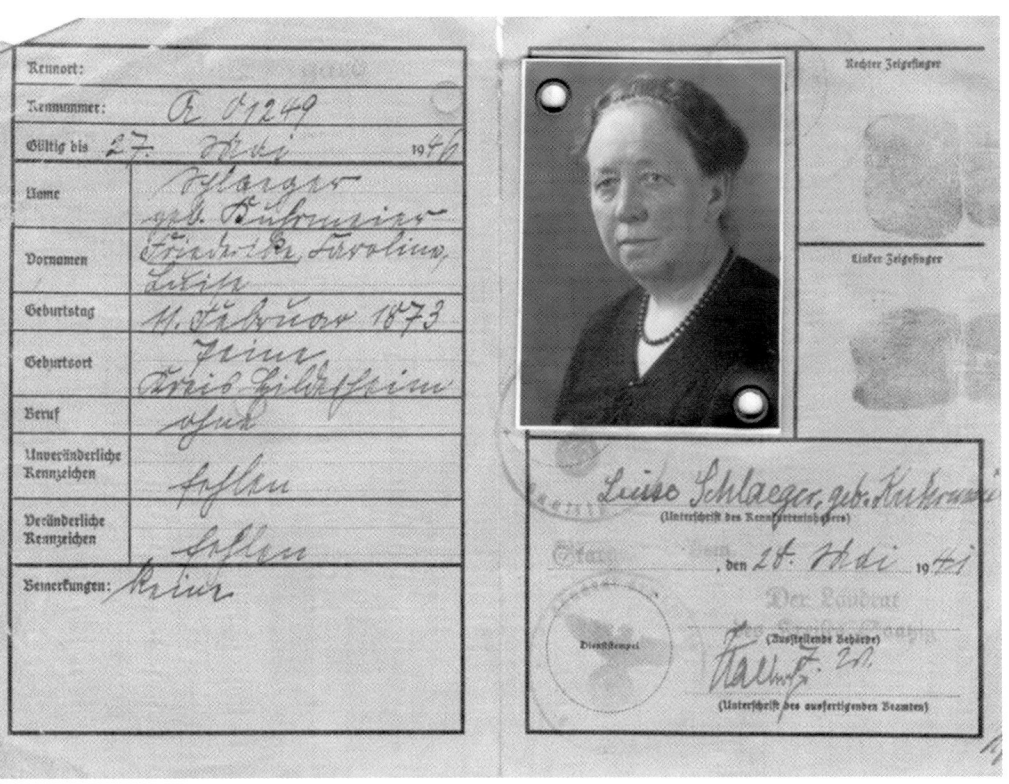

Luise Schläger's identification papers.

Officer-Joachim Schläger.

Ruth's nephew.

View of Klein Pobloth Manor House, 1944.

Side view of Klein Pobloth Manor House, 1944.

Barn at Klein Pobloth before 1944.

The Ice House at Klein Pobloth, 1944.

Left: The von Kaphengst Crest.

Below: Dolores Meissner, Max Schmeling and Anny Ondra with friends in front of Klein Pobloth, 1939.

Right: Ruth Meissner and Anneliese Hertel, 1941.

Below: Ruth Meissner's identification papers.

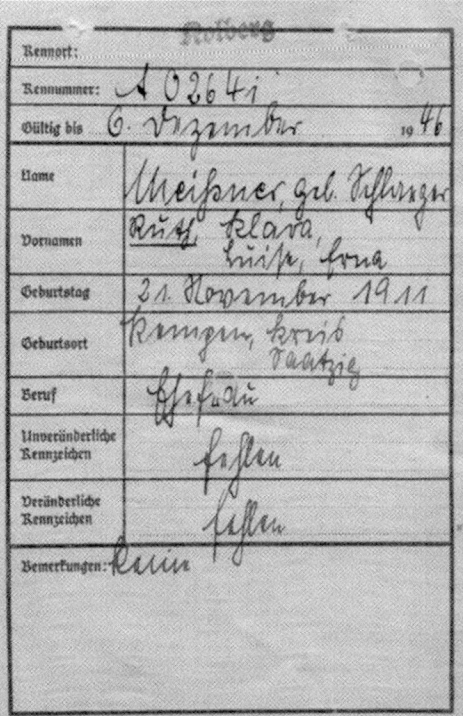

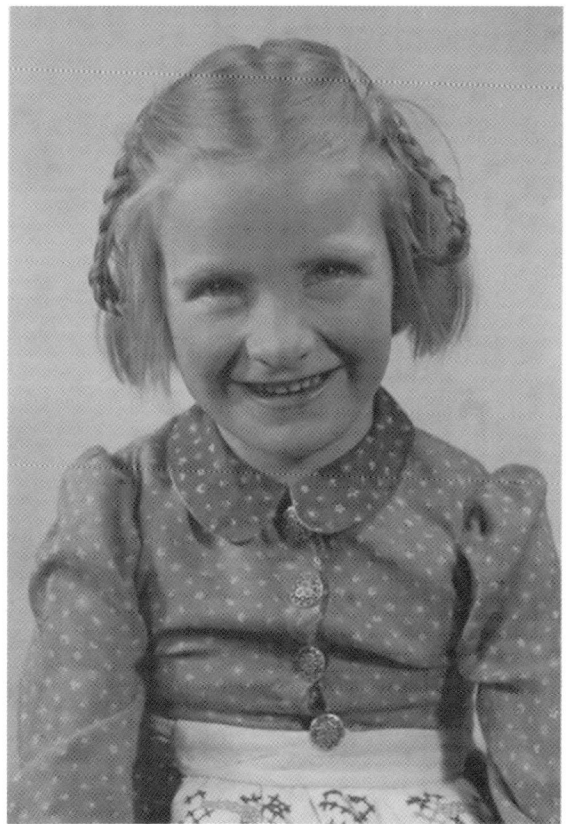

Above: Hans-Georg, Dorlies, Ruth, and Susanne Meissner, 1944.

Left: Susanne Meissner.

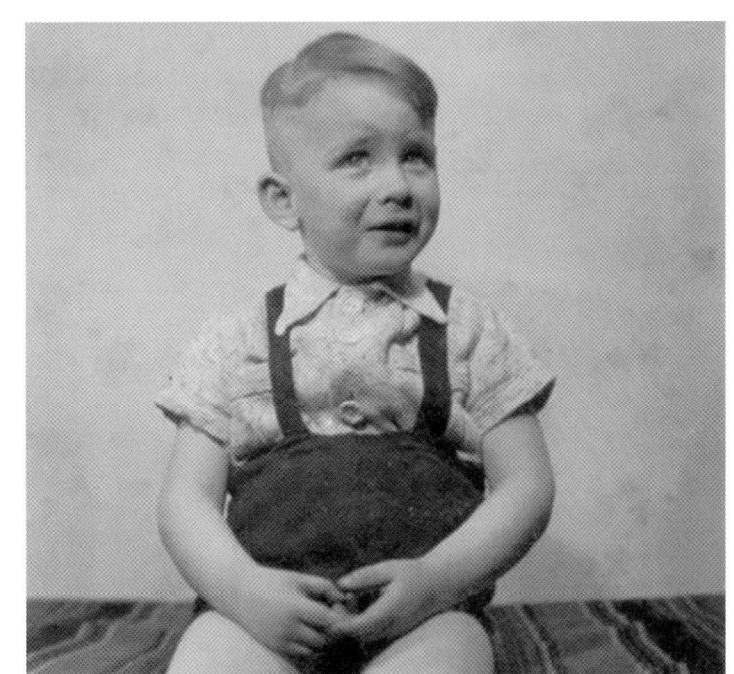

Right: Hans-Georg Meissner.

Below: Dorlies Meissner.

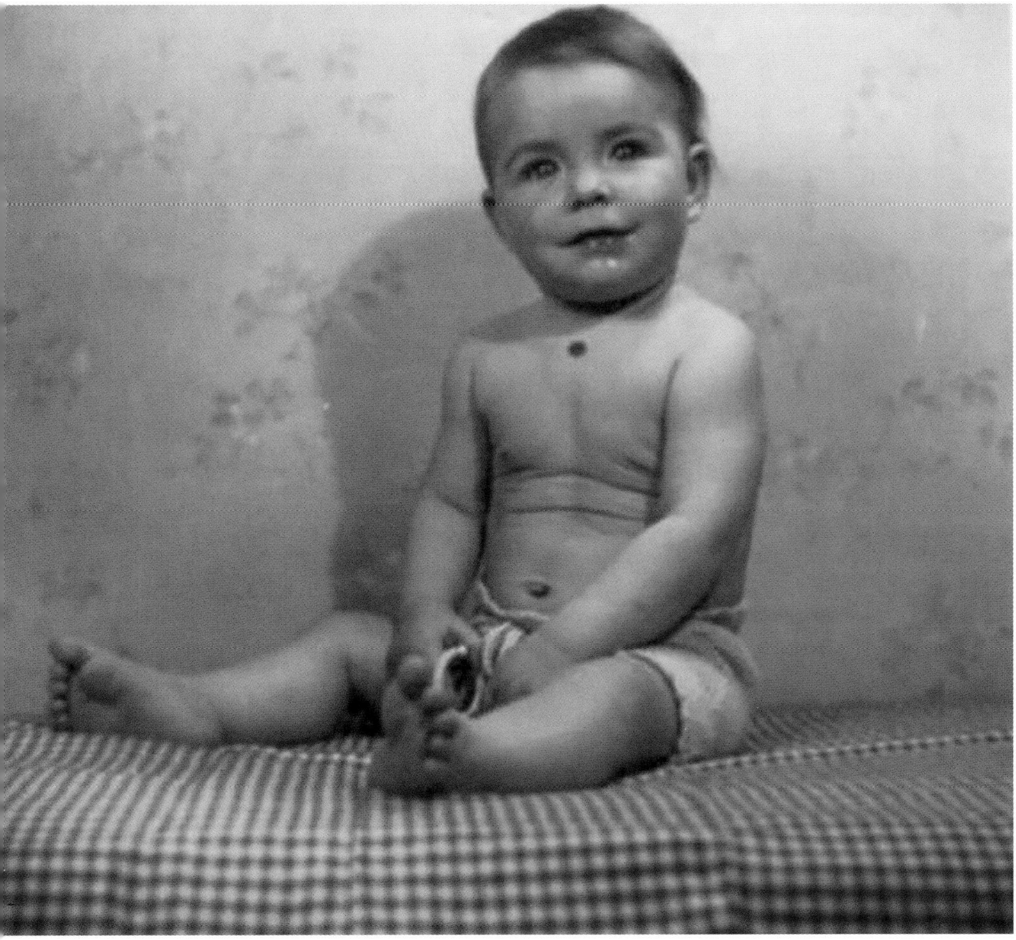

Above left: Hans-Rudolf Meissner as a young soldier.

Above right: Hans-Rudolf Meissner in 1952.

Below: Luise Schläger holding granddaughter, Dorlies Meissner.

who was too overwrought from stitching up the soldier. She freshened up her three children with dripping water next to the road and stood beside the tiny stream to rinse their hands and faces. With the hem of her skirt, she washed Hans-Georg's temple, thinking of nothing else other than the safety of her children.

The truck driver was also moving along the bank, searching for any food or items that could be useful, and meandered over to where Ruth and the children washed. He swished his hair back with his grimy hand aimlessly chattering away, as nervous energy worked overtime. He stepped beside her, staring at the children and making her uncomfortable. Then, the driver moved closer until Ruth placed little Hans-Georg between the soldier and her. He stood tall up to expose his best look and projected his personality. Ruth could barely comprehend what he was saying but soon she understood his words and their meaning too well.

The ripe-smelling driver spoke directly to her. "Lady, what do you think? Should we go on living as husband and wife?" He clasped Ruth lightly about her shoulder and moved closer. Trembling with passion, his sour breath upon her, he blurted out, "My name is Paul, Frau Meissner… I love you. I love you. Will you marry me? I will take your three children as part of my family also."

The driver's attempt to sound sincere combined with his genuine, heartfelt voice as he choked on his words fell on Ruth's ear. As he spoke, he must have been reeling with emotions after what had occurred earlier. A blush rose on her cheeks. A flood of astonishment came to her mind. She must be insane. *This man could not have just proposed marriage to me.* He stumbled as he added again, "I will look after your children also." Her caution was well-founded. It was one thing to hitch a ride with the soldiers, but making them believe women had no interest in the men was potentially dangerous.

Immediately, she thought, *Oh my, this is one of those problems that needs to be solved before it gets out of control.* There was nothing further from her mind than anything to do with romantic emotions. All Ruth wished for was to keep her children alive. She stared at him. She did not laugh at him but choked back tears. His proposal should have humbled Ruth, incredibly filthy as she was and reeking as if she had crawled out of a rat's nest.

The delusional man knew the answer to his question. He was not amused. When Ruth silently gave him her absolute rejection, she felt as though she could see the steam of embarrassment rise from the depth of his pride. With that, they finished their conversation.

Her earlier decision to get a ride with the caravan returned to haunt her. Ruth quickly freed herself from the clumsy man. In haste, she tugged at her children to return to where the other two members gathered. Once there, Ruth turned her head to see the man return to his group.

Without realising it, she almost stumbled over her sister-in-law. "Your face is as crimson as the evening spring sky," Anneliese teased.

Placing her hands on her face, Ruth touched her hot cheeks. They felt as though they were on fire. "No matter how tragic life is, there is something humorous that often happens. Anneliese, sit on this rock beside me to help me sort out what I just experienced."

"How can you be smiling after all that has happened? All I ever seem to do is scratch those darn itchy painful welts from the lice bites on our skin."

"If you will take a moment and let the children play in the fresh trickling stream beside the road, I will tell you the absurd incident that happened to me a moment ago." Ruth glanced about to ensure Anneliese was the only one who could hear her."

Delayed fear of the soldier's words struck her, and Ruth laughed hysterically under her breath.

"Ruth – Ruth, are you alright?" Anneliese huffed. "You have not told me anything I find amusing."

"Sorry, I do not know why I am so hysterical. I am releasing the emotions I experienced with the truck driver, including the miracle that Susanne is saved along with the unexpected surgery I performed." Ruth glanced at Anneliese, then chuckled as she related her recent proposal.

After Ruth confided in Anneliese, an icy voice suddenly barked instructions to the group. "Get back in the truck. It's past time we're on our way!"

The doctor and the two men who had held him down hoisted the weighty injured soldier onto the truck while Ruth's family followed. Once the soldier was settled, the doctor waved from his jeep and then sped off to catch up with his unit.

"What are we going to do with our dead?" a weary, voice asked from beside the road.

"We must leave them behind to save our hides," the driver bellowed.

One of the soldiers in the group shouted, "We don't have an extra blanket to cover their bodies. This is simply unconscionable, simply unacceptable."

A stream of grievances erupted from the crowd. Wordlessly, the soldiers around the truck gathered brushwood mixed with leaves for a makeshift grave to give homage to the dead men who, a few moments ago, sat in the same vehicle they now occupied.

After hearing the bellowing call for the second time, everyone hastily clambered onto the truck out of fear of being left behind. Once back in the vehicle, the stench of urine and sweat overtook the passengers, adding to the absolute fear of being attacked again. Each released their fears in their own way. The German soldiers were ready and willing to give themselves up.

Less than fifteen minutes passed when the familiar roar of the truck began to sputter.

Ruth's nerves were too raw to keep silent, causing her to chatter unendingly. With as soft a voice as she could manage, she quickly finished her story for Anneliese. "Thank heaven I did not have to say anything to this broken guy. But his proposal was ludicrous among these radical changes to our lives, not to mention these horrific times. I will never forget this moment because the timing was tragic since several soldiers from our group perished. These deaths must have hastened him on…"

Numerous trucks were still in flames. Thus, in his suffering, the frightened man had produced this preposterous marriage proposal. Ruth believed his delayed confession of his love for her was his way of making it through the terrifying insanity to which the war had exposed him. With his overflow of emotions, Ruth was certain his angst at the moment, not knowing if he would see another day, had brought on his outburst.

Ruth placed her hands over her face and yanked the hem of her skirt into her eyes. "On the other hand, for me to be a part of his sudden flare-up was a bizarre feeling. Particularly when death knocks at the end of every breath we take."

Now, Anneliese needed relief. Bursting out in fearful snorts at Ruth's story, she clasped her hand over her mouth and said, "Oh, we must keep silent after the dreadful ordeal we have just encountered."

"Naturally, you're right. I shared my prickly ordeal with you to release it from my mind. Besides, the Russians are historically known for their reputation of being ruthlessly unrelenting. Their philosophy of life is unbridled self-gratification as far as their treatment of women is concerned. However, this German soldier was sincere in his proposal."

Sitting in the truck's rear gave the two women time to make crucial decisions. Anneliese was so deeply immersed in her fears that Ruth felt compelled to speak up. "If our group were to be abducted by the British or the Russians, the aftermath you and I would endure would be unbearable. We must make a pledge. As my uncle did, we must be determined enough to kill our children and ourselves." She added in a hushed tone as she choked back tears of anxiety, "You know perfectly well they prefer little girls, as well as small boys who have not been touched."

Anneliese whispered, "Ruth, I know you are right in this. Besides being extremely frantic to escape their attacks, I am more determined than ever. "This is uncharted territory for us. Nevertheless, we know the Americans or British troops will not put us through the agony the Russians are known for."

Ruth paused to ponder. "Most importantly, we know we are in the last few days of the war."

Chapter 19

THE MEADOW

Ruth peered out of the back of the truck to study the sky. When she spoke, her voice reflected her disappointment. "The monstrous, angry skies will bring heavy rains this May as they did in April. With Germany's wet climate, why should this season be different from others in the spring? How will we ever keep the children from not catching their death from the cold? If not from hunger, then from the Russian, British or American soldiers invading our homeland?"

Turning to the soldiers under the darkness of the canopy, Ruth asked, "Do one of you soldiers know what day this is?"

One of the soldiers smiled, "This is May 7 or 8, not sure which, but I am fairly sure it is 8 May 1945."

Ruth had to make a great effort to smile, but one came forth. "I have lost track of time. Thank you, soldier."

Several soldiers were now attempting to sleep in the burned, uncovered back of the truck, and they kindly passed around their jackets so the two women and children could cover themselves while they slept.

"It is a pity that you boys must suffer because of us. But we are profoundly grateful," Anneliese smiled sweetly.

The people in the vehicle fixed their eyes on the inkiness of the night, only now allowed to reveal its secrets by the clouds unveiling and letting the waning crescent moonbeams to throw silhouettes onto the horizon.

Abruptly, their small green canvas military caravan unexpectedly drove into the intermittent sounds of voices – out of gasoline, shortly after the truck sputtered to a halt and a small amount of gunfire that became apparent in the area. As their vehicle approached the mayhem, the restless soldiers, women, and children became startled by thundering tanks and intermingled waves of voices. The repeated gunfire was of no avail in keeping hordes of people under control.

"Shhh, children, one of the soldiers is saying something that might be important," Ruth calmly warned, trying not to terrify the children more than they already were.

One of the young soldiers beside Ruth called out, "Who must we escape from now?"

The explanation was to the point. "According to the extensive rumours I heard while encountering other soldiers," a soldier breathed deeply, "the rumours are

The Meadow

true. With their army equipment, massive Russian troops have arrived near the vast meadow we are approaching, pushing their way from the east. With its machinery in tow, the British army is also a stone's throw away from here. I can only suppose this is the situation."

The caravan of fatigued German soldiers with whom Ruth and her family travelled came upon a big meadow. Both women were shocked by the unexpected sight of the multitudes of German soldiers in the same area their convoy needed to pass through. Pandemonium was taking hold of everything, human and beast. The caravan of soldiers, Ruth and her cluster saw the sight unfold just beyond them. The soldiers buckled their helmets and bolted from the vehicle, dashing in every direction to disband and abandon their duties. Within seconds, the truck was void of any military inhabitants.

The power of the moment overtook Ruth's family.

The soldiers' horses had become a hindrance. It appeared that the other soldiers in the crushed brown-green meadow with horses and wagons must release their animals because the counteroffensive was headed toward them from all directions.

The women knew they must immediately get the children out of the truck, but where could they find shelter away from the madness in which they found themselves? The soldiers snaked their way under the nearest abandoned German trucks and wagons in a bid for survival. The German soldiers were defenceless. There was no longer hope in counting on their assistance. Some other soldiers could not conceal themselves while their comrades were racing for their lives. Others pushed their way into the trucks and wagons to avoid the onslaught of horse hooves. Some in grey-green woollen uniforms struggled to melt into the earth like the sheep they had hoped to eat but had consumed years earlier.

As the desperate tried to escape the warring sides, panic developed among the other refugees surrounding them, trapping them inside the vast meadow. In the dusk, it was challenging to differentiate the foe from their countrymen.

Ruth recognised their truck driver's voice shout, "On one side of this vast meadow are British soldiers who appeared from the western side of the field with their heavy machinery lined up to battle to the end. As far as my eyes can see, on the other side, several rows of Russian soldiers with enormous tanks are supporting their own position."

The Russians made a stronghold on the eastern side of the field, lined up with their heavy equipment as far as the eye could see. Both armies were at a standoff, the perfect canvas for the devastation of the meadow. Both armies moved like beasts pouncing to cause havoc in their wake.

The intended standoff of the two armies on either side of the meadow caused Ruth's small family to freeze in their tracks, terrified of getting shot. Before they realised what was happening, her little family had been locked between two antagonists.

Ruth's tears poured forth – love for her country now that her nation was torn asunder. The German people would be in mourning for eternity from Hitler's gruesome atrocities and those of his henchmen who took part in them. Would the history books, together with the storytellers, look cruelly on her country as they had after the first big war? Or would the world look kindly on her people with the realisation and the knowledge that most of the German people were not responsible or approving or aware of the twisted violence the Nazi Party created?

The comprehension of their future hit Ruth like a dagger in the heart. She was once again cut to the quick. There would be no returning to the Klein Pobloth Estate for Rudi, who cherished his home. Now, all was lost, never to be seen or experienced again. The Kempen Estate was lost in the dusty path left behind by the Russians. Ruth's soul was jabbed to the core whenever she heard or thought about her own family. Desolation struck her when the realisation pounded at her. For weeks, she had not heard from her dear mother, Luise Schläger, her sister Elizabeth, Margret and their families. Was Peine the town where Ruth hoped her mother found safety lost also? Ruth did not know if her siblings or mother were alive or dead. If her family members were lucky, they would have escaped from the wrath of the Russian army and all would be well in her world. She feared the Russians had plundered her childhood home and burned it to the ground, the beloved home she adored, where she and Rudi were married and Susanne was born. They lived there with Susanne until the young family moved to Klein Pobloth, where Hans-Georg and Dorlies were born.

The personal losses of the countless letters left behind and the photographs taken of loved ones – Ruth would never see them again. Now, they must be etched in her mind. These small and large articles would be the most profound losses for anyone in the same situation. Ruth's children would not get to appreciate what their grandparents, including other relatives, looked like. Instinctively, Ruth placed her arm around the children to protect them from unseen hazards. Without expecting an answer, "Among the uproar we find ourselves in, what can two women do to safeguard our family?"

The atrocities the SS had conducted over the period when Hitler was in power had become increasingly despicable. Outside of Ruth's realm, the horrific loss of life worldwide was overwhelming.

The moon was like a lantern in the sky when the mayhem escalated. Out of the darkness, swarms of liberated prisoners of war flowed over the crest of a hill and then streamed down to the vast meadow where Ruth's family was tightly huddled. It was apparent to the refugees gathered there that the prisoners of war had no instructions for where to go after they were released. Their only option was to join the masses amid the German soldiers and the refugees who had previously gathered in the meadow. The onslaught of naked, troubled, ill, crippled and insane people

The Meadow

was a horrifying sight, thoroughly alarming the collection of humanity already gathered at the foot of the small knoll. Without consideration for the welfare of the native society, the liberators released the prisoners of war, not taking the time to screen them first. Consequently, convicted criminals, people with mental health issues, prisoners of war from various countries and religious groups were released simultaneously.

Although danger awaited them, Ruth peered about the meadow. She could not close her eyes. Within seconds, Ruth saw that the field was an anthill of pandemonium. German men and women hid amid the abandoned German military equipment. Then, a new form of devastation unfolded in their path with new fear as the enraged POWs neared the family group. While life within her family ebbed, her spirit was still strong. As if the bowels of hell had swallowed them, countless refugees stood in the field, helpless, bound with sorrow, weeping bitterly. Containing her own grief, Ruth stared into the fearful groups. She could not utter a sound as she flung her headscarf over her shoulders, and her brown eyes glistened with tears. Ruth gloomily thought, *This is the end! This would be the crushed key to our destiny now that the war has reached its final hour.* Still silent, she made a fist, 8 *May 1945, the date will go down in history.* Breathing deeply, Ruth curbed her fears, gently touching Anneliese and repeating her oft-spoken projections. "We have been chosen to survive," her grip tightened. "We must survive to care for our children."

Like panicked rabbits weary from their perils, Ruth's family cluster was huddled on their little patch of the meadow with the other masses of people somewhere between the small seaside town of Travemünde and a stone's throw away from the larger bombed-out municipality of Lübeck.

Under hostile conditions, the next day, Ruth and Anneliese, with their children, spent their time in anxiety, alternating between hope and fear. Terror dominated their every thought. However, the children did not understand. They knew something had changed in their mothers' demeanors. Nonetheless, the two women steadied their nerves and resolved to plunge ahead despite their misgivings. Lübeck was out of the question. The constant massive bombings had obliterated the town over a year ago. With the destruction of their country, the most significant old cities, such as Dresden, Leipzig, Leuna, Berlin, Hamburg, Hanover, and Lübeck, among countless others, had been annihilated, bringing their nation to its knees.

They would be no better off there than where they were now. Alarming to the family was the potential danger lurking in every Allied authority figure.

While staying at Schloss Prüsen, the women had heard news snippets over the shortwave that a POW camp for officers, Oflag. X-C was located near the city. Lübeck was attacked by the Royal Air Force on 28 March 1945 and persevered until 2 May. Without opposition, Lübeck had been occupied on 2 May 1945 by the British Second Army.

The burden of Germany's collapse into a black, miserable pit of unmitigated disaster was brought on by Hitler and his collaborators into their current, every day, miserable lives. Ruth and Anneliese comprehended much of the rumours of the German soldiers' atrocities. After the Great War, Ruth understood, "To the victors go the spoils and woe to the vanquished." Ruth also understood that as the Allied objective was achieved, many of these rumours were outright propaganda by the opposing forces. The hostile situation was created by military forces striking at the centre of Germany. The eastern countries had coveted this vital central European territory for centuries. Their military troops had gained a foothold in the land and the Baltic Sea. Atrocities by these groups were rampant and hidden.

Chapter 20

THE HORSES

Ruth's family cluster had been thrown into the midst of the thunderous clamour occurring on an enormous meadow near where a POW camp was located. Their best chance for survival was to surrender to the British, who occupied the western lines along the enormous pasture.

With the anticipated release of the prisoners, the German political factions had been eliminated. Thus, it was difficult to understand the social and political explosion when the new military forces' prisoners were freed, and they did not comprehend the type of individuals being released. Many were criminals, mentally ill people, and starving people who had not been fed properly by the failing German guards. All were ready to attack anyone in their path for protection and a bite to eat.

The demilitarised German military, along with their equipment, horses and wagons, found themselves trapped in the meadow between the Russian and British armies. In a desperate bid for survival, the soldiers left their military wagons and horses and abandoned their posts to escape their inevitable fate.

Among the individuals in the meadow were German mounted troops, their minds clouded with uncertainty as they tried to determine whether their best options were to flee or surrender to the British army, which had established its outpost along the western length of the vast meadow.

Given that the meadow was filled with dangerous choices, the chaos heightened. The high number of horses mixed with humanity intensified the danger of the surrounding expanse by closing the gap and causing extreme apprehension among the family.

The night sky darkened the horizon, triggering a few sizeable searchlights that scanned the meadow and beyond the hill in the direction where the released prisoners ran wild. Enormous torchlights were added and placed in various locations to allow both military forces to see clearly. Appeals for law and order bellowed out from both sides, only to fall on deaf ears. Restlessness once again increased, potentially causing more harm to befall Ruth's family.

Survival again intensified the name of the game for the family with the deep thunder of machinery mixed with horses' hooves galloping free and ringing through the meadow throughout the night.

Escaping the Russian Onslaught

At dawn, Ruth and Anneliese ached from the lack of sleep, allowing themselves to get carried away believing they could snare two horses from among the countless running loose in the meadow. Parched, hungry and grimy faced, each searched the other's expression for approval. Ruth could feel her heart beating faster and faster in her chest. The calculated plan evolved hastily, expanding with excitement building within her until she thought she would explode. As Ruth regarded Anneliese, she said, "I am not a coward – neither are you! I have never stolen anything – this is not the time to think about that." Sternly, each mother instructed the children to watch out for one another. With great zeal, they stripped off their coats, stepped out of two layers of skirts, leaving only their undergarments on their shivering bodies and dropped their clothes on the cold ground to add to the golden fleece blankets for the children to sit on.

Without thinking clearly the two women rushed to where the horses ran loose. Realising the British and Russians were openly eyeing them. They acted quickly. The unrealistic moment lying before them was eerie since their undertaking was extremely dangerous.

Quickly, the power of unadulterated concern for their family empowered the two women to attain the unthinkable. In striving to give their family more security, the two women behaved as if they were in mortal combat. They did not relish being injured but recognised that there might be no other choice.

The two small women snuck over to where a large, wooden, covered buckboard stood, along with two horses grazing nearby. The animals and the equipment appeared to have been abandoned by the German army. The women nodded at each other in agreement, understanding one another's meaning. Each woman pretended to have food hidden in her hands. They had learned long ago to make the click-clacking sound to get the attention of horses they tagged as their own. The wild horses were like the ones in the American Wild West, and the women were like the wise indigenous Americans stalking their prey by coaxing a black and a tan horse their way.

Anneliese attempted to seize the larger black mare when the horse approached and grabbed the mane on its broad black neck and enormous head, but the animal was determined not to be captured. Anneliese cried out in pain, but Ruth could not hear her over the fierce racket in the meadow. Her plan to melt away into the dusty afternoon sky was foiled. After several unsuccessful attempts, there was a fierce struggle to capture their horses right under the noses of the Allied forces as if they were already seasoned thieves.

Ruth grabbed onto the mane of the elegant tan gelding. Since the meadow was still as full as the night before, the horses fought the two women out of fear from the dreadful racket. Their pilfering would have been easier if the two women had blankets to throw over the horses' heads to temporarily blind them. As it was, they only had one blanket between them, and it now covered the children.

The Horses

When Ruth took hold of the mane, the smaller tan gelding twisted so that Ruth wrenched her wrist until she was forced to her knees with a cry of agony. However, she did not let the animal loose. Instinctively, she grabbed the horse with added force to bring herself up with her free hand to hold the tan horse, only to find herself entangled in the mane. Ruth's sudden strength startled her. She found the gelding attempting to struggle again and nipping at her shoulder. She was determined not to concede but whispered to the animal in a soft, soothing tone in hopes of helping to relax the frightened animal. Ruth began to caress the tan gelding's smooth, slender neck with tender, firm, yet gentle strokes. Slowly, Ruth controlled the animal. Biting her lower lip, she wondered if this beautiful, unfortunate animal had been abused.

Ruth glanced over in Anneliese's direction before doing anything else to jeopardise their plight. She saw that Anneliese had had an easier time getting control of her black horse. The black horse must have been accustomed to labouring as a farm animal and was familiar with being handled.

Anneliese felt Ruth's eyes bore into the back of her head, then turned in Ruth's direction to see the anguish on her sister-in-law's face. "Are you all right?" she asked.

Ruth did not hear the words, but the meaning was clear. She nodded sideways, conveying her dilemma. Anneliese had her hands full with the large animal she had picked out and could not be of any assistance.

Soon, salty sweat ran down Ruth's forehead, making it difficult to see. She felt like her entire body was exploding from the sheer force of her emotions. She wished to cry out in pain but did not. Instead, Ruth bit her lower lip until ruby-red liquid oozed out between her teeth. *Above all else, we cannot have the enemy think we are thieves.* The thoughts of being caught ran rampant up until, in the end, she became indifferent. *We've lost the game. Our families will be placed in the depths of Siberia so no one will ever discover our whereabouts. Now, none of this type of thinking. I have children to worry about!*

Ruth instinctively bit her lip harder. This time, she tasted the warm gooeyness of the ruby-red blood. Although determined not to succumb to the attack of her unruly horse or disentangle from her grasp on the horse, she assessed her fate, tightened her hold on the aggressive animal, and then swiftly sputtered out the bloody rank taste of rage.

Ruth looked around to see if she and Anneliese had been found out. They had not. She and her sister-in-law worked side by side to gain control of the horses. Each woman captured the prize for which they were striving. Anneliese shot Ruth a glance of approval. The two women immediately turned toward a wagon they had eyed earlier within arm's reach of their children. Each had acquired a horse to tow by its lengthy mane and set out to grab the sturdy, bonnet-covered wagon with a worn-out neck yoke, plus two sets of harnesses still dangling from the wooden bench.

When Anneliese touched Ruth's shoulder and shook it, Ruth soon returned to reality. Both women, who grew up around horses and buckboards, knew what to consider when pilfering the horses and the covered buckboard. Everything had taken place so rapidly that they had gained two horses and a wagon before they knew it. What struck Ruth most was a strange euphoria at realising their accomplishment. Her earlier objections to her sister-in-law and the many disputes they had had before and at Klein Pobloth quickly evaporated. Anneliese's provoking attitude towards Ruth had disappeared in the dust surrounding their battlefield.

Without their knowledge, these two stalwart women belonged among the countless fearless women of the world's history. They had the most essential items to exist, yet they were still vulnerable. Nevertheless, they needed one another to survive these wretched, difficult, unyielding times. Surviving the horrific ordeal and avoiding recollections of the home they loved became necessities. Hopefully, they would learn to live without personal disputes and leave them behind. The journey had allowed the two women to keep their children and their most sacred part: their souls.

Chapter 21

THEIR LIEUTENANT

The blackness on the horizon changed the light from the British and Russian searchlights into a golden glow, giving way to the drowning sun. Lying on the rough, crushed pasture, the children were huddled together, finding solace in pressing their dirty little faces against one another and seeking to avoid being spotted by the many vagrants running free in the enormous meadow. Susanne, Hans-Georg and Klaus-Dieter were sniffling out of the utmost concern for their mother's safety. Little Dorlies' big blue eyes and the other three children solemnly absorbed the furor around them. Dorlies was the youngest of the three other children; therefore, she was the most sensitive and traumatised. Her lack of understanding of what was happening hid her speech behind a veil of terror.

Both women struggled to have their horse attached to their rickety old army wagon. Sweat dripped from every part of their bodies. Ruth took her battered right hand to rub her brow, leaving a trail of dirt mixed with tan horsehair behind. She glanced at Anneliese, who skillfully controlled her animal. Subsequently, she did not have to struggle, thus finding the reins easy to fling onto the rusty iron wooden spokes of the large wheels and secure them. Soon, the two women securely harnessed the tan gelding to the other side of the wagon.

Anneliese put her hands to her waist to crack her injured back into place. Ruth bent to tie her undone shoelaces. In doing so, her back screamed from the pain. Their aching feet could barely carry their throbbing bodies back to their brood. The women heaved their youngsters into their new home and scuttled in after them. Too weary by this time to tidy up, they found solace in their new surroundings. The mothers explained that the wagon was their new home now, yet as usual, they huddled as they had become accustomed to, protecting one another. The children watched the greenish canopy quiver with the breeze, creating a mumming thud. Nevertheless, they took comfort in their new surroundings. Ruth tenderly adjusted the children's outgrown coats, loosened their tight shoes, and pulled up their threadbare socks. She spat on her hand to rub some dirt off Dorlies' and Hans-Georg's tear-stained cheeks and forehead. While tidying up, Susanne flipped her thick blond braids over her shoulders as Ruth spat into her hands once more to wipe her grimy, tear-stained cheeks.

Anneliese said, "Did you see the British soldiers eyeing us? I really don't care because, for the first time in two months, the responsibility of hanging onto our rucksacks and small suitcases have become the obligation of the horses and wagon that are our chariot to freedom."

Ruth smiled at Anneliese sheepishly. "Did you see them? When I looked at the soldiers, I felt the British soldiers' eyes boring into us, and I knew they were intently observing our battle with the two horses and wagon."

Within a few moments, the cluster was sound asleep, resting in their newfound home.

The setting sun glowed upon the wagon. Ruth stirred and then bolted upward, pressed her index finger to her lips, and shook Anneliese's shoulder. "I hear someone coming close to the wagon." An adrenaline rush hit Ruth as she rose hurriedly, shaking her head to make sense of her new surroundings. She had always been a person who could go to sleep at the tilt of a hat and wake easily.

A brief silence fell on the interior of the buckboard.

As the two women snaked forward to the opening of the canvas, the old wooden army wagon creaked, sending shivers of fear down their spine, trembling with panic that soon turned into self-assurance. Ruth straightened her shoulders. With the unabashed authority of ownership, the two women quickly leaped out of their new home to plant their feet firmly on the ground of the trampled pasture without thinking twice. Their brood huddled together in the wagon's back, hanging on for dear life.

Little did they realise a young British officer had been eyeing them, including the buckboard, for some time. The young officer was eager to prevent further aggression against the little family. Merely concerned for their well-being, the officer had meandered over to their buckboard.

Out of trepidation, Ruth puffed twice at her oily mahogany hair creeping from under her green headscarf as she fidgeted by the wagon. Ruffled and grimy as they were from their ordeal, the two stalwart women inched towards the animals to try to divert the soldier's attention from the children within their wagon by stroking the horses' broad necks and speaking sweetly to them.

Finally, he spoke in a low, commanding voice. "Why are you taking these two horses and this wagon?" Out of anxiety, they clasped their grimy hands together behind their backs to keep their hands from shaking.

Ruth studied Anneliese, who stared back at Ruth. "Engländer?" Overcome with joy, the two women discovered that they, indeed, were confronted by the British Military, known to be extremely civilized compared to the Russians.

The young man's gaze was intense, and his answer was short and to the point. "Yes, I am a British officer and investigating the goings on."

Jolted, they jumped back three steps when the soldier posed the question, strained not to be afraid, but their rigid bodies would not have it any other way.

Their Lieutenant

Ever feeling threatened, Ruth could not understand the young man since he spoke English. Still, in her mind, the officer was articulate. He motioned to them to take the children out of the wagon so he could examine the interior. Ruth sensed that this man, by the tone of his voice, excelled in goodness. However, he also exuded power.

Ruth could not understand him. She felt her heart pounding in her throat. She backed against the buckboard, where she grabbed onto the wheel in order not to topple over. Ruth found the heavy iron rim cold, released her grip on the wheel, thrust out her palms, and shrugged up her shoulders, indicating she did not understand.

Ruth noticed the officer's nose crinkled while a soft smile played at the corner of his kind eyes, and soon a chuckle came when he saw her petite little girl, Dorlies, whose infectious smile softened everyone's heart. His eyes appeared to be filled with empathy when he saw her daughter's big blue eyes. After the British officer saw little Dorlies and the other children, he exhibited compassion that only a young parent could understand, beaming affectionately at the children. Thus, Ruth felt the officer understood their apparent dilemma.

Although the sun was setting, Ruth could see the colour drain from Anneliese's eyes, which appeared as large as the eyes of the horses. To Ruth's way of thinking, the end of their downfall would be the two different languages clashing.

The British officer questioned them again, stroking the tan horse with surprising tenderness. When the horse refused to respond to his touch, he said, "I believe these are military horses, including this wagon?"

Ruth's knees rattled under her woollen skirt. The officer's words blurred her mind because she did not understand English.

Anneliese was irritated with the whole business. Her blue eyes became vibrant, and her forehead furrowed. After struggling to find the words to explain, they initially came forth in German and she finally spoke up in frustration, with unbounded energy and a self-assured voice. There was a brief pause. English words began coming from her quivering lips, her voice cracked, and she insisted, "These are our horses. The horses became entangled between the horses the soldiers released in the meadow. Perhaps we did not have them secured to our wagon properly."

Ruth's brown eyes stared in confusion as her jaw dropped in astonishment and she staggered back when her sister-in-law found her voice and spoke to the soldier in English. So absorbed in Anneliese's assertiveness for their defence, Ruth became rigid like a piece of dried wood. Ruth hung her head and muttered under her breath, *Gott im Himmel. What is she up to? By speaking to this British officer, her actions might entangle us in a new, dangerous situation.*

Ruth's throat became dry when she heard Anneliese's use of the English language. In all the havoc, she had forgotten her sister-in-law had spent six years learning the English language, including history classes at boarding school. *How convenient is this?* A fleeting depressing thought came over her. *It is time for me to help. But what can I do to assist Anneliese? I am a strong female. Now, it is time to put it to use. I can no longer stand the degradation and will not begin to sob in a hoarse voice. I must control my raw emotions. It is for our future, our children's potential.*

Hoping to resolve their plight, Anneliese stumbled over her words. "Please. Oh – officer, please help us out of this painful situation," Anneliese begged. She half expected herself to do the same in her native tongue.

Joining the younger officer, an elegant-looking, higher-ranking, older English officer sauntered up to the wagon, and for a long moment, he studied Dorlies, the three other children and the two women who were protecting their children like mother hens. The older officer leaned into the younger officer. "Lieutenant, you know a little German. Please help me ask this woman to purchase..." he leaned forward, casting a smile at Dorlies, who studied him continually. The big-eyed officer hoped for ownership of the young child. Soon, the older soldier asked the younger officer, "Bargain with the child's needy mother to purchase the charming baby girl for me." He pulled out his wallet, fanned out a handful of crisp English bank notes, and then explained, "My tour of duty will be over in a few days because of my past injuries, and then I will return to London. My wife and I could not have children. Therefore, I feel that taking the gift of a darling baby girl will make my tour of duty worthwhile and make my wife happy upon my return."

The officer seemed appalled at what the older, higher-ranking officer was asking of him. With a grave look of concern, he explained the situation to Anneliese, who did not need to explain the older man's request to Ruth. Her appalling frown revealed the outrageous request when she glanced at Dorlies.

Stunned by the unexpected, outrageous offer, Ruth was appalled by the proprietary state of the older officer's demeanour. The Allies were attacking her family's sense of morality. Now in control, this greedy officer wished to buy her daughter. Ruth froze in disbelief for a second, gritted her teeth, and clutched onto her little daughter for dear life, revealing her motherly attachment to her darling daughter. Ruth's resentment took hold: she felt her dark eyes flash with hatred. Her breath was knocked out, her knees buckled, and she felt faint. The long, arduous moment for her did not pass lightly. Repulsed by his offer, her wish to kick him between his legs subsided when she realised nothing good would come from her rage. Ruth's joy of being rescued by the British made her feel regret that soon turned into apprehension. For the offensiveness of this man's suggestion, it would please her to see him burn in hell.

As he laughed rudely, the older officer realised his mistake and reflected it in his behaviour. He held his nose snobbishly high in the air to indicate his pride was shattered and he needed to regain his composure. He lifted his chin higher and pressed his lips together, clicked his heels, and returned to the line of British troops.

Once the older man was on his way, their young English officer profusely apologised to Ruth, with Anneliese translating for her sister-in-law. "I am appalled by my colleague's actions." The young officer's attempt at pacifying the two women did not take hold so easily.

Ruth's eyes were still filled with tears, and her temper flared. Trembling from this British upstart's audacity triggered Ruth's tears to spill over. Ruth lifted little Dorlies into the covered wagon. The other children scurried to the big wooden wheel hub, with the women showing them what to do. They stuck out from the middle of the wheel as if it were a stepladder designed for each child's safety. One by one, they scampered to their hiding place under the protection of the green canvas tarp in the wagon, huddled together in one fearful, shivering bundle. Ruth climbed into the wagon's back with her three children. After the sharp pang of her near loss, she kissed her three little ones on their temples one by one and embraced them close to her breast as if to reassure herself that her family was well. The rest of the world could go to hell in a handbasket, but she and her children must survive this miserable war.

The British officer pondered. His mouth and forehead still showed the frown he had worn earlier. Without hesitation, he spoke his mind, "I am willing to help you get the horses under control. The disorder in this meadow most certainly has frightened these unfortunate animals. I will get a couple of my fellow soldiers to help also." The officer turned to his troops on the far west side of the meadow. The young officer asked Anneliese to ascend to the wagon. She did as ordered. Then, he lifted his right hand to beckon two younger soldiers over.

From the wagon's bed, the women could see two young men in British uniforms immediately run to him. Once by his side, he gave them orders in English. Finally, with assistance from the British officer and the soldiers, the two horses were hitched to the groups new living quarters. However, he informed the women that the horses should have new equipment to secure the wagon more safely.

With the broadest smile she could muster, Anneliese leaned out of the wagon to speak English to the British soldiers. "Thank you, young men, you are too kind." The men took off their caps and bid them a good day.

Ruth's resounding voice echoed from within: "Danke – Danke." Then, she jumped to the floor of the brown meadow. She stretched her right hand to the British soldier and said, "Danke."

Before Ruth realised what had transpired, Anneliese clambered up on the wooden bench and threaded the reins between her fingers. The young British officer assisted Ruth in ascending to sit beside her sister-in-law. Exhausted and bewildered by the whole ordeal, Ruth sat next to her without uttering a word.

Escaping the Russian Onslaught

Anneliese tapped the reins and clicked her mouth to guide the horses to a haven. The black horse was willing to cooperate, but the elegant tan gelding reared up in protest, spooking the other larger animal. In their haste to take the two horses, the women did not take the time to size them up to see what type of horses they were. They did not consider that horses must work together until they coordinated their stride to trot securely on one side or the other as a team. They also did not realise the black might have been accustomed to pulling a wagon where the tan was only comfortable having a man on his back.

Consequently, the two horses they seized did not match up as a team. The long-legged tan gelding pulled and tugged at the yoke to the right while the heftier black horse was accustomed to pulling the wagon's weight. However, Anneliese successfully moved the buckboard to a more secure meadow area. The women felt God was good to them on this day, as they gained a mighty advantage over many of the other unfortunate refugees. In the end, the result of their brazen bravery gave them new hope.

After resting for a while, the two women set to work with great excitement and anticipation to search for what might be hidden in the ditches. The hours between darkness and dawn would be the best time for the family to forage for desperately desired items. While the rest of the family foraged, Ruth ordered Hans-Georg to stay in the wagon and to keep his little sister occupied.

Anneliese, Klaus-Dieter, Susanne, and Ruth quickly scrambled to pick up as many effects as possible, abandoned on the ground by other refugees who could no longer carry them. Nonetheless, this only amounted to a few pots, pans, and one blanket.

Like two mother hens, they gathered up their chicks and scurried them back to the wagon, heaving them into the bed under the protection of the canopy with strict instructions to stay put.

Once Ruth and Anneliese saw the children safe, they busied themselves by rescuing their meagre belongings from the German army truck they had abandoned earlier. In the darkness of the night, the two women moved like wild animals hunting, creeping along the cold ground as low as possible, and made it safely to the truck they had occupied earlier. The women peered into the bed of the vehicle. To their astonishment, the wooden planks were still there. Ruth swung her leg onto the fender and slinked into the bed. Anneliese followed her sister-in-law. Ruth crept to where their treasures of odds and ends were concealed among the boards in the rear. She snatched the few pieces of clothing used for snuggling.

In their weakened state they took all they could carry on their backs. Although the load was light, it took an effort to haul their possessions the small distance back to the covered wagon. They lifted their skirts, and Ruth helped Anneliese pull herself back into the safety of the wooden wagon, where the canvas cover helped protect them from the elements and nosy bystanders.

Ruth stretched out her small hand to caress Hans-Georg's back with slender fingers. She said in a hoarse, exhausted whisper, "Now, no one can disturb the restful sleeping children in the wagon. I think, at last, they feel safe even amid the thundering hooves of the horses mixed with the shouting of the people who are still out of control. They need to find peace in this darkness. So far, I sense the children feel protected by their new home."

Anneliese's voice was no longer energetic, yet she was compelled to speak. "I hope we can get some rest despite the cries from the desolated souls still scattered on the meadow." Out of fatigue, both women stretched out. They dozed off on the cold wooden boards of their new home, their wagon. Their exhaustion, along with their suffering, finally took its toll.

Chapter 22

A NEW FRESHNESS

The first rays of spring sunlight gleamed through the small cracks of the canopy covering the wagon, waking them and giving them time to collect their thoughts. The sun had a new freshness that Ruth had not seen for a long time. She felt she should take a few moments to tidy up their recently acquired quarters.

She sat up, rubbed her eyes, and realised how her body throbbed from the ordeal of the day before. Glancing at her new surroundings, she determined all would be well. She smiled and whispered to Anneliese, who drowsily placed her elbow under her chin: "Regardless of the quantity of rubble I saw earlier lying about, I think it would behoove us to collect as many items as possible. We do not have a heavy enough pot to cook in. Most of all, we must have a fire to cook with."

"If this made any difference," Anneliese barked out of indifference. "We do not have one potato between us or a drop of water to make a soup for the children."

Ruth struggled to keep her displeasure under control. "After such a daring gallant effort, at the very least, we need to try. The three older children can help. Hans-Georg can once again keep a watchful eye on Dorlies. Odds and ends are scattered about in the ditch others have discarded because they have gotten too weary of carrying their belongings and left them behind."

With the sun climbing higher in the sky, the two older children and their mothers emerged from their wagon, their movements synchronised. In hushed tones, the mothers instructed the children to be as quiet as possible, turning the task into a game of finding hidden treasures. The women, in turn, focused on more practical finds, their collective efforts a testament to their shared responsibility.

The horse's neck yoke was worn, posing a safety risk. The day's most significant hunt would be for much-needed newer equipment, a crucial step towards keeping the horses secured to the wagon. The undeterred women began to strategise, their determination to find the necessary gear a prerequisite for their journey west.

Soon, the sun crept over the horizon, awakening the crowd. Although the women felt they could load the wagon with more belongings, they soon discovered that masses of horses and people were still causing havoc in the meadow.

Ruth found the chaos debilitating until she could no longer stand it. She alerted Anneliese to the other dangerous entrapments in the meadow. They scooped up the two older children just in time, placing them into the wagon before other horses bolted toward them.

A New Freshness

When the family returned to the wagon's rear, their fatigue was unbearable. Unconsciously, Ruth brushed her face, fingering the dried grime from the sweat she had endured during her battle yesterday with the tan horse and their encounter with the British officer. How long had it been since she last washed her face, took a hot bath, and brushed her teeth? The dried blood around her mouth would need to stay there until some precious water could be found.

Ruth studied Anneliese. Still drained, she glanced at her sister-in-law and realised what her own appearance must be like. Her cheeks turned pink out of embarrassment. Anneliese scrutinised Ruth's actions and quickly understood her thoughts. Both women chuckled despite themselves.

Great thirst was upon them, yet Ruth and Anneliese gathered a bit of saliva in their mouths and spat the liquid into the hem of their tattered skirts to attempt to rub the grime mixed with horsehair and dried blood from their bodies. They stared at their torn, filthy fingernails and hurriedly hid their hands under their skirts. They endured one another's bitter oaths out of concern for their mutual suffering.

Ruth spoke. "What has it all come to? We are struggling even to feed our children. But for now, we are alive and under cover of darkness, we will draw ourselves up below the heavy canvas for protection."

Ruth felt herself dozing off when she awakened abruptly but knew not why. Apprehensive from the events of the days before, she lay still, struggling to decipher what had roused her. She reached over to stir Anneliese, who struggled to wake.

Out of the moonlit shadows, they heard deep, vibrating, rumbling, horrific sounds spreading in every direction. Some of the racket poured over a nearby knoll's crest. At first, tentatively. Then, shouts of panic suddenly brought Ruth and Anneliese back to reality, shattering any dreams of homesickness they might have harboured during their sleep. Ruth's family immediately peeked out from under their protective coverings. They could hear the extraordinarily high, ugly laughter reverberating down the incline to where their wagon rested.

Ruth shivered, "This is more terrifying than anything we have yet experienced."

"Ruth, what on earth is happening now?" Anneliese endeavoured to understand but her panic only added to the hysteria they heard outside.

Ruth answered, "Something has set the whole meadow into a renewed rage."

It had taken no time for the children to be awakened from the first restful, sound sleep they had enjoyed for weeks. The sleepy little ones were too terrified to move. The women stood next to the wagon. They saw men, women and some German soldiers descend from different confinements into the open meadow.

The multitude moved toward them for endless moments, wedging together until the meadow was covered again. The pressure on Ruth's emotions was beyond belief.

Anneliese spoke out of frustration: "The masses add to the confusion already taking place. Now, there is little room to stand. I wonder how many people the British and Russian armies plan to squish into this meadow. We thought we were going to manage to get away. Some look like wild animals."

No more rest came to them that night. The strange, disturbing noises surrounding the meadow were more daunting than they could imagine. The blaring noise kept the children awake. Muttering softly to Anneliese so the children could not hear her fear, Ruth said, "I am left to wonder if there will ever be a chance for happiness after all that has happened during the last few months. My spirit is being challenged to the core. I wish Rudi and Achim were here to help us sort out the many decisions we must make at a moment's notice."

Midday arrived with fewer worries other than the overcrowded situation in the meadow. How were the two women to feed the children, no less themselves? Dehydration, along with hunger, would be their biggest enemy now.

They saw the young British officer who had assisted them earlier walk over to the wagon. He realised the two women with four children were in dreadful danger.

By now, they felt he could be trusted. Ruth remarked before the officer was upon them, "He must have left a sweetheart back home or a wife and children, a man who is sensitive to a woman's needs and trained to scrutinise a dangerous situation. It's all I can do to stop myself from having you ask him about his family. I must give you credit, Anneliese, that you had the nerve to speak with him in English."

"I am stunned to receive a compliment from you, Ruth. Everything has gone awry. I am so frustrated about our situation."

All Anneliese could do at first was to stutter and then speak again when the officer was within hearing distance. "Oh, Herr officer… Herr officer." She beckoned him over with a little pleading. She stretched out her hand. "I beseech you to please… you remember me. My name is Frau Hertel. Sir, you were kind enough to help us the other day. Now, this time, we do not understand what is happening. Are we in more danger today than yesterday?"

"Yes, I recognise you and your family, Frau Hertel." The young, dark-haired, brown-eyed officer looked like he had been born into a warm family atmosphere. The handsome officer profusely apologised. "No one knows what happened, but the rumour is that many more prisoners of war were released today. Among them are ill people from the camps around here who were not freed earlier. You, ladies, must be aware that these people are alleged criminals. Other undesirables might have blended in with the mob. They might mistreat you. They showed their joy since they came in hordes, converging onto this full meadow. I would, of course, suggest you keep your family in the wagon. Do not show yourselves."

Ruth noticed the young officer becoming aware of the long distance he had left between him and his troops. She glanced over to his group, which was exhibiting some nervousness. The young man beside them breathed deeply, trod a few paces back, tipped his cap, and said, "Ladies, perhaps we will meet again."

The two women nodded their heads in responsive gratitude.

Chapter 23

MAY SUNSHINE

The day's last sunshine was struggling to send its beams over the horizon when Ruth noticed the two horses' heads jerk upward. Their ears flickered back and forth as if they were antennae listening to something undetectable to the human ear. Before the family saw them, the multitudes of hysterical individuals gathering on the crest of the hill were surging in the distance, the sun hidden by people gathered there.

Out of the wagon's rear opening, the two women could see mayhem caused by more released POWs, who were disfigured people dancing in the dirty haze, causing great dust billows to rise. With the Allies saving them, their joy overflowed.

With tears welling up in her eyes, Anneliese questioned, "I can see what is happening now. How are we to survive the day's destruction with all this mayhem? It is as though we must defend ourselves against hundreds of fanatics?"

"Mutti… Mutti, Mutti, I am frightened!" Whimpering, Susanne tugged at her mother's skirts to protest the ugliness in front of her young daughter.

"Hush, I know, Susanne, I know. I am frightened also," Ruth whispered back to her elder daughter. She raised her daughter's chin. "To keep ourselves busy, we will play a game. You can count your buttons to see how many beautiful buttons you have on your sweater that I knitted for you before the snow fell this winter." She ran her fingers through her daughter's hair. "Your thick blond hair has grown so much in the past months, so I will tidy it up by re-parting the back into two wonderful new braids. I think you will enjoy it like this." Ruth soothed again after seeing Susanne's lower lip buckle and quiver since she did not wish to participate. "I know you must miss your lovely room with all your clothing and many lovely dolls and bears remaining at Klein Pobloth."

"Oh, Mutti, I do not miss my dresses as much as my farm animal friends and the folks still on the farm."

"Our friend Pinnow and the other families are looking after your pony plus the red ox you enjoy. Remember fluffing their small tufts of curls on top of their strong, big heads. Well, now, we will count the buttons…"

Before Ruth finished her sentence, Susanne cried again, "Mutti, I am afraid." The continual roar streaming toward them startled the youngsters, who were crying uncontrollably. Susanne, Klaus-Dieter, Hans-Georg and Dorlies were ashen from their terror. The uncontrollable, despicable masses were emerging in such droves.

To the adults in the wagon, the new masses appeared to be made up of thieves who were immediately ransacking the other refugees' belongings. Susanne lost her place in counting, just as she was ready to start counting again. Once again, her blue eyes were drawn to the racket. She yelled out desperately when one of the younger men poked his head under the canvas. Susanne was ready to smack him. "Mutti, they are climbing into our wagon." Screeching, her little six-year-old hands batted at the intruder, "No. No. Oh, no! How dare you – this is all we have left!"

Ruth pleaded with her child, "Please just sit still. No, better yet, back up and snuggle close to me." Susanne did as told. "Let them take what they want. We can find more useful things later in the day. We can think of better times and happier moments since we have sacrificed so much. We will not bother ourselves about these people. Above all else, do not start to fight them if they take something we wish to keep." Ruth tried not to appear too alarmed. All she wished to do was scream for help, but no one could come for support. *Oh, Rudi, please come and help me.*

More intensely than before, Susanne sobbed, "I don't understand Mutti?"

Ruth gathered her thoughts to soothe her daughter. "I understand if you think this is unacceptable, Susanne. You are not old enough to realise what is happening. In many ways, I do not know either. Hopefully, you will understand someday when you are grown."

"But to just let them take things and not to say anything. It is hard to swallow my anger." Susanne tried to hold back the tears spilling over her pale face.

The two women and the children's eyes became wide, filled with terror, when they saw a woman turn her gaze towards the children. The toothless woman spoke over her shoulder to the man, who heaved himself down from the wagon to wait for the woman. "Do you think we can sell these children if we take them from these stranded women?"

Ruth could feel her stomach flip-flop and then tasted the green bile on her tongue.

The woman's comrade in arms shouted angrily, "Fool! We do not have time to drag them along. Ignore them! They appear too small to bring us coins for a meal." Lifting his fist, he shouted, "They are not old enough to work. Let them be. Leave them behind!"

The woman snorted back at the man in disagreement. "What about the two women?"

"We can't take on baggage like that. These women seem like they haven't done a full day's labour. They must be from the nobility. Just glance at their soft skin with their dignified manners. They would not be strong enough to pay for their own food. Let them be. We will move on."

As unexpectedly as they had rushed into Ruth's family's wagon, the vagabonds abruptly moved into the semi-darkness. Ruth's eyes followed their every move.

She felt dreadful for the refugees in the buckboard sitting close to theirs as she saw the group climb into another wagon. By the exclamations creeping through the canvas covering, she knew that the thieves were ransacking their way through this wagon. A blood-curdling cry suddenly erupted from what sounded like a young woman in excruciating pain.

Ruth and Anneliese looked at each other in a questioning way. However, the two women did not dare reveal themselves for fear that these vagabonds might change their minds and snatch one of Ruth's young daughters for their pleasure.

Susanne again lamented, "These people stole just about everything we have gathered together."

Ruth desperately struggled to quiet her family when suddenly, in the blackened night, she heard new footsteps. They had a distinct resonance, an all-encompassing sound of authority. "Hush, children. I believe the British officer might be coming to speak to us again."

Inside the wagon, the sudden silence was uncanny. Anneliese peered through the canvas opening and then enthusiastically spun around to confirm Ruth's prediction. "You are correct – our British officer who befriended us earlier." She hastily lifted the greenish canvas. When her eyes adjusted to the outside light, she saw a friendly face smiling.

The officer tipped the brim of his cap and quickly spoke his mind. "Because of the number of people flowing through the area, there is little we can do. Ladies, I do regret your circumstances."

"Well, yes," Anneliese snapped her fingers out of frustration. In her fragmented English, she said, "Oh, yes, these people are stealing the only belongings we have left. They are treating the other refugees in the same manner."

Eager for Anneliese to translate to their officer in his language, Ruth added her frustration in German. "What is still more astonishing is that the British are allowing the havoc to occur."

Anneliese quickly translated for the officer.

Catching the two women's distressed gazes, the officer tipped his cap to them, turned on his heels, and hastened to his troops to gather as many soldiers as possible. Galloping down the slope on their mounts, the British soldiers surrounded the masses within five moments.

Three soldiers rapidly placed Ruth's family cluster into a holding position while they stood guard on their mounts. The handsome young officer made his way to Ruth's family again and said, "For the time being, you are safe. I sent the British troops to protect the rest of the German refugees." His assurance was a Godsend to Ruth's family cluster.

After considerable restlessness, Ruth suddenly heard Anneliese begin to breathe laboriously. She discovered her sister-in-law had found sleep. Ruth rolled to her side and then noticed Dorlies' backside, seeking to snuggle into the warm recess of her mother's spooned body. Ruth closed her eyes and recalled how she and Rudi slept in the same delightful position. Soon, she discovered the tranquillity she so desperately desired.

The following morning the two women discovered their hopes to move on were in vain. The two horses they had harnessed became willful and would not pull the wagon. Instead, they trampled the brown, dry vegetation under their hooves. The women would need to find grain and water for them somehow. The black mare was willing to pull her weight, but the tan gelding was a racehorse and was becoming too unruly to pull the wagon. This panicked state frightened the two women battling to control their buckboard, the horses reeling to escape each other's side.

"You take hold of the tan horse, Ruth, and I will work with the black horse. They are powerful enough to topple the wagon."

"Perhaps we should have the children get out for the time being!" Ruth screamed in the direction of her sister-in-law. Quickly answering her own question, Ruth spoke her mind. "If we do, we will once again jeopardise the children, risking them being kidnapped by some refugees who have lost their own children."

An expression of terror came over Anneliese's face as she considered her sister-in-law's words, "You're right. We cannot take a chance on the safety of our children. We have seen that such stories are true."

Ruth yelled as hard as she could, "I do not know how long I can fight this beast due to the chaos. Fear is panicking these animals, causing an alteration in their behaviour."

Their young British officer had his eye on their dire situation. He was willing to assist them once again. He rushed over to where the family's wagon stood in the meadow. The officer gazed at Dorlies' bewildered eyes and then saw her recoil, not knowing his intentions as he stretched out his right hand to finger the blond curls at the back of her head. "I cannot allow this to happen," he ordered with authority only an officer could use.

The young officer took control of the wagon and the family within. "I am the father of a little girl about the same age as your little blond one. I cannot allow this dreadful fate to take your family's wagon and topple it over."

With one jerk of his large arm, the most uncommon event occurred. He instinctively grabbed the black horse's halter and calmly took control. With self-assurance only an officer could achieve, he tugged at the horse's harness to get Ruth's family cluster to where the British soldiers were camped.

Too astonished to respond, no one within the wagon made a sound. The women leaped out of the buckboard in exhilaration when they learned that they were safely on the British side.

Elegantly, he took hold of both women's rough, battered hands, bent over slightly, then one at a time tapped his soft lips on their calloused grimy hands, "From now on, you will be safe."

Both women glowed with profound gratitude for the British officer's valiant actions to save the women and children from destruction.

Ruth beamed. "It is as if he is fulfilling an obligation. You do not have to translate his words for me. His actions speak volumes. I am still petrified. There is no one to help drive the challengers off or continue to help us after the care the young officer gave us. Yet, my dear sister-in-law, by nabbing the horses and the wagon, you and I have succeeded in doing what might seem impossible to other women."

Ruth and Anneliese sat transfixed on the rough oak wooden bench, not understanding why, out of all the refugees, this young British officer, with so many emotions, consciously aided in saving their lives.

The officer rushed back to his troops. As the reality of their situation hit, Ruth's family felt incredible gratitude for him. This young officer made it possible for their wagon to be one of the first to cross over the meadow into the border area where the British held their position. Ruth's family greatly respected this compassionate young British officer and the other soldiers responsible for saving their lives.

Chapter 24

FIRESTORM

The family cluster soon learned it had been a bittersweet victory for them. After the family's arrival on the British side, a firestorm broke out between the British line and the Russians in a decisive move that neither force could squelch. The Russians torched the buildings in the area.

Within seconds, the bystanders' screams resonated in the rig. Overwhelmed by the light of the orange and red blaze setting the canvas of the buckboard aglow, the family clung to each other inside their wagon.

"The horses. The horses, we must rescue the animals!"

Ruth lifted her skirt and sprang out of her spot in the rig, with Anneliese right behind her. In one leap, both women were planted beside their harnessed animals. Anneliese tossed her navy blue and white polka-dotted blouse over her black farm horse's eyes, which were terrified by the blaze. Ruth's attempt at persuading the tan gelding was not as successful.

Ruth click-clacked her tongue, but the creature could not be controlled as the animal reared on its hind legs, its forelegs pawing wildly into the glowing atmosphere. The animal whinnied in terror, flinging its head and mane toward the ground long enough for Ruth to throw her skirt over the horse's panicked eyes.

Stroking their horses, the women shivered in horror while the multitude of refugees silently stood, observing the blaze with debris fluttering in the heat of the firestorm until it was lost in the updraft.

In no time, the area was an inferno. Smoke billowed up to touch the clouds now dusted with fragments of glowing red, deep-orange and black charcoal bits drifting through the heavens. The silence in the area was broken only by the dust crackling from the blaze.

"You and I hated Hitler while others followed him like blind sheep. This division in our nation has backfired for the next thousand years Hitler and his Nazi Party had in mind to conquer for our homeland and the world." Salty tears tumbled down Ruth's cheeks and along her neck. She turned to Anneliese, whose eyes were also rimmed in red.

Another shrill cry erupted from Ruth. Soon, her 4 August 1933 recollections overwhelmed her. *These events have shaken me as deeply as when I was forced to relinquish my firstborn baby daughter, Annerose.*

Firestorm

The violent upheaval continued in front of their eyes, drawing Ruth and her sister-in-law closer together in some mysterious way, even if only temporarily, overcome by the carnage occurring during the past few days. They were unaware they would soon reach a pivotal turning point for humankind. Still quaking, Ruth's family cluster and the others in the area were hit repeatedly and more powerfully than the unbelievable was true. The reality was that the foremost leaders of the liberating countries, the United Kingdom, America, and Russia, were bent on a quest for revenge against Germany and its people.

Reports leaked rapidly, so the two women heard glimpses of information to confirm the rumours beginning. Throughout the last months of the war, the other nations had shaped Germany into a living hell for its people – questions of why and the wrong of it all lay heavy on Ruth's heart. Yes, Hitler and the Nazi thugs were ignorant madmen with lofty goals and corrupted beggars working with the devil. These uncultured oafs were mistaken and misguided in their crimes against humanity and God. They pushed the vast majority of the people of their nation into being cynical and callous. However, not all levels of German society entertained the same philosophy as that hideous tyrant and his followers to deserve all the atrocities and crimes now being perpetrated.

The two women embraced. "Anneliese, my soul has been ripped out of my body." Both women shook in each other's embrace. "Yet I am grateful to manage to get away with our lives," Ruth murmured as she and Anneliese sank into deep despair. "I empathise with all men, and I know our nation will no longer have enough men left over after the war to heal itself. We can no longer be thin-skinned about the criticisms already cast at us. We must rely on our judgement in dealing with how to survive."

Ruth and Anneliese were among the thousands of refugees who could not stop themselves from viewing the destruction in the immense landscape stretching beyond their view. After Germany had surrendered on 8 May 1945, German soldiers and many younger and older men who might again rise, believing in Hitler's ideologies, were herded together like cattle to the slaughter.

Ruth flinched at the thought of the many German men hiding among the refugees for protection so the Russian or the British soldiers would not take them to a new POW camp.

Ruth said, "The occupying military has destroyed our country. Anneliese, you and I crossed this volatile border because we have small children; therefore, we were saved. Sadly, no one realised Stalin was as much a monster as Hitler."

The next half an hour was like a black hole, a mystery as to what was happening.

Thwacks could be heard against the wagon after the firestorm, causing extreme family anguish. When a young questioning face stuck its head under the wagon's canopy, Ruth and Anneliese pushed the children under their covers to protect them from the intruder. Gasps of dread emerged from the entire cluster, but they were too terrified to speak.

The young soldier nearly made his way into the wagon's back when he caught Ruth's eye. He crawled up to her and muttered, "You must help me?" The young, blond-haired, blue-eyed, terrified man pleaded while knowing he was in a very questionable position of entering as an intruder. "I am terrified of being captured and then thrown into prison." He implored Ruth for her mercy. With mournfulness, he studied Anneliese. "My name is Steffen..." Bitte – Bitte, I need help. I can quickly discard my trousers and disguise myself as a girl if you ladies can give me a blouse, skirt and scarf so I will not appear to be a soldier." The youth rushed on, hoping to make his point. "In this way, I can come with you, belong to your family... be one of your daughters."

The childlike German soldier studied the two women with intense pleading. He was filthy and agitated. "The rigid Russians, the main culprits, are targeting the young men in hopes of placing us into prison camps. After that, they order us to Siberia for a hard, punishing labour life."

Ruth's family soon realised that having a young man would greatly help them gather foodstuffs and relieve them of caring for the horses. The women saw the young man's point of view most clearly. In moments and without hesitation, the two women agreed that Steffen would become part of their family cluster and allowed him into the safety of the wagon.

The chaos continued for several days as Ruth and Anneliese determined they must be strong and think clearly. "There must be a way for us to get a hold of some of the cinders left behind by the firestorm. I believe Steffen has been sent to us for a reason. Anneliese, you and I will make a necessary request of the youth."

"I do not understand what on earth you are dreaming up this time," replied Anneliese in bewilderment.

"If you will simply think for a moment. The one thing we need is an ember of fire to make our lives easier. We can ask Steffen to fetch several small pieces of wood still smoldering with a slight amount of fire ember. He has military training in hiding among the opposing forces. Just think how this fire could make our lives easier," Ruth urged Anneliese into her way of thinking.

Ruth took it upon herself to ask Steffen the vital question. Once it had been posed to the young man, he recoiled with a terrific reaction of unabashed horror. He backed away from Ruth, "No... You cannot ask this of me. I have been in the worst situation of my life for the past years. Now, you ask me to mingle among the same forces who would imprison me?"

Ruth's feminine, motherly charm oozed out as if striving to seduce a skeptical foe into submitting to her way of thinking. "Yes, I suppose it is a crazy idea. Since we saved your life, you are now part of the family. You might consider this your part in helping us to stay alive. It is still spring, so the nights can get mighty cold near the Baltic Sea."

Steffen melted into Ruth's palm just as she hoped he would. "If I go out, it must be tonight because tonight there might still be live ember. Besides, the moon might give me enough light to find my way through the darkness to achieve the impossible."

By what the two women guessed, close to three in the morning, Steffen finally crawled quietly back into the rear of their wagon.

Chapter 25

SHATTERED DREAMS MAY 1945

The darkness was replaced by the dusting of greyish crimson, announcing the dawn. Ruth and Anneliese were awakened by the rattle of tin cans on the rickety small wagons in the endless files of carriages. They craned their necks from under the gold fleece blanket to see what was around. The chill touch of the morning air caught the two women off guard. Ruth felt her heart palpitate at seeing the bedraggled humanity again making their way westward.

Presenting a more immediate threat were two women and one young man struggling from starvation and to take care of their children. With every passing hour, the acid bile was building from hunger. The infestation of lice caught from the other refugees feasted on their thinning bodies, but they could not lose hope now. Both women's nerves were as raw as last fall's butchered meat, yet they had to work together as a team. Like the others, the two women bundled up the few belongings left to them and pushed on their way among the rest of the disgraceful migration.

During the many weeks on the road, the women had little luck finding a place to wash and clean themselves, much less the four small children. Before getting underway again, the two women busied themselves by covering their hair in miniature printed multicoloured scarves that they learned to knot into a turban to hide their unwashed, mussed hair.

The morning sunbeams rose over the horizon, casting a welcoming glow on the meadow, filtering its light onto a small stream, casting the promise of spring. To freshen herself, Ruth stepped near the icy water. Suddenly, Ruth was consciously aware of her being and sniffed her underarms to smell the rank odour, instinctively yanking her head back. The last bath or washing machine available to them had been at the castle with Irene. She had run out of the scented powder in the first few weeks after leaving Klein Pobloth. The prized bars of soap were also gone. Immediately, she fanned herself to get the stench away from her nose. Her feet, socks and shoes smelled like Limburger cheese. She would gladly exchange her smelly footwear for a bite of the tasty spread, a delicacy in their country, no longer available because of shortages.

Dismissing the ugliness of her feelings, Ruth needed to make sense of which garments to wear for the top layer. The underlayers of everyone's clothes were extremely nasty by now. Ruth dropped her three shirts to the cold, damp, weed-covered soil. Then, she stepped out and picked them up with the striped multicoloured wool skirt and the beautiful fawn-coloured leather suit her dear departed father had given her as a gift, placing them in her suitcase. She layered the dark brown skirt to cover the two she favoured most. Her bodice was covered by a dingy, cream-coloured blouse that she kept hidden with the threadbare, dingy green sweater, alternating with the jacket from the leather fawn-coloured jacket. Ruth was glad for the heavy brown woollen coat she had decided to take on their journey. Sadly, being worn day after day by someone unable to wash her garments, the coat also reeked of an unpleasant odour. These garments could rest in the wagon's bed in warmer weather.

A sudden burst of what sounded like a chuckle erupted from her. How silly Ruth had been when she shoved her belongings into her suitcase. Ruth had been vain enough to match all the items as during her younger years, even when she packed only a few belongings.

Ruth resembled a mother stork making nests to house its brood as she struggled to settle the children in the various hiding places in the wagon she and Anneliese had prepared earlier.

As the multitude moved along, enough water with which to clean themselves was provided by the farmers they passed, but not much more. Any bit would do. How would she keep the children from breaking out in a rash? Unfortunately, infection, influenza and dysentery were among their many problems. Without the necessary water and soap, soon their skin would turn into coverings of brownish-grey patches where bacteria were thriving. This ugly trademark had been a sight on many of the refugees. Sadly, her family cluster, too, soon might unwillingly wear this same obnoxious characteristic. For Ruth, as a mother, the worst was when she could not keep little Dorlies from having a raw bottom. The children learned to go in the nearest ditch or behind a bush and then use the weeds beside them to clean their bottoms. Naturally, this made her baby girl bellow with pain when the blisters became too large and then burst.

Chapter 26

TO LÜBECK OCCUPIED BY THE BRITISH

The blighted northern portions of Germany fell into British control, and the country struggled to establish order for the refugees. After leaving the meadow, the family's weary wagon carried them to Padelügge near Lübeck. Ruth and Anneliese, their faces etched with exhaustion, took in the unfamiliar surroundings. It was a brief respite from their arduous journey, a moment to catch their breath before they continued.

Then, they moved on to Lübeck. Ruth's stomach lurched at the sight. They saw what was left by the bombing a year earlier. After the bombings, intermittent publications had been printed. While living at Klein Pobloth, Ruth had read the accounts repeatedly in the Kolberg newspaper until she had practically memorised the words. Only a waxing crescent moon could be seen on 28 and 29 March 1942. There was little light to be thrown at the bombers to keep them hidden from view on the ground. So, this was when the Royal Air Force bombarded the city of Lübeck by night since the moon's light was a shining beacon for the fliers to see the historic town by the Baltic Sea. When the British finished dropping their hailstorm, the Hanseatic League city, built in the Middle Ages, was turned into a firestorm, sending the city's active business centre into ruin.

Decidedly emotional, Ruth and the refugees saw hundreds of buildings that had been obliterated into a thousand pieces by the British Royal Air Force. All that was left were demolished buildings, another reminder that the fabric of their country was torn asunder, a lingering image that the world had gone mad. Ruth's strong resolve crumbled. She and the other fleeing refugees stood in the field as if held down by the ashes covering the city. With tears, the two women did not know they still possessed. They stood in utter speechlessness. Ruth's heart wrenched with dismaying sadness as she and other German refugees studied the bombed city destroyed by a virtual firestorm. The refugees' tears fell like cascading salt spouting out of fountains that should have dried up months earlier.

In the few months the family had been away from Klein Pobloth, Ruth had become someone she did not recognise. Destroying the traditions built up for hundreds of centuries in only twelve years, Hitler and his henchman had earned her hatred and added to her disdain for the Nazis.

Gagging in agony, Ruth confessed, "Up to this point, our heritage was the pride of all Germans."

Ruth and Anneliese could not fight back their tears. Agonising sorrow drowned Ruth's attempt at speaking, and she felt hollow in the pit of her being. Ruth, Rudi, and Anneliese were born when the Kaiser was in power. They grew up having pride in their male offspring in the army, navy or air force. In earlier days, to devote one of their young men to military service was a noble privilege. German citizens were always proud of their highly technologically advanced and powerful German military. The horror lying before them was proof of how their current government had deceived them. Seeing the city was a terrible realisation, a wake-up call for what the German people were to endure from there on out.

The two women let their tears flow over the vast destruction within their broad view. Their ardent spirits smashed, they and the other spectators knelt and stared at the obliteration of the city and their hopes. Bowing their heads and with heavy hearts, like small children, they wept and begged for God's help. Seeing their mothers carrying on in such a manner triggered the four children to wail. There was no other noise, no movement, nothing but sobbing from the others standing and kneeling at the horrendous sight in front of them.

The fact was that there would be no more rich land and edible crops to feed the masses. Thus, everyone realised this was the end of everything. Germany, as they knew it, was destroyed. There were no more illusions, no more hopes. Their livelihood was annihilated: the spectacle before them sealed their fate. Among them, there was no doubt that, from this point, they were defeated, and their lives forever changed.

By 11 May 1945, south of the outskirts of Lübeck, there remained no misjudging of the temperament of the immense homeless masses. With general uncertainty for their future, Ruth's family was thankfully protected by the British soldiers who turned the large area into a makeshift camp. However, the military was utterly helpless to feed so many families and meet their countless needs. There was nothing to shelter the enormous number of migrants from the need for food or the damp spring days, not to mention the cold, humid, unfriendly nights. Ruth's family felt fortunate to have the wagon they had bravely appropriated.

Now posing as a teenage girl, Steffen did not need to shave regularly since his peach fuzz was still a part of his rosy complexion.

Ruth smiled gratefully. "Steffen, you have helped us restrain our unruly horses with your strong young muscles. Cloaking yourself in a hit-and-miss-matched fashion with the combination of Anneliese's and my clothing has proven useful. It is not as cold with the spring air, so we can shed off some of the layers of clothing we walked away with."

"That reminds me gnädige Frau Meissner and gnädige Frau Hertel, perhaps it would be a good idea to find me a girl's name."

"Why, naturally, you are correct if you are to survive and live among us. We must find you a girl's name. What name would you like us to call you?"

"Now, let me think." He hesitated momentarily and said, "My sister's name is Gretel. How would you like an older sister for your two girls, Frau Meissner? After experiencing the harshness of war, I am thankful to pose as a caretaker for the youngsters and occupy them with childish, cheerful games."

"Gretel, it shall be. You have been re-christened."

"Yes, Gretel, we are grateful to have you among our group, particularly your joyful diversion for the four children," Anneliese explained.

"Danke schön, Steffen... No, Gretel." Ruth smiled thankfully. "You are an official part of our family, so you should address us with a familiar first name. Anneliese will become Tante Anneliese; you can call me Mutti as my children do. We might be found out if we do not follow a normal family conversation, which would endanger us."

"Ja, we agree," a chorus of childish voices from the group's three older members said.

Curiosity got the better of Anneliese, so she heaved up her courage to speak to a befriended British soldier to gain information. Anneliese's fractured English had improved over the few days the British Military protected the family. Through her understanding of English, she discovered that Russian troops had attacked Berlin on April 1945. The Americans had infiltrated Nuremberg on 20 April 1945 and thousands of infantry divisions had taken over much of Germany's western part.

The hostility between the refugees subsided when the British Red Cross cooked enormous pots of food for the multitudes. Still, the masses remained in lines with tin containers they had found on the side of the byways or carried with their belongings. The migrants also felt protected from the Eastern forces, making them feel less paralysed with the dread of being swallowed up by the Russians at any moment.

In the early morning, folks gathered, especially where the Red Cross from the British forces who occupied this area was set up to assist the refugees. Everyone tried to get a bite to eat. At best, soup with lots of water, last year's cabbage and potatoes was welcomed. At worst, the soup was water-thickened with flour and a little salt. It temporarily stopped their hunger, warmed the refugees and lifted their downtrodden spirits.

The British soldiers informed a small group of refugees outside of Lübeck that there was abandoned German military airport housing in Vorrade. So, the houses were empty. If Ruth and Anneliese, with their children, wished, they could live in one of the small bungalows. The British would inform the family when these houses became accessible.

To Lübeck Occupied by the British

One of the large farms where Ruth's family stayed overnight was supplied with too much milk since the farmer had no assistance to get the milk to the next town to be sold. Nor did the farmer have a way to store the milk. The farmer was beside himself that he would be forced to throw his splendid dairy products away. Thankfully, the farmer gave away as much creamy whole milk as possible. Naturally, the refugees were overjoyed to receive the bountiful farmer's gift. Unbeknownst to the masses, the milk was too creamy for their malnourished stomachs because they had not eaten rich foods for months. To their dismay, everyone became extremely ill with diarrhoea.

The family unhitched their wagon and slept in the friendly farmer's farmyard, but nothing could help bury their past dreams. Now, the only option was to deal with their unwanted hunger. Finding oats for their horses and food for the family became their goal. Ruth's and Anneliese's newly found barbaric natures forced the two women to burrow through the food intended for the animals in the barn that belonged to the farmer who put them up for the night. At every opportunity, the two women and Gretel pilfered what they could, sifting through the oats meant for the farmer's horses and giving the remainder to their own horses. Saving some oats for food for the family, with calloused, filthy hands, they extended their skirts to hold the grain to cook for the family's meal. The children were instructed to help sift through the oats, find the mice droppings and toss them out.

Ingeniously, Gretel caught on quickly, grabbed a feedbag from one of the horses, and then ran outside, where he spotted a rain barrel on one side of the barn. Within minutes, Gretel returned with a scoop full of water to add to the oats. There was a place outside where a fire could be built. Ruth placed the oats and a large amount of water in the only tin available and boiled the mixture over a makeshift campfire for hours to sanitise the mush as much as possible.

"Without salt or any other spice to add flavour, the mixture will have little taste, but it will warm our tummies." Ruth glanced into Hans-Georg's eyes as if the consoling message was meant for his ears.

Gretel had become accustomed to watching the entire area surrounding their location where the family chose to rest. He made his way back to the family in a flash. "There is a huge crowd of soldiers gathering nearby. It looks like something is going to happen within the hour."

It was heart-wrenching to hear the drunken shouts from the British soldiers. "It is more than I can endure," Ruth choked. "On the one hand, the German people will be glad the conflict is over. Nonetheless, I feel our hearts will wrench in pain for the rest of our lives."

Once again, the bitter tears would not flow from Ruth's eyes. She heard Anneliese moan with pain as the two women clutched onto their children. The family stood at the crossroads of history as if they were accused of some monstrous crime. Ruth's, Anneliese's and Gretel's shoulders were slumped with humility, "Well, now, no tears." Ruth demanded.

"What is happening out there, Mutti?" six-year-old Susanne asked.

"Darling Susanne, it is simply too difficult for me to explain now," Ruth calmed her daughter. "We should return to the warm barn and eat our oat porridge."

They sat by the open-pit fire. Ruth ladled out small portions of the so-called soup. Hans-Georg dipped his spoon into the hot liquid, hungry as ever. He pulled a dollop: "Oh, Mutti, the soup looks like long stringy hairs are growing from it. Besides, some types of little brown shells remind me of little animals floating in every bite."

"I know Hans-Georg. But getting the hard shells from the oats without the proper tools is impossible. Mutti cannot help it. Do you understand? This is all we have to eat tonight, so if it helps, close your eyes, breathe hard, and then swallow quickly. The porridge will not scratch as it goes down to your belly. It will make your tummy stop hurting and will make you feel cosy and warm."

Ruth glanced around at the others, who wore the same expression as her son. Tears welled up in her eyes. *I will not let them drop. I will not let them fall.* She then pulled back her shoulders and began eating the porridge as if it were made for a queen. Anneliese and Gretel followed her lead as the children gulped the soup through silent swallows of discontent.

The unyielding, deafening vibrations from the celebration roared through her mind like thunder. Ruth felt she could not endure the euphoric behaviour of the British soldiers any longer.

She tugged at her grimy, fawn-coloured skirt, so loose-fitting it could almost fall off her slender hips. Ruth wished so badly that she had thought about bringing several safety pins. They were such small items but so useful. Her thoughts ended when she heard Dorlies whimpering and tugging at her skirt for attention. Ruth realised she had been so busy attending to the never-ending needs of the family that she had not noticed that her daughter, who would be two in June, had not uttered a word for weeks.

I still do not know if Rudi is alive or lying somewhere under the rubble in an unmarked grave like countless other soldiers. But I must move on. I must survive, even if only for the sake of my children. Besides, things could always be worse. We might have ended up on the Russian side.

The Lübeck area became the British border, while the Russian border encompassed the area of Mecklenburg-Vorpommern, Brandenburg, Berlin (excluding West Berlin, held by the United States on July 1945, Britain, and France), Saxony, Anhalt, and Thuringia. The United States zone, the Rhine Regions, and Eastern Germany became the Russian zone; Britain held Schleswig-Holstein, Hamberg, Lower Saxony, the province of Westphalia, and the North Rhine area. France, along with the U.S. and Britain occupied a zone in Western Germany

To Lübeck Occupied by the British

encompassing areas like the Rhineland, Baden, and Württemberg-Hohenzollern. During this short time, the welfare of the refugees was largely ignored.

Countless wagons with refugees had already crossed over to the British side. Ruth's family and their buckboard would not have survived the massive overcrowding of refugees wishing to travel to the British side had it not been for their young British officer. Many other wagons and people pushed carts with their belongings, some on crutches, others almost crawling to get across to the British side.

Once more, Ruth's gratitude for their British soldier was apparent. "Just think, we could have been among the other German refugees sitting in the big meadow, not knowing where to go or what to do. But we have our wagon next to us, with the officer in control of the horses," she said.

With life-challenging struggles at every turn and the need for survival, Ruth grew as close to Anneliese as two dissimilar women could. After fleeing from the end of February to the end of May and on the road for so long the two women had settled into comfortable familiarity.

Chapter 27

THE BEACH HOUSE, 15 MAY, VORRADE

The political red tape took time to untangle before any normality could exist between the refugees and the British soldiers. During the war, the German military had acquired the small beach houses that the liberating British forces now secured for several women with young children in the beachside hamlet of Vorrade along with several uninsulated structures that stood only as vacation homes.

It was late afternoon, and Ruth's family's spirits were elevated when they discovered their name was among those chosen to live in one of the little beach houses. Anneliese took the reins as they pulled up before the painted greenhouse. Ruth was delighted to see a welcoming window with white wooden mullions like a Swiss cottage. She was pleased with the welcoming atmosphere of their new home, but at the same time, her heart sank when she thought about the thousands of victims who suffered from not locating a roof over their heads.

Turning to Anneliese, Ruth said, "I am pleased the British army is providing houses for us and food for our horses." Ruth took a moment to glance at the overcast spring sky, still glowing from the bright but diffused setting sun. "It would be difficult to keep the animals with us while living here if it were not for the army." Ruth felt a moment of concern watching the horses as they came to a halt. "Sadly, we cannot let the horses graze freely without being stolen."

Ruth lifted the children from the buckboard from the rear of the wagon. Unshed tears of joy came over Ruth as she bent over to pull Dorlies, Hans-Georg, and Susanne near her, close enough to give them a proper kiss on their heads. She hoped to secure their placement in the new home with as much love as she could conjure up in her waning spirit.

After Anneliese stepped off the seat, she held Klaus-Dieter high above her and kissed his freckled cheeks until he giggled.

Since their husbands had entered the war, the women had been the only constants in the children's lives. Currently, they were clinging to their mothers' spirits, which for far too long had been shattered, so broken, so torn that mending seemed beyond hope.

The Beach House, 15 May, Vorrade

Ruth was the first to peer into the front window and discover the house was furnished with a small desk, one small wooden table with four mismatched wooden chairs, and a small bedroom with a mattress on the floor. The sickening fear and absolute abandonment they had felt for so long diminished as they approached the green entry door. She felt a vague cheerfulness that allowed her to do her level best to make a concentrated effort from now on not to replace their former life but to make the most out of what was given to them.

Her body cringed and shook as she yanked the door handle until the fragile, summer-weight windowpanes rattled. Entering, she wished to pull her upper lip over her nose like an upset chimpanzee. Through gritted teeth, Ruth said, "Anneliese, the inside is covered with dead and live creeping vermin. Please tend to the horses while I see if I can find a way to get this new home of ours clean."

Under the circumstances, the family was willing to spend one or two more nights in their previous home, the wagon.

It was time to find some grasses and twine them together as a makeshift brush. Staring over the coastal dunes' lowlands, Ruth noticed the grasses she intended to pull reflected a hint of vibrant, pink dusk now beginning to darken the horizon. She also caught sight of numerous seagulls gliding in the sky where the beach might be.

If only the children could play on the beach so near yet far away. Breathing deeply to catch the brisk spring air, Ruth smiled once more. Her hopes ran high now that she thought the ghastly days might soon end.

They had mingled with countless strangers after leaving the Schloss, infecting the family with lice. The following day, the army fumigated the beach houses with the disinfectant known as DDT. As in the past few days, one more night in the back of the wagon would be tolerable.

In a rough tone, the soldiers ordered the women to lift their dresses, skirts, and blouses and the children their tiny little clothes to expose their skinny, small bodies. With gritted teeth, they exposed their dishevelled bodies to the soldiers who used handheld bellows to pump the white powder up their skirts into their clothing so that it could kill the varmints but might also absorb into their bodies. "First the front, then the back," Anneliese understood the orders too well. She could do nothing but show the group what to do. The rest of the families in the group followed her lead. She understood the next stern bark, "Bend down, lower your underpants, and then you will get a blow of the white powder everywhere."

"To say the least, this was humiliating beyond belief," Ruth grumbled to her sister-in-law. "What must the sweet little girls think? Not to mention the boys who are sensitive at this tender age."

"Never mind the humiliation," Anneliese whispered. "The rumours I have heard are sizzling. The white powder is a disinfectant called DDT. This horrible stuff might harm us for the remainder of our lives, particularly children, yet we must stand here, enduring what is dished out to us."

Escaping the Russian Onslaught

It was inevitable that this time would not be the last. Rumours flew in every direction: If the refugees did not follow orders, food stamps would not be allotted to those unwilling to submit.

The last thing they expected came a few days later. The refugees remained in line to receive shots to prevent typhoid. The injections were administered close to the neck in the chest. They were extremely painful for the refugees, especially the children.

Their day was not at an end because the horses and wagon needed a safe place to prevent being stolen by other refugees. Although tired beyond comprehension, the women were required to safeguard their few valuable belongings. With strict orders to the children to remain in the wagon, Ruth and Anneliese went to secure their next necessary acquisition.

Once among the British, Anneliese became more proficient in using their language. More than once, she saved the day. With Ruth as her companion playing the innocent, incapable female, Anneliese bravely sauntered over to several British soldiers. Five soldiers were taking a cigarette break by a pile of unwanted half-burned wood left behind by the truck driver when the soldiers gathered in the meadow. Ruth soon imagined the leftover wood built into a shelter for their two horses and the wagon. She shoved her sister-in-law and drew her eyes to the woodpile beyond the lads. Anneliese caught her meaning.

Clearing her throat, Anneliese began, "Gentlemen... gentlemen... my sister-in-law and I have a problem we cannot solve by ourselves. Your generosity blessed us with receiving one of the lovely beach houses. But now, unfortunately, this leaves us with another problem we do not know how to handle." With superlative wisdom, she and Ruth pleaded for help, making certain the men believed it was their idea to construct the needed lean-to.

One of the soldiers suggested, "I have an idea to solve your problem. After supper, we could spend the evening building an enclosure for your two horses. The men have offered to help me build the lean-to from the wood left behind from the burned-down buildings. We will build a shelter where your horses will be safe."

With her rough hands over her face, Ruth was overjoyed that her cleverness had succeeded so well. But without Anneliese, the plan would not have come to reality.

One of the soldiers added, "Both of you women must be beyond exhaustion. I will find another lad to give you a hand cleaning out this filthy, bug-infested cottage and carry your belongings into the house." The British soldier beckoned to his companion, and within a few moments, the soldiers assisted the two women in unloading the wagon and placing their belongings into the beach house. Once in the house, the new soldier found Gretel attractive, sending "her" a broad smile and a meaningful wink from his twinkling brown eyes.

Ruth noted his flirtatious approach. Pulling her sister-in-law close, Ruth whispered her wishes to Anneliese, who quickly understood Ruth's rapid observation.

The Beach House, 15 May, Vorrade

"Now, now, none of that, my good young man. Gretel is far too young to be placed into a situation with a handsome British soldier like yourself."

"Yes, mam. I understand. It will not happen again."

With a sympathetic smile, Anneliese added, "Bless you for your understanding. When you go out to your companions, please thank them for the welcoming support they have shown us throughout the past few days. Without their help, we would not be alive tonight."

The young soldier beamed as bright as the stars beginning to make their way through the night sky.

"My sister-in-law and I will bid you goodnight now. If not, our bodies will fall where we stand."

The soldiers saluted the two women and then bid good evening to the remainder of the household. Both women stood inside their new home's entrance and watched the soldier stroll over to his chums. They saw him pick up a wooden plank to aid the others in building the promised shelter for their horses.

Ruth's family's safety felt assured by the chatter from the soldiers working just outside their new home. The British soldiers refrained from making the family feel like they needed to cower down. The soldiers smiled while measuring food portions for them with a little cup of hot British breakfast tea. The family could not remember the last time they had sipped anything hot or felt how quickly relaxation would overpower anxiety.

The nourishment did not need to be forced upon them. With sheer humility, like street urchins, their endless hunger allowed the family to use their dirty dishes just as they were and then stand in lines receiving rations so they would have at least a small bite to eat. The family stretched their eager hands to the food the Red Cross provided and then gulped it down. Eventually, the pain in their empty bellies would subside. The refugees were exceedingly pleased to have the help so generously given.

They were under British control, so Ruth felt it was important for Anneliese to teach her to say *thank you* in their language. It would also be wise if she tried to learn a few more words. Thank you would not be enough for her to get by, but she would put the plan aside until tomorrow.

Without warning, the Allies had all the refugees on their hands. Beyond anything else, hunger grabbed hold. Thus, the agony had become a part of the family's lives for such a long time that everyone moved at a snail's pace. Ruth became aware that little Hans-Georg was becoming particularly undernourished. His situation was exceedingly difficult to perceive since her dear son had such an angelic nature about him. For now, there was nothing more she could do about their hunger.

After what had occurred, both women's nerves overwhelmed them, and sleep came quickly. Ruth awakened with a start, yearning for the security of Rudi's arms around her, but it seemed like she had been an eternity away from him.

Escaping the Russian Onslaught

When chatter woke the family, Ruth hurriedly asked Gretel to fetch as many small branches as possible and a long, straight stick to make a makeshift broom. Gretel was also sent to find a tin can large enough to use as a bucket for fresh water. Once found, they ripped apart one of the garments to use as cloths to wipe up the filthy table, chairs, and floor.

The women hauled the disinfected mattress as far away from their home as possible fearing it would be stolen. They left the mattress lying where it was to air it out, otherwise they feared becoming gravely ill from the germ-infested bedding. No matter what, Ruth's family was determined to make the best out of what they were given. Thus, they would eventually spruce up the bedroom with the mattress and their golden blanket on the floor and the other as a makeshift living room, doubling it as a playroom for the children. A tiny desk was in the sitting room since it had been used as officers' quarters during the war.

Once the house was bug-free and aired out, the women rushed to see if the mattress was still there and were pleased to see the mattress was where they had laid it. By stomping on the mattress, they used their tattered shoes to create a brown and black dust storm with dead varmints flying like a pepper shaker being used in the open air. The two busied themselves, brushing off the heaps of annoying pests and creating a small pit to entomb their enemy. Undeniably, good fortune came again to Ruth's ever-growing family. A British soldier saw their plight and volunteered to help clear their new home so that it could be habitable.

The housing search remained problematic for many others. Despite the challenging circumstances, Ruth's family, forced to keep a low profile due to the young German soldier in their midst, adhered to the strict instructions received at a general meeting for the refugees. They were resilient, adjusting to the muddle under which they were forced to live. Their resourcefulness was tested, and although they received food stamps, the amounts were never enough. They had been hungry for a long time, so filling their empty stomachs took twice as long.

Undeterred by the scarcity of resources, Susanne, always resourceful, delved into trash barrels sitting on the side of the road next to the housing the British soldiers were occupying. She found some old, discarded food in one of the trash cans but could not identify the big white crusted stuff with green fuzz.

"Of course, I will inspect your find. It is British bread," Susanne's auntie explained. "It is just lighter and fluffier than anything we have seen. If you wish to eat it, I suggest we cut off the mould."

Ruth chuckled to make everyone feel better. "And in this way, we can have our first taste of food we do not recognise."

With the assistance of the young soldier who had aided them the day they moved into the house, Ruth acquired a few packages of seeds from the British, who passed them out. Planting a vegetable garden would help the refugees have a more regular diet. As expected, the formidable women chose to be as self-sufficient

The Beach House, 15 May, Vorrade

as possible and to put some civility back into their lives. Without the constant chaos about them, the new silence around their home was a pleasure with which to become acquainted.

When the spring sun was high in the sky, the warm air returned, giving Ruth time to put her knowledge of planting a garden into action. Within a few weeks, the earth gave them a bounty of much-needed fresh vegetables: a few large radishes, a basket full of baby spinach, and a few carrots, which they boiled in salt water. This gave them something nutritious to eat. Ruth silently wished she had the herbs she had planted at Klein Pobloth to enhance the soup.

Anneliese shook Ruth's shoulders with unabashed joy. "The aroma… there is an aroma drifting throughout the house." Taking another deep sniff, "Children, just smell the delicious meal we will eat for luncheon. Without your mother's gardening knowledge, this fine meal would not have arrived at our table."

Thus, Ruth could provide the family with the necessary food and Anneliese with the communication needed with the British soldiers. In this way, two women who had been adversaries before the war worked well together to keep their family cluster safe.

Chapter 28

TWO NEW MEN IN THE HOUSE

After living in Vorrade for a few days, the women decided it would be better for Ruth to care for the children while Anneliese walked for one hour both ways into the bombed-out city of Lübeck and took her place, standing in broad bands of refugees waiting for the family's food stamps issued by the Red Cross twice a week. Her eyes constantly swept the crowds, chatting with anyone who would speak to her, desperately requesting information from whoever was eager to share. She was only one of the many people who probed strangers gathering around a building where word was posted from anyone they might know from their homes.

One day, as she walked through the refugees, she let the former unrest she felt vanish when she saw someone. With multitudes being displaced in Pommern, loved ones were impossible to locate. Nonetheless, a tragic figure soon appeared, and he looked familiar to her. To her astonishment and delight, Anneliese spotted Horst Schumann, one of their neighbours from the Lübckow Estate, aimlessly wandering the streets of Lübeck. She recognised his unique stride. Horst's mother, Klara, had been Dolores's best friend for years. Horst and his older brother, Friedrich-Wilhelm, spent hours playing with Anneliese and Rudi as children. Then, the three boys and Anneliese attended the same boarding school, Staatliche Genehmigte Private Oberrealschule, near the Tyrolean Alps.

With his dirty, shabby attire hanging from him as if he were already dead, Horst ambled about. Seemingly delirious, moaning, and babbling to himself with a great emptiness in the enormous purple shadows under his expressionless, hard hazel eyes. He was wearing grey trousers, which he must have stolen off a dead man, for they hung on him like a potato sack. He, too, was scanning the hordes of passersby in hopes of finding someone who seemed familiar.

Astonished to find someone who lived across the street from Klein Pobloth, Anneliese began to shiver as she walked with purpose toward him. His once-tall frame stumbled, and his eyes took a long lingering look of disbelief at seeing her. She rushed toward him. At first, his jaw clenched when he recognised Anneliese, his former neighbour, playmate and friend. She caught hold of him in a strong and relentless grasp. He flinched and drew back momentarily, distrust in his dull eyes.

Two New Men in the House

Anneliese yelled out his name in a cry of delight. "Horst. Horst Schumann is it you, Horst?"

Horst Schumann lunged toward her, but his body was too weak to move quickly, yet soon, the two scooped each other up in their arms. Anneliese smiled warmly at Horst as she pushed his shaggy, dark hair from his suffering face. In that instant, Horst recognised her girlish smile. After a lengthy embrace of welcome, the two sat down on a nearby rubble of concrete mixed with red bricks that had been scattered by shellfire. Striving to hold up his weak hand, Horst's weary hazel-grey eyes stared in surprise, and his mouth opened in a tired cry. His fears of being alone in this world had dissolved in her arms a moment ago.

Horst's recognition that there was a familiar face in the crowd after the horrific experience he had endured as a soldier was unfathomable. Before the dreadful war, Horst had a jovial sense of humour. The sight of a familiar, friendly neighbour diminished his state of agony from roaming about in an unwanted world mixed with homesickness.

Anneliese told him about their excellent fortune in finding the little house. Even though seven people lived there, he would be welcome. She told him how the two women had become shrewd and strong-willed in pilfering the two horses and a wagon that carried the family to Vorrade.

His eyes glistened with tears as Horst said, "I am embarrassed along with being a scoundrel for being so blunt. Nonetheless, times have changed, and so must we. May I come to live with you, Ruth and the children?"

Anneliese wrapped her arms around his waist. "Here. Come lean on me."

He raised his eyebrows in desperation and said to her, "In this world that has fallen apart for all of us, I do not know where my family is."

Arrangements were quickly adjusted to accommodate him. Saying no was out of the question. Having someone from Rudi's and her childhood along with them would make life more tolerable. While the women used the small bedroom, Horst was happy to sleep in the house's living room with Gretel and the four small children.

The British had constructed a small barrier between the refugees and the soldiers. The adults pilfered the only two rusty nails sticking out from the divider. The ever-growing family used the golden blanket and two nails to build a divider to ensure privacy between Horst and the children. The tiny dwelling appeared more like a vagrant's camp than a temporary summer vacation cottage.

After resting from his ordeal of fighting in the war, Horst told Ruth, Anneliese and Gretel the stories of his hardships. He had hidden in the rubble for days to avoid being captured by the Russians. When the zones were divided, Horst was grateful that he happened to be on the British side of the border. He rambled on aimlessly to drive the point home of his thanks for living under their roof. Horst explained that he could help with the horses.

"First things first," Ruth insisted. "We must put some meat on those bones before you fall apart on us."

Anneliese practiced her conversation skills with total strangers standing in enormously long lines to redeem their food stamps. Thus, she remained accustomed to speaking openly to everyone on the street.

Ruth had a timid personality as a child, so when she raised the children, she became clever at finding ways to keep them occupied with spoons and tin cans as drums. Creating a meal from what Anneliese could find with the stamps, combining them into something tasty, was difficult, but she became efficient at cooking those few foods scraped into a nourishing meal for the many occupying the home.

Within the week, Ruth took her turn on the one-hour track heading towards the city. Weak from hunger, she aimlessly walked, accidentally bumping shoulders with a man who shouted out in fear before recognising her. Turning angrily on his heels, with his untidy dark brown hair and bearded face to follow her, he recognised the gaunt woman ready to walk away. Albert Westphal graciously said, "I beg your pardon, gnädige, Frau Meissner."

Ruth's ears perked up at the familiar voice calling her name. She whirled where she stood in her thin brown leather-worn shoes and recognized Albert Westphal on the road. Although Westphal wore a look of undernourishment with a hard hollowness, they fell into each other's arms, embracing openly in the middle of the walkway. The former Lady of the manor and the farm labourer could not believe God was blessing them in finding someone else each knew from Klein Pobloth.

Inviting Albert Westphal into Ruth's family cluster was the only right and honourable act. While walking back to Vorrade, Westphal explained to Ruth that he did not know his family's whereabouts. At Klein Pobloth, Westphal had overseen the cows and the horses. Now, he was accepted as part of the family and everyone called him "Onkel." Uncle enjoyed being in a family atmosphere a more than being a soldier in the German army.

Thus, Ruth's extended family cluster grew in the tiny two-room summer vacation household to four children, two women and three men. Ruth's little family had swollen, and feeding everyone's bellies became challenging, yet she found joy in the extraordinary relationships developing in her cluster.

After Albert regained his strength, with the Red Cross's help, Westphal discovered his lovely daughter, Hilde, and his wife were still alive but had not been able to escape the East Zone in time. The Red Cross informed him they might not have escaped Klein Pobloth before the Russians entered Pommern.

Three young British soldiers who had their work duty assigned around the cottages during the next few months were not permitted to speak with the Germans. However, they sauntered around and lingered for periods of time. The family members observed the three soldiers for a while and realised they differed

Two New Men in the House

from the others. At first, the family thought they were just curious about their sad state. They looked to be simple, honest, good guys, but it seemed as if this group of British soldiers had second sight as they gazed candidly at the needy family. As if they could read the children's minds, the men strolled past them, smiling in delight.

The crisis of their pitiful state tapered off when, finally, spring was in full swing. The bounties of their vegetable garden lessened the family's desperation. The night skies deepened, and the stars could be seen more clearly than in many months. The dust from the bombing began to settle back into the earth where it came from. The atmosphere was calm, the sky equally so, Ruth and Anneliese stepped out of the house needing fresh air, where three men and four children crowded their space.

This evening, the three men were resting beside the stoop. At the same time, the two women tucked their tattered skirts under their derrieres and then sat on the edge of the splintered wooden steps leading to the beach house. Astonished at what she saw, Ruth nudged Anneliese and said, "If my eyes do not deceive me, I believe I see a jar of red jam sitting beside the fence waiting for us."

Delighted, Anneliese smiled, "If I am not mistaken, I know who gave us this mouthwatering treasure. The British guys miss their little ones, and their kindness will make our children extremely happy."

Ruth swiftly tucked the jar into her makeshift apron as they chuckled in delight.

The following day, three soldiers came strolling by and tossed several tea packages to the women at the front door. Often, gentle, tender, fleeting noble glances passed their way. The soldiers received their rations and shared them with Ruth's family; however, her family could not speak to these unusually generous men even as they edged into their lives.

After a few days, one morning as daylight was approaching and everyone was still cuddled close, a thumping was heard at the house's front door. The family rose in alert. Overwrought for so many months, at this point, they were aware of every strange noise coming in their direction. The thump at the door brought anxiety and trepidation into their shaking bodies. The distinction between insecurity and survival had been unconscious and unplanned, brought on by the war. They were in constant effort to survive extinction from the conflict surrounding them. The feeling flooded Ruth often as if they were in a dark, ravenous cloud, dooming them to failure. In the spiral of the vortex of the war, the enemy had been the seawater whirlpool, determined to drown them. Thus, they had been slow to accept others' helping hand in their plight.

Westphal opened the door with great effort and peered out to see what he could observe while directing the others to stay where they were. He was following his instinct, which worried him that something might be amiss.

Schumann's uneasiness grew until his curiosity overtook him, so he jumped up from his place on the floor to join the alarmed man at the entrance. Finally,

Westphal shrugged off his apprehension and opened the entry even further while Schumann reached for one of the wooden chairs close to the table.

Westphal happened to be nearest the entry. A shaft of light made its way to the front entrance as he began to decipher what was at his feet. Cautiously, he opened the entrance further. As he pulled the door ajar, he saw a brown paper bag on the ground and pondered if he should take the chance to collect the package and examine the inside.

"The British soldiers have left a brown paper bag at the front door."

"What do you see... what is in the brown paper bag?" Schumann's voice could be heard coming from behind him.

Westphal peered close. "I can see a white loaf of bread, some luncheon meat and spring apples in the bag. The young soldiers gave us their leftover rations."

The family joined Onkel on the small wooden step. They stood there, nodding politely and throwing much gratitude and admiration with their smiling eyes to the soldiers, nothing more since no words could pass between them.

Within a few weeks, more soldiers were infatuated with the children, so they attempted to speak. Slowly, the children's shaking little frames steadied. Nonetheless, their eyes were wide, and they stared at the soldiers, who struggled not to chat but spoke a few phrases. Yet, the children were still terrified by the unfamiliar language on the strangers' lips.

As time passed, the soldiers became even more familiar with the children, for they reminded them of their homes. From then on, they often brought luncheon meat, tea or whatever they could spare. The soldiers knew they could and would be reprimanded as adults if they broke the camp's rules. After the children were settled in bed, calmly recuperating from a long day while sitting on the front stoop became a welcoming pastime for the adults observing the British soldiers' behaviour.

Sipping her hot, well-used tea leaves the English soldiers had thrown at their front door, Ruth thought of what they had endured in the past few months. "Of course," she began, "so many small things are forgotten, probably for good reason since this allows us to move on with our lives. Yet, some trivial things can eat you alive. We have no control over much, so time does not seem important. Somehow, Anneliese and I know we were doing the right thing by moving westward."

Teasingly, Westphal suggested, "To me, it sounds as if you need strong *schnapps* to calm your nerves."

"My dilemma is that I have not heard anything about Rudi for months. I know Anneliese is as worried about Achim."

"That is a fact. There is nothing we can do about it now, Ruth."

"No, I suppose you are correct, Anneliese. Nonetheless, I have a little story about Dorlies, who is about to be two. As you know, she considers Onkel Westphal as a surrogate father figure. You can see he is responsive to her need

Two New Men in the House

to cuddle. Dorlies toddles up to him in her strained attempt to make herself understood, so if you watch her closely, as she sends him a pleading glance, you can see him melt under her charms. Naturally, he takes the time to sit in the room's only chair and hold her to his warm body. Sweetly, she asks him in her fragmented, odd way that only they could understand, 'Onkel, please, can I sit on your lap?'"

Like a big cuddly bear, Westphal blushed and chuckled at his embarrassment.

Ruth said, "I simply do not have the time for her. Besides, Dorlies began to speak before we fled. She has been so traumatised by the effects of the war that she has not begun to speak correctly again. Hopefully, she will learn again after being settled for a few months. As the soldier told me while in the meadow trying to buy her during our flight, Dorlies resembles a little well-mannered porcelain doll."

Chapter 29

AFTER THE WAR

Mail delivery was sparse during the summer of 1945; thus, throngs of people were still struggling to discover their loved ones' whereabouts. The adults in Ruth's family were forever stopping strangers on the streets to see if someone would recognise a name. They would ask them if they came from the Pommern area or if they might have seen or heard the whereabouts of a loved one. People were using each other as messengers. A hastily handwritten note in pencil on a scrap of paper would be given to strangers passing by who would tuck the note into a cap or the side of a woman's shabby shoe.

People were writing notes: their names, dates, where they could be found, or for whom they searched. They posted messages on bombed outbuildings or on store walls that might still be in some working order. These were notes to search for loved ones and were posted in places where people would gather, standing in line to have a moment to read a list of names and locations where they might be found. Another record was posted for people still missing. When these folks read the name they were searching for and saw a loved one was listed, the earth beneath their feet seemed to tremble. Ruth gazed about and saw other people who felt like her and who struggled desperately to know their family member's whereabouts.

Ruth readied herself to work in the garden at daybreak before traveling about. She glanced around to locate the best spot to plant the bits of potato sprouts she had received from one of the nearby farmers. Wearing a tattered blue cloth tied around her waist as a makeshift apron, holding the ends up so she could carry the cuttings, Ruth dug her toes into the soft soil as she stepped out of the bungalow to labour in her favourite getaway.

As she studied her tiny garden, she looked up and recognised a former Gross Jestin man, who had been a ditch digger and now worked in the army as an officer. In her bare feet, she hoped that he did not recognise her. The officer and his wife walked past the garden and recognised Ruth as the former Lady of Klein Pobloth. To get Ruth's attention, the man cleared his throat.

Glancing up to meet his gaze, Ruth's face reddened. She silently shrieked as the couple approached and she dug her toes firmer into the brown earth. The man, with his newly found authority and his wife, strolled up to Ruth.

After the War

Still playing the part of an officer, the same gentleman as during the war, his training had taught him to be extremely polite. He started to bow, said, "gnädige Frau," and then marched over to kiss Ruth's hand while his wife dropped a deep curtsy. The couple had scarcely finished their niceties when the officer's wife scowled at Ruth's weathered hands and bare feet. The stress of the war had rapidly transformed Ruth into appearing as if middle age had been pounded into her frame and she had developed into someone unknown to her. In their seashore home, the thread binding the family together was humour filled with tenderness towards the children – only attainable within those walls.

Aware of the wife's dismayed expression, Ruth quickly hid her grubby fingernails behind her back, her shoulders slumping awkwardly out of humiliation. In her mind, Ruth strengthened a conversation between the two acquaintances before she spoke. She was imbued with a new belief that the whole world was turned upside-down. Dignified as the Lady she was bred to be, her frame rigid with indignation, she sought to regain her composure. Ruth had lost everything other than the loved ones in her cluster. Her spirit was trampled, yet her soul remained unscathed. She quickly strengthened her reserve. *These people do not understand, nor do they choose to. They do not know we have very little to comfort our empty stomachs. I am not one to spread the news.*

Her shoulders once again lifted in pride, her head upright, Ruth suggested, "Now, under these circumstances, gnädige Frau and the kissing of the hand are no longer necessary."

The couple noticed Ruth's surroundings.

Ruth's eyes followed their scrutinising glance. She silently sighed in relief when she noticed grey soot billowing out of the chimney. "Ah, Anneliese must be heating water for tea and a sweet. Will you come in and join us?"

Mercifully, the couple declined her offer with an awkward smile, "Well, perhaps some other time."

Rushing into the hovel, she felt she was given a reprieve for telling lies to the officer. "Oh, Anneliese, how did you pull off this small miracle?"

"What on earth are you talking about, Ruth?"

"Why, stoking up the small bricks we call our stove, making it appear we have plenty of coal and wood to feed a fire? A former acquaintance and his wife saw the smoke. I offered them tea so politely, knowing we do not have any."

"Oh, well, yes, you see, I could see your hands behind your back and your bare feet struggling to dig their way to China in the wet dirt the heavens blessed us with. You were aiming to tell me something."

"I suppose I was. It was fun seeing the smoke spiral upward."

When the small beachside village lay in darkness, the adults again sat on the front stoop. The reality of the situation with her former acquaintances struck Ruth with humour, and then her expression changed. She pressed her calloused hands over her mouth to hold back her laughter. Despite her efforts, a squeak escaped her lips, and her shoulders began to heave involuntarily.

The others quickly recognised her state and a sympathetic understanding crossed their faces. Abruptly, the mood changed as they lightheartedly recognised their situation. Within seconds, the three men and two women sat in front of the cottage in hilarious laughter until salty tears of joy dropped onto the damp spring-green grasses below.

The family was grateful to be able to keep their horses in a nearby farmer's meadows as spring turned into warmer summer days. The farmer was thankful to have the two horses and the three men working in his field.

At the beginning of June, Ruth spoke to the friendly farmer in hopes of picking the strawberries growing in his beautifully kept garden as a surprise for Dorlies' third birthday.

The dawn was radiant. Her timing needed to be right to make it to the farm before anyone else. True to his word, the farmer was waiting in the garden for Ruth when she arrived. No doubt, his wife was not a part of the plan. He pointed to the garden patch, indicating seven plump, bright red berries. She picked them up gently and placed them into the tattered handkerchief she had brought along for their safe journey back to her home. Ruth nodded a thank you. Then back home again.

Ruth sliced the beautiful red berries into a bowl. She hid the treasure on top of the only cupboard in the house and draped a damp cloth over it to keep the berries fresh. After the others in the house rose, Ruth called them to participate in Dorlies' party. Ruth brought out her surprise at breakfast, still covered with the white cloth. She tugged at the fabric to unveil Dorlies' surprise. To her dismay, the children had no idea what they were seeing. This was something new, and red did not bring inviting thoughts to their minds. As in one chorus, the children began to weep.

It took two strong men, one middle-aged teen and two women to convince the children that what they saw was a sumptuous fruit none had tasted for some time. Dorlies still refused to partake of her sweet treat, so the other eight people in her household enjoyed the berries.

Struggling to think of something to give the children a bit of continuity and joy in their lives and to remind them of their father's humorous antics at Klein Pobloth, Ruth gathered her brood. "Come snuggle next to me. I want to share a funny story about your father and Tante Anneliese." Four beams of delight were sent her way. Thus, Ruth knew she had found a way to make them temporarily happy.

Chapter 30

QUEST TO FIND RUDI AND ARCHIM

The cold September winds blew their way in between the cracks of the small dwelling. While standing in line for food stamps, Anneliese Hertel turned to face the man behind her, who also longed to locate his family. He mentioned getting his papers for permission to travel to Rosenheim, a small town near Munich, the capital city in Bavaria. Anneliese knew her mother's first husband's family, the Krauses, lived in the area. After the first war, Dolores's brother-in-law, Rudolf Krause, had been the manager at Klein Pobloth Estate. In their youth, Anneliese and Rudi had travelled with his mother to Rosenheim on several occasions to visit the Krause family farm, Eulenau Estate. Fortunately, the stranger Anneliese befriended agreed to take a note with him. She then gave the stranger directions to the Eulenau Estate. He placed the message securely into his brown Beret hat and then traveled on to the Rosenheim area.

The Americans supervised this area of Germany. Everyone knew these soldiers were tough to get along with. The American soldiers interrogated the man as he entered their territory and searched him thoroughly. The American soldiers did not find the note hidden in the lining of the man's hat. Afterward, he walked to the Krauses' farm to find out if Rudi was living with the Krause family. If not, perhaps they would have information about where he might be.

The sun rose later in the mornings, making it more problematic for Anneliese to make her way to Lübeck to stand in the long food lines and get back home again before dark. The three men walked in different directions to secure any available labour and did not return until dusk.

With the garden no longer producing enough fresh vegetables, Ruth faced putting a meal together with less than they had enjoyed during the summer.

The older children played chase outdoors while little Dorlies busied herself with dried greens and clay, combining them with sand to build a sand house.

Ruth mused, *It is challenging to keep up my spirits, put on a cheerful expression for the children, then pretend all is well.* She realised then that she had been daydreaming. "How long have I been sitting at the window staring out at the light spilling over the house, drawing itself onto the frostbitten ground?" The chill in the air caused goose bumps to rise on her arms.

Ruth worried about Anneliese's late returns. After waiting at the window one night to see her coming, she sank into the nearest chair. Ruth said to Anneliese, "I can only guess, but I have been considering the last five years as all over Germany, in the towns, villages and farms, this time has belonged to the women responsible for the families and property welfare. Men, as well as boys of all ages, were fighting on all fronts of the war. As women, we are becoming accustomed to making the most difficult decisions ourselves. Thus, we became stronger and learned how to survive after making important, sometimes life-changing decisions."

They hurried the children indoors when the autumn October winds became too cold for them to bear. The children had gotten on Ruth's nerves, so she had closed herself off in selfish silence. She had refrained from speaking to the children for the rest of the afternoon because she might use too many harsh words towards them. Klaus-Dieter, with his unruly red hair, Ruth found appealing on most days. But his actions sent shivers down Ruth's spine when he provoked Dorlies, who was too young to defend herself.

With the hem of her skirt, Ruth wiped the day's grime off her forehead, released the edge of her clothing, and then dropped to her knees. Pummelling the coarse wooden floor the actions created pain in her palms, and the aching travelled up to her wrist. Before long, she clasped her wrists and gazed at the ceiling, "*Gott in Himmel*, what am I to do? I work as diligently as possible, yet there is still not enough food to place on the table to feed all nine. What am I to do?" After her plea to God, she realised her cramped limbs also ached out of agonising frustration and fears of the future. Her worst anxieties were well-founded. She still did not know if Rudi was alive or dead.

To calm her nerves Ruth sat down to write her mother a letter with a little ink and some borrowed paper. She hoped her mother would receive it if she were still with her relatives in Pine.

9.9.45

My dear Oma!
In my short note, you probably got in the meantime. Today is Sunday, so I have time for a longer message. It is wonderful that you had company from Hoenes, our former neighbour from Kempen. Did they know anything of the other families? Many families from the Kolberg area were killed or stayed there and are now chased out by the Poles. They had to be out in ten minutes or get injured. Hans-Rudolf's mother is still there. I wonder how she is. I have not heard from Lilla or anything from Hans-Rudolf.

Tante Clara wrote that living in their apartment did not work out for them. The renter does not want to move. So, we must stay here, which is not easy with winter coming, and here the building is made from wooden boards, with no insulation. We are already cold, sleeping two in a bed, and do not have enough blankets. I have a golden wristwatch I want to exchange for bedding. I traded a diamond ring for some bedding. I have two nightgowns for three children, and Susanne has no skirt for her pullover. I have nothing with long sleeves for the winter. I can pay for it or give you a gold topaz or silver ring with amber. Not much money is left from home, with 30.00 Mark for me and 15.00 Mark for each child I do not get far. How do you live since you do not get any money from Kempen? Do you have to pay something to Tante Lieschen? Do you get along with money from welfare? Did you get to take some of your clothes and jewellery along? I have no warm clothes, no jacket or sweater. Does cousin Hannelore have any clothes from her daughter that Dorlies could have? Especially a coat or long pants. We can use anything, including underwear for my children.

I would love to have toys or books for the boys. With winter almost here, they do not know what to do. Susanne misses her toy corner and will miss school. Hans-Georg is very patient. He plays for hours with a piece of wood and imagines it to be a truck, car or cannon – if I could get each child at least one article for Christmas.

Should it turn out with Hosüne [Tante Clare Schläger], I will go without Anneliese, and we won't get along for long. I am the maid, and she is the madam.

Your Ruth

Chapter 31

HANS-RUDOLF RETURNS

By late on 11 September 1945, Anneliese had not returned from Lübeck. Ruth could not understand what took so long with every task her sister-in-law attempted. Her walk back from Lübeck was a case in point and her late arrival concerned Ruth for her safety. She should have been back before dusk. At dusk, Ruth nervously paced the floor, waiting for Anneliese's return.

As Ruth twisted her fingers nervously, she noticed the children were ready to eat the meagre meal she had prepared. Naturally, the men ate the chief portions since they worked for the farmers within walking distance. The children finally ate picnicking on the floor as had been their custom. Ruth joined the three men, who were squeezed around the small table. She had difficulty turning over the wooden stump pilfered from the side of the British soldiers' housing. The other stump was empty for Anneliese to use as a seat upon her return.

The chill drifting through the cracks of their hovel sent the four children to sleep directly after the meal. They huddled together in one small lump of covers. Ruth bent to kiss their foreheads and then scooted closer to lie beside them. In her soft, soothing voice, she told them of one of her childhood adventures, anything to put a happy giggle in their hearts.

The adults were sitting and having dinner when Anneliese finally could be detected strolling in their direction. Once the children were sound asleep, Ruth rose and cracked the door a few steps to allow the fresh night air to calm her temper, which had built during the day. She hoped the wafting fragrance of the salty sea air entering the hovel would calm her nerves.

"Anneliese, come sit. Supper has been waiting for you."

Ruth lit the only kerosene lantern, walked to the front window to glance through the middle mullion, and saw a stranger meandering up to their walkway. In alarm, "A stranger walking in this area at dusk is uncommon. I hope he is not one of the British officers giving us some radical orders again!"

When the man studied their hovel, everyone at the table stood to fix their eyes on the man's stride. Ruth observed the man more intently. "The way this man walks appears vaguely familiar." Shivers ran down Ruth's spine, and her body shook uncontrollably, but she did not know why. Her words trailed off as she stepped away from the window.

Hans-Rudolf Returns

Speechless for a moment, Ruth realised only then that the figure was her dear husband, Hans-Rudolf. The figure could not be Rudi. The man was much smaller in scale and with a hunched back, and he was struggling to make his way to the entry of their hovel. The kerosene light shone onto Rudi's gaunt, weathered face. Ruth was so shocked at the sight of her dear Rudi that she could not walk to the door. Suddenly she found her words and screamed, "It is Rudi! Study the man. It is Rudi!"

The sight of Rudi flashed through Ruth's mind so fast that she scarcely recognised the man she saw as her husband. She did not know if he remained a figment of her imagination or if, indeed, Rudi's life had been spared. "Yes, Rudi is alive!" Exceedingly haggard, eyes surrounded by purple and sunken into the depressions of his face, the look of death leaked from his semi-recognisable form.

Knocking over the makeshift stools, Anneliese, Schumann and Westphal scrambled out of the house so hastily that they terrified the children, who began to cry.

Ruth stretched out her arms to receive her husband, who tumbled into her open embrace. After a long moment, Ruth pulled back from the frail man to search for a smile that did not come from Rudi, who was too weary. The muscles of his face had taken on a lifeless form, his body struggling to keep his stance with the onslaught of loved ones vying for his attention. Once again, he strained to make a slight smile at the adults rushing out of the door to him.

Ruth stepped into the house, gathered her three children and then returned out into the open air with the children hiding behind her skirt. She swung her arms about Rudi's neck and held the ninety-eight-pound man toward her slender body. Then, ever so tenderly, her arms moved past his shoulders down to his waist. Once her fingers found his chest, the lean frame clung to her like glue. Holding onto his shoulders, Ruth slightly pulled Rudi back from her so she could see his face, studying the man who was her husband.

Still in her arms, Rudi was too weary to respond to Ruth's joy. The only way he could express his emotions was to weep openly.

Extremely concerned, Ruth said, "Come lean on me, then I will help you walk the rest of the way into our new home."

Ruth turned Rudi into the hovel where the kerosene lantern shone onto his decrepit body. The children saw the man who was supposed to be their Vati, but they would have no part of this stranger who entered their home. Instead of greeting him with open arms, they silently crept into the adjoining room and hid in the farthest corner out of fear of this stranger.

To Ruth, her husband appeared twenty years older than the last time she had seen this battle-weary man standing in front of her, scrutinising her as she, in return, did the same. Rudi's cheeks had sunk deep into his face, causing his blue eyes to turn into grey crystal foggy emotionless shadows. Before the war, they were brilliant, sparkling with fire and life until she could not resist his charms. After four years in the war, Rudi's eyes had turned into icy grey crystals of horror. Behind them was a vast buildup of dread she hoped to shatter. It was like a part of a never-ending nightmare. Now, only warmth could burn off the bitter distress of war.

Anneliese announced, "A hot cup of water will do him a world of good. I will place a can on the bricks and then stoke the fire." Eventually, she placed the hot can into his grimy, cold grasp. "Now we must find you something to eat." She drew a chair near where the men supported him.

Ruth seated herself beside her husband. In absolute silence, she studied his every move. Ever so gently, Ruth helped Rudi wrap his fingers around the can to help him sip the water and he lifted his eyes in gratitude.

Soon, Anneliese returned with another can containing some broth with a few carrots swimming like little goldfish, ready to help fill his stomach's emptiness. Once he downed the broth, his body seemed to turn to gelatin and slipped slowly to the floor.

Westphal and Schumann were quick to grab hold of his underarms while Gretel seized his feet. Once safe in their care, they carried the ill man to the nearest pile of straw and then surrounded him with the warmth of the dry stalks. The adults kept an ever-vigilant eye on Rudi while the children kept their distance. Rudi's breathing soon relaxed, and twisting his tired body, he closed his eyes out of fear of the night and the constant nightmares and did not awaken until mid-afternoon two days later. It took a week before Rudi could sit upright. Plus, another few days until he began to stagger about the house. He felt well enough to take in the fresh air his frail body desperately needed by the second week.

One evening, while sitting on the stoop chatting about his struggles, Rudi recalled what had taken place a few kilometres away from the beach house, "Outside of Rosenheim, while on my journey, a train stopped to fill the engine's cooling tank with water." A small, familiar chuckle escaped his lips. "People were pilfering from a supply train belonging to the American soldiers going to who knows where. I joined to find my share and grabbed as much as I thought I could carry. Once secure, I stashed the goods around the warm green grass surrounding me. I stopped to open a can of hash with my Swiss pocketknife, but I was not strong enough to make a dent in the can. There was some wonderful-looking bread and luncheon meat, so I made a sandwich. Wouldn't you know it, my stomach could not hold the food's richness. I turned to the nearest bush and heaved everything up.

"From there, I bagged my goods into my jacket and slung it over my shoulders. I was pleasantly surprised when the group I was with helped each other onto a train going in the direction I hoped to go. From time to time, I dozed off on the train. One of the women from the group travelling with me knew I was headed for Lübeck. When she saw the city's outskirts, she nudged me to wake up. A smile of delight must have crossed my lips. The woman smiled at me and said, 'You're welcome, soldier.'

"I stood to open the window and then carefully threw my precious bag of goods into an outcropping of trees next to the tracks. As speedily as I could, I rushed to the door and jumped as close to my food as possible.

"The day before I found you, a few kilometres outside of Vorrade, I became too weary to carry my foodstuffs any farther. I walked up to a farmhouse that appeared friendly to me. I needed to make friends with the old farm lady who opened the door to a needy soldier. After sharing food with her, I asked her to conceal a stash of goods under the barn to protect my wonderful food. She promised me the goods would be safe so I could surprise my family."

Rudi's thrill showed in his voice. Being reunited with his beloved family once more revealed his deep feelings for them that were beyond comprehension. His eyes still lacked the intense and unusual vivid shade of blue, plus he continuously seemed worried. His forehead wrinkled in a familiar furrow of concern, but then Rudi's eyes brightened. "Can you three men help carry my belongings to the house?"

When they entered their hovel again, they carried a carton of canned ham and several cans of jam under their arms. Rudi's valued food was totally devoured within a few days after his findings were presented.

The two women, four men, plus four children spent their time eking out a better living for the family. With so many people in the house, Ruth, Rudi and the three children were not able to familiarise themselves as a family unit. Gingerly, Rudi attempted to reacquaint himself with the children who had forgotten their father. What might have been a lovely reunion only served as a reminder of how hungry everyone was.

As the couple was chatting one evening, Rudi pulled Ruth aside and then suddenly grimaced with pain in his voice. Sulking a little, he said, "I do not know what is worse, the ache of having the love of my family compromised, or if every bone in my body is broken from the hardships of war or the American POW camp."

Ruth's heart quickened at his words as she rested her hand lightly on his frail, outstretched fingers. Feeling his grasp as she nestled into his embrace, she whispered into his ear, hoping to soothe his fears, "We will make it all work out after you have rested and gained some of your weight back. That is more important than anything else."

It took Rudi many weeks to regain his strength. Conditions had hardened his character, a defence mechanism to survive. All Ruth could get out of him was that he had been in an American POW camp on the Rhine after the Battle of the Bulge. The POW camp robbed Rudi of his freedom but not his enjoyment of nature.

Ruth reacted to what she saw in Rudi's behaviour and saw that his boyhood playfulness and his gentleness had been snuffed out of his character. Would she ever get the man back with whom she fell in love? Who fathered their three children. This shell of a man sitting beside her was her husband, who still had his integrity. She knew this was no time to hesitate or even think of what the changes might mean for the future. Ruth and Rudi managed to cling to one another, not knowing precisely who the other had transformed into during their long separation. They studied each other steadily and then found it difficult to hide their shock at all the things they had taken for granted as the people they had been before.

Ruth and Anneliese were the women of the house, and the other men had not been prisoners in a war camp. The harsh cruelty soldiers like Rudi had endured in the POW camp remained beyond their comprehension.

On the other hand, after fleeing from Klein Pobloth, these two stalwart women had endured their own battle to fight daily to keep their families alive.

However, the four men in the house, on the losing end of a war, had given the best years of their young lives. Ruth understood that their dear Pommern remained lost for eternity. However, this awareness did not turn into a deep depression, for their only thought was to survive the life dealt to them. For the two women and the children, it was now a constant tiptoeing on what seemed to them like treading on a mirror so that the men's frail temperaments, including their perplexing minds, would not shatter and break into a billion little pieces. Fear of doing anything that might erupt into a meltdown for any of the men kept everyone on guard. The two women questioned everything these strange men were doing while the children tried to stay out of the way.

When Ruth and Rudi studied each other from across the room, the adults recognised that the couple needed to get to know one another again. The men quickly found some excuse to take the children to find firewood or rummage for food. Alone, Ruth supposed they should not dwell on the delightful, peaceful times of the past, with the details becoming dim and teetering on distortion. Now, it was a most complex situation. Conflict about how to show their emotions toward one another struck Ruth. Rudi's heart nearly broke with embarrassment. It was too painful for them to yet enjoy each other. Sadly, both minds were too devastated, their bodies too weak, and both had lost so much weight. They were far too undernourished to fulfill the typical desires of earlier years. Both Ruth and Rudi were humiliated to admit this failure in their relationship. They did not know how the others managed to cope with their issues.

Rudi attempted to shut out the horrifically agonising period in the American POW camp that Ruth could see flashing through his mind. While sleeping, her husband screamed out, breaking into a sweat and causing every member of the household grave distress. Regardless, Ruth attempted to keep up an endless understanding in their conversations, trying to impact a sense of what the children had suffered and hoping Rudi would reciprocate by telling her about his experiences. In a rough tone, his answers were always the same – too soon – not now – perhaps later.

He attempted to tolerate the children and the crowding in the little house, but the POW camp had blemished Rudi beyond understanding. The camp had driven a stake into his self-esteem that Ruth had not seen in him before, a coldness, a hardness about him.

Early on, their relationship had been filled with explosive passion and extraordinary understanding. Now, when problems arose even the smallest situation caught them in total conflict without understanding why their relationship had become so out of balance. Yet there were other times the two still seemed to cherish one another. Thus, Ruth sought an excuse to place the children out of harm's way at every opportunity.

Chapter 32

ACHIM RETURNS

Rudi made every effort to help put right what the war had put asunder. More than any other man in the house, he became proficient at scavenging minor items to make their lives more tolerable. His intellect and ingenuity put his findings to good use.

When Rudi repaired the stove in the so-called kitchen area, Ruth could enjoy cooking the fresh vegetables she had painstakingly planted during the summer. They had stored them underneath their hovel to keep them fresh yet not frozen. The men had dug a hole into the cold, damp earth using small kitchen utensils and lined it with straw to create a necessary root cellar. They were rewarded for their efforts by saving various fresh vegetables.

After Rudi's return, Anneliese's loneliness accelerated. At supper, she sobbed, choking on her words. "Here it is, October. I am so upset because no one knows of Achim's whereabouts, so I cannot write to him."

Through the endless conversations in Lübeck, Anneliese had discovered that her husband, Achim Hertel, was a prisoner of the Russians. Being only too familiar with what happened to men who were Russian prisoners of war caused her great trepidation, fearing greatly for her husband.

Anneliese hurried to the cottage to relate her heartbreaking news to the others in the house. "From the way the rumour was related to me, several German soldiers were able to find their way out of the terrible conditions they found themselves in." She breathed heavily and added rapidly. "The eyes of the man on the street I spoke to were the same as Rudi's, glazed over with uncertainty. I presumed he must have been a soldier. He babbled a few words, and I could not understand him, so I had no choice but to say my husband's name repeatedly, 'Hertel… Hertel, Hertel, do you recognise the name, Hertel?' With a deep rumble from within him, he repeated my husband's name, Hertel.' For that fleeting moment, his eyes hinted at recognition. I questioned the man further, but there was no response."

Faithful as always, Anneliese made her way to Lübeck to stand in line and then wait patiently for the family's essential food stamps. She began to familiarise herself with the many people waiting in line, the gift for chattering away making the time pass quicker.

Achim Returns

Come what may, by the end of October, Anneliese was determined to ask the Red Cross in Lübeck to inform Achim's elderly father in Hilbeck, Westphalia, of his family's whereabouts. The Red Cross in the area would help inform Achim Hertel where to find his family. Once he received word of their location, Achim could have the Red Cross forward a message to the family in Vorrade.

One day, she received a telegram. During these dreadful times, a telegram usually meant bad news. She unfolded the single piece of paper doubling as a letter and an envelope with quivering fingers and eyes filled with tears, she screamed waving the sheet high to the sky. "Hallelujah! Hallelujah!" She screamed again, "At least, now I know my dear husband is alive. Just think, after all this time, Achim is alive. I know he will be clever in finding his way to Vorrade."

The trains were running again, although not as punctual as usual. During the middle of October, Achim found his way to their hovel to join the ever-growing family.

While having his cup of hot water to help him get warm, he told them, "I was severely wounded in the Russian-occupied parts of Germany. After spending weeks in a Russian camp hospital, one of the doctors took pity on me and informed me that it was too expensive to keep me alive. So, the doctor signed my release papers and sent me on my way. I hitched a ride on a train travelling to my boyhood home. For four months, my father helped me recuperate."

Achim appeared to be at war with himself. Like most soldiers, he also fought his inner demons. He kept most of his experiences to himself, spending many silent hours alone and having difficulty integrating into the family unit. Filled with anxiety, the family searched his face in the hope of his revealing any of his former self. However, all they could see was death staring back at them.

Everyone was willing to sleep on the floor, to press their face into a secluded corner of the room so Achim, Klaus-Dieter and Anneliese had a place they could call home. Every morning, they sat around the makeshift table with their food stamps, deciding as a group what the best investment would be so the food would last longer and reach further. They knew potatoes keep the stomach fuller than a slice of thin, white British or American bread.

The liberators had disparagingly called them "krauts" during the war. Now, after the occupation of their country, they made sure they ate as much sauerkraut as the Allies could dish out. The household pooled their resources to cook heartier meals for the children and the men who had fought fearlessly in the war.

Within four days of his arrival, Achim announced that he had found a train route to take his family to his father's home in Hilbeck, where he and his family could live until they found their own place to live.

When Anneliese and Achim announced their pending departure from Ruth's family, Horst Schumann and Steffen decided it was time to find their families through the Red Cross. With Achim able to find his family, the other men contacted the Red Cross. Within a few days, Schumann and Steffen received word of where to locate their loved ones. Steffen was too choked up to speak, so Horst began, "The war placed us into a loving family atmosphere that helped us recapture our fundamental status in life, and for that, we will be forever grateful to you, Ruth, for bravely choosing to flee and welcome us into your home. Words cannot describe how grateful we are. But now we must find our families and our way in life."

Anneliese choked on her words, "Ruth and Rudi, I am sorry that we must leave you behind. With the winter coming on, you can't remain in this beach house." She smiled at Ruth. "I am eternally grateful that you found it in your heart to take Klaus-Dieter and me on your journey at the last moment."

Onkel Westphal asked, "Ruth and Rudi, my family is behind what is now known as the Iron Curtain. I have nowhere to go. Please, can I live with you a little longer?"

Ruth and Rudi embraced Westphal, and Ruth said, "Onkel, you are welcome to join our family as long as you like."

Ruth did not find her words easily. "Anneliese, at first, I was hesitant to have you and Klaus-Dieter travel with us. But you have been extremely helpful as a partner in achieving my goal to escape. I am eternally grateful that we have become friends and spent these arduous times together. It is difficult to say goodbye."

Chapter 33

WINTER COMES

The problem of finding a different home than the musty little beach house, which would not be warm enough for the winter, finally became a fact. Although the family could get enough wood together for cooking, their challenge came when they tried to find enough firewood to keep the house warm.

Fortunately, there were ample farm gardens that belonged to the original owners. Rudi and Westphal had been unrelenting huntsmen, which gave them an edge in being great at gathering food. Thus, the men in the house learned to pilfer from those gardens during the night.

Westphal happened to stumble upon a farm field with an abundance of cabbages. His findings showed that cabbage had been served to the family in every way possible with water and salt for weeks.

It was truly remarkable when Rudi found a potato field ready to be harvested. He asked if they could dig in the field after the farmer and crew had finished harvesting. The farmer agreed. "If any potatoes are left, you are welcome to them." Rudi was grateful the farmer gave his consent. He knew what the farmer's next move would be. As was the custom, the farmer took a torch to the dried potato plants, which poked their heads above the ground. Without further delay, everyone living in the house, even the small children, dug through and gathered this unwanted crop.

Hans-Georg and Dorlies were particularly pleased since Ruth made it a game of finding the potatoes in the field: "If you find several to place in your bucket, you will receive a prize." Ruth's little ones beamed with delight when their little tin bucket was filled. Now, it was time for their mother to make good on her word. Ruth thought for a moment and whispered to them, "When we get back to the house, I will make you a Sugar Baby. Would you like that?"

They nodded with much enthusiasm.

The women and children returned to the house before the men left the field. Once at home, the children remembered their mother's promise. Dorlies tugged at her mother's skirt and rolled her tongue around her lips. Ruth understood what her daughter desired. "I will find the condensed canned milk and the sugar the nice English soldiers gave us, and I will take a little spoon and some sugar, then trickle a bit of condensed milk on top. Then you three can have your goodies, as I promised.

Sit at the table, and I will prepare it for you." As Ruth guessed, her little ones grinned with delight at one of the only sweets they had ever tasted.

After Ruth and the children left, the entire field was an anthill of people. Many potatoes had a blackish brown colour where the hot flames had charred them. No matter, these potatoes would be eaten first, for they would be the initial ones to rot. If it were not for the charity of the farmer and this wonderful potato field, many of these people would undoubtedly have perished.

By nightfall, the men had found enough potatoes to fill a gunnysack full of potato pieces. Once the men tried to return their precious treasure to the house, Rudi and Westphal found they were too weak to tow the sack of potato pieces home.

The family had two horses and their wagon, so they drove to the farm to carry their sack home in the back of the rig. When the other families in the beach houses saw the horses and wagon, the men kindly offered to take their findings back with them. It was a considerable haul the men had made during this day. The family was thankful for their precious cargo and a portion of staple food to eat for many weeks.

After Rudi and Westphal returned for the evening, Westphal lamented, "Oh, Ruth, I am afraid we must throw these very badly blackened potatoes out. They will most likely have an extremely bitter taste to them." Ruth thought hard as she was not ready to discard the potatoes.

"I see this problem now, but we will not waste food. So, this means we must be very clever about having the children eat something they do not care for." Ruth placed her hands under her chin to think. Then, she snapped her fingers as she smiled, "I have it. We need to play a game of sleight of hand or quicker than the eye can see."

Ruth placed a clean plate in her eating area with the bottom blackened. She rubbed the bottom of the lower plates with the blackened potato skins. Setting the table, as usual, but on the bottom of each plate, Ruth blackened the plates with the blackest potatoes. She placed the adults' plates on the table. The children always picnicked on the floor and seated themselves in their assigned seats when it was time to eat. Unbeknownst to them, their plate was also blackened on the bottom.

"Mutti, what is this that we are supposed to eat?" Susanne questioned in an unpleasant tone.

"Why, my dearest daughter, they are the potatoes your Vati and Onkel were able to retrieve from the kind farmer. Just take your fingers, pull off the blackest part, and place them on the side of your plate."

Grimaces soon appeared on the faces of both the adults and the children. Before long, Hans-Georg piped, "Mutti, if these are potatoes, then I do not care to eat anymore because they taste bitter." He huffed and pushed his plate to the centre of their picnic area.

"My dear son, eat just a few more bites, then Mutti will surprise you."

With much chagrin, Hans-Georg did as he was told.

"Now that you are finished, we will play our game. Just watch and do as I do."

"Now, I will pick up my plate and show you how clean my plate is. Then you must follow my instructions."

The adults, as well as the children, were happy to play along. "The secret of this game is that no one is to make a single sound during our experiment. Does everyone understand?" Nods travelled about the room. "This means you, Vati, and Onkel Westphal must play along with the children and be silent the whole while."

Dragging her forefinger over the back of the plate, Ruth then pretended to draw stripes and circles over her cheeks and nose. "Now, you must do as I have just shown you."

Turning her plate around, she showed the family her plate, and all were satisfied that Ruth's plate was clean. With a sleight of hand, Ruth quickly slipped her clean plate onto her lap and placed the blackened plate where the other had been.

The other children and the adults soon followed her lead. Like the others, Ruth ran her fingers over the blackened bottom and painted her face.

Everyone followed her instructions. Snickers, mixed with laughter, were beginning to escape everyone's lips. Hans-Georg pointed to his mother and giggled loudly in delight. "Look at everyone's faces!"

The ruse was up. The children looked at each other and then at the adults, who had black soot on their noses and cheeks, with hardy laughter ringing throughout the house.

"I must say these old black potatoes did not taste as bitter now as when I first bit into them," Westphal happily announced. "You agree, Rudi?"

"Yes, indeed," Rudi was quick to answer. "Ruth, I must admit you were extremely clever in your sleight of hand."

Another burst of laughter erupted from the group, making the evening one of happiness.

Chapter 34

REGISTERING THE HORSES

The telegram Rudi received from the authorities in Lübeck concerned him, so he read it to the family. "We have been informed your household has two horses, and they are required to be registered with the British government overseeing the area."

"Why are we required to register our horses?" Ruth asked with concern.

"Receiving a telegram like this is never good news and is something of a mystery. I do not like the smell of it," Westphal assured.

"I believe it is because the area around Lübeck has been inundated with refugees from eastern Pommern, with too many horses and wagons. Perhaps this increase made the authorities believe there would not be enough hay to feed the animals in the winter months ahead of us," Rudi replied. "Westphal, can you think of another reason for their actions?"

"No, that seems as logical as any other answer," Westphal replied.

A cloud of concern hung over the household, but Rudi and Westphal hitched the horses onto their wagon to do what the authorities required. They rushed into town to the big auction building, where they were ordered to assemble. When the men arrived, they were given a number for their two horses. After distributing the tag with their number seven, the men in power instructed them that they would call out the numbers individually, then ordered them to take their horses and enter a large hall to register their tags.

Confident in his friend, Rudi suggested, "You stay here with the horses. I will see what is going on in the large outbuilding. I want to find out how this registration will proceed. The men appear harmless enough. Nevertheless, I would like to have all the facts straight on what is happening in the barn. For some reason, I smell a rotten fish in our midst, and I cannot decide where the stench comes from!"

Teasingly, Westphal smiled, "Rudi, it is nice to see you in the supervisor role as I was used to seeing you at Klein Pobloth."

As was the norm, Rudi's curiosity got the better of him. He sauntered into the large hangar as if he belonged there, moving about unnoticed. Suddenly, he overheard one of the British officers talking with a German official. As they chatted, Rudi eavesdropped and tried to keep an open mind. He glanced about the hall and realised that additional British soldiers were sitting around

Registering the Horses

the room, attending to their worktables. He and the British officer spoke for a moment. One of the horse owners was called to report the ownership of his horses whereupon the German representative also in charge inspected the horses to appraise the animals. The German walked to the man who owned the horses. Then, calculatingly, they informed the owner that the British would pay sixty Marks for one of the horses, adding coldly that they were willing to pay him one hundred Marks for the other horse.

After realising what had occurred, Rudi was sure the authorities wanted everyone to sell their horses to the governments in charge. He could see Westphal from where he was standing. At a close glance, he noticed one man dressed in the same uniform as the men who were part of the organising committee in charge, standing on the same side of the room as his friend. At first, Rudi stood back and watched, pretending not to notice what was happening. As he stayed to observe the goings-on, what he saw quickly solidified his resolve to understand the entire situation.

Determined not to fall into the same trap, Rudi blocked the man who sold his horses to the authorities. "I am curious about what is going on in this hall?"

Angrier than a hornet's nest, the man quickly reacted. "I notified the men in charge that I did not wish to sell my horses. Unfortunately, they gave me no other choice!"

Observing the heated conversation, Westphal secured the horses to a nearby post and rushed to listen to what the man was saying to Rudi.

The two men heard the rest, "Even worse, the British are ordering every one of the refugees who have horses to sell them to the government. The group gave me no alternative other than to sell the horses. I was encouraged, 'Just think how useful this money can be to help your family."

Rubbing his eyebrow, Rudi replied, "Yes, just think about how long this money will last for your family. Selling our horses would be a devastating loss."

One of the men in charge walked up to Rudi and Westphal. The man's tone toughened as he assessed the situation. "Sir, you must also sell your animals."

Rudi yelled. "No! You and the other officials gathered in this hall can go to hell!"

The official's expression indicated he understood what Rudi was expressing.

Rudi stiffened at the man's comment, snapping, "I feel a conspiracy is happening against the people who were forced to flee and have nothing." Rudi's wrath for the establishment raged at the feeble amount of money they suggested bestowing on the people who had already lost everything. Rudi responded to the man in authority, who was trying to keep Rudi's anger under control, "Oh no! No, never, under any terms. If necessary, I will kill the horses and drag the meat away for dog food."

The man in charge cautioned, "Shut your trap! What kind of trouble do you intend to cause us? Please exit the area immediately and wait until your number is called."

Rudi did not bother to question the man any further. He felt the man's gaze follow him as the two men rushed back to where the horses were waiting.

Anger welled inside Rudi until his entire body shook. "We are trapped in the hangar with our horses because there is a fence around the building. Desperately, I wish to be gone from this place! As far away from these crazy men who want to take away the only means of livelihood we have left to us."

With his anger ignited, Rudi challenged the government when their number came up, marching into the hall, the two men determined not to sell their animals. In the centre of the auditorium, his fists thrust to the ceiling to raise as much havoc as possible, "I insist these two horses are the only item of value we have left. They are the only means by which we can work or get a job!" Rudi's fists knocked on the table. "With the horses, we can work for the farmers by ploughing their fields or something comparable. The money you want to give us is insufficient to buy a loaf of bread because the German Mark has been so significantly devalued." Rudi's fury mounted until his blue eyes were filled with fire when both fists slammed into the conference table again.

A hush fell throughout the large hall. "Sir, you must get yourself under control."

"I must demonstrate my resentment of what your people are attempting to do to the suffering refugees. To those who have lost everything, now you are robbing us blind of the only thing we have left. I would rather spit on your shoes than turn over my horses to you!"

The man who questioned Rudi had no answers to give him. The only thing the British officer could do was shrug his shoulders.

Rudi hurried back to Westphal, still holding onto the two animals waiting for him. With great wrath still boiling over, Rudi informed his friend of the official's intentions. "I cannot force myself to put the horses up for sale. Before I sell these wonderful creatures that have saved our lives repeatedly, I would rather take my blade and slaughter them. At least, by doing this, we would have the meat to feed our families. We have not become so vulgar to resort to eating horse flesh, but I am blasted if I am going to hand over our livelihood to these idiot government officials."

"Truthfully, Rudi, I do not remember seeing you in such a rage," Westphal said gruffly, "but it is well-founded, that is for certain."

"Above all else, we need to devise a plan to keep our horses," Rudi quickly added.

After hearing the loud voices, one of the officers rushed over to the two men. The officer behind the table stood rigid. "Hold your tongue – be quiet – calm down."

To Westphal, Rudi hastily added, "These thieves do not want the other people to get all roused up and then get the same aggressive ideas we have."

The officials pulled the two men and the two horses to the side. One of the officers spoke to Rudi in a hushed tone, "If you promise to be out of this area in a

Registering the Horses

week, you can keep your horses." The officer sent the two men a stern scowl, "on one condition. You must not spread any rumours or cause an uproar of complaints among the people living in the area."

"Germany is small now, although not that small. We will find another place where we can go to find work and food for our animals," Rudi assured. "We must think about our family's needs. We will manage to arrange something. Do not give us another thought because I am revolted by the vicious corruption oozing out beneath every rock. The corruption is even among the troops the German soldiers fought beside." Rudi spat his words at the men in charge. "I can well imagine that by the time our country gets back on its feet, it will be sliced into a thousand pieces and our people right along with it." He thrust his right hand up in the air until his fingers touched his large Adam's apple. Then, Rudi dragged his fingers across his throat. "I have had it up to here!"

After the terrible threat of losing their livelihood, the two men, with their belongings, returned to the little cottage in Vorrade, realising that this day forecast a situation with grave consequences.

Chapter 35

TO OSNABRÜCK

After reporting to the large outbuilding where the horses were to be sold, with battered hearts, Westphal and Meissner hesitated to enter their home since each man's thoughts swirled with the many decisions confronting them.

In the murky autumn night air, Rudi ranted to his friend. "We can at least tell ourselves now that we tried to make every effort to be prudent. To my way of thinking, the disillusionment in our nation is now complete." Then, he shivered slightly out of rage and partly from the chill that crept more deeply into his being.

Westphal scoffed. "The cold has taken on a greater sting from when I first saw the two women standing in the doorway of the small hovel we call home." He stammered out of rage to Ruth. "The ignorant thugs running the country tried to make us sell our horses."

Grumbles came quickly from those who lived in the little beach house as Rudi closed the door behind him. The icy breeze took hold of the ember in the small stove, igniting the flame, now doubling as their only heat and cooking source. As the group closed the door behind them, Rudi's keen sense sent his eyes to the stove, where he saw the ember practically crumble into lifeless grey ashes. At a second glance, he still detected a glowing fragment of wood, enough to stand by and warm his hands.

While sitting and relaxing around the small table after their evening meal, the adults determined the British Government Officials, with the aid of the German Officials, were backing the refugees who had horses into a corner.

As Rudi had done in the building hours earlier, he struck the table with his fist: "We have been pushed around enough! We suddenly find we need to become bolder than before the war. We are nothing more than scapegoats to whoever needs to untie our own evilness."

Pushing more intently, Westphal added, "You can't trust anyone these days."

"We are humiliated and disillusioned once again by our own countrymen because they attempt to trample on us, which increases our isolation and unimportance," Rudi insisted. "We are beyond exhaustion, so we should get some much-deserved rest."

No sooner had Rudi finished his sentence than Westphal doused the lantern. Soon, soft, smooth, deep breathing hovered above the floor where everyone slept.

To Osnabrück

Plagued by nightmares, Rudi found himself gasping for breath during the middle of the night. He awoke the following morning with thoughts on how he could solve their dilemma. He voiced his worries to the other men over a white slice of English, five-day-old bread. He grumbled into the hot water, "Ruth has always been resourceful, but this terrible new way of life is putting her through trials and hardships she could not have imagined a few years ago. She has wisely traded a gold watch for an old bicycle, questionable condition as it is. I believe I can make this old bicycle serviceable. I must use the ingenuity God blessed me with. Tonight, I will hand-carve a new wooden seat, but I am annoyed I do not have a scrap of old leather to cover the seat so it can protect my rear end, giving me a place to sit without getting splinters into my skinny rump."

Early the following morning, Rudi shoved the finished wooden seat onto the bicycle and bid his goodbyes to everyone in the cottage. Then he started toward Hamburg, pursuing his goal of finding some place for his family to live.

Rudi hoped to pedal from village to village, pleading here and there for work and a place to house his family. On the first afternoon, pedalling the bike gave him the perfect vantage point to notice his surroundings and see firsthand the deep destruction his Fatherland had endured because of Hitler's regime. Rudi had taken the train and hitched rides from Rosenheim. However, on this journey, the rawness hit him to the core, negating the space between loneliness and happiness.

After peddling for longer than two hours, he needed to stop, get off the bike, and let it fall where it may. Finding the nearest group of bushes, his knees fell to the cold, damp ground. His guilt gave way to his needs. Perhaps it was his weakened state, or possibly it was the rawness of what he saw. Perhaps his longing for his home of Klein Pobloth caused him to be ill. Rudi did not know. The pasture beside him was abundantly filled with blue bachelor buttons and white daisies, too inviting for him to overlook. He rolled over, closed his eyes, and passed out from exhaustion.

At daybreak, Rudi found himself on the road once more with a new determination that the world would not get the better of him. He was here to lick the world. When Rudi reached over to hold his bike, his body evoked a new grit of strength he did not have before this moment. So, onwards, he pedalled day and night, stopping at every village hoping to find employment and lodging for his family group and the two horses.

Several days passed, and Rudi was almost on the verge of tears out of complete exhaustion while fighting his hunger mixed with frustration. Suddenly, he heard strong winds behind him. Rudi turned around to see where the strong winds were coming from. When he saw the blackness and the clouds quickly closing in on him, an eerie feeling of doom came over him. Before he could find shelter, gushes of rain mixed with sleet pounded about him, slamming directly at him. At times, the water was so deep his bike left tracks in the water. Preoccupied with finding a position and new housing for his family, Rudi trudged on. The deluge worsened when the storm pummelled him from the opposite direction. The surge hit his weathered face so sharply and then into his eyes, making it impossible for him to see the road. Naturally, he was drenched to the bone, hanging onto his bike like a limp noodle.

As abruptly as the storm had flung its deluge upon him, the rain ceased, and the sun filtered through the clouds several times, drying him as he rode in the wind. Unfortunately, the wooden seat on the bike displayed its wear and tear from the constant weather changes. Because of the rain, everything went awry, making it impossible to maintain his momentum in pedalling the bike.

Anxiously, Rudi glanced at the sky for a break in the weather, "Oh – ignoble fear or not, I have found no work of any kind. Dagnabbit, I will not be defeated. Has the world gone fickle?" Rudi cursed into the sky, lashing out at himself and his Fatherland. His eyes brimmed with tears, and Rudi cried out, "I have been dragged through the war. I fought in the spearhead in Russia during Operation Barbarossa on the Eastern Front. Within a few days, I was sent to what the Allies call the Battle of the Bulge. I nearly starved to death while spending months in an American POW camp. I lost everything! What a deceitful machine Hitler and the ruthless Nazi Party were. Now, the Germans are hated by the rest of the world. I do have the tenacity to try to pull off such a feat as finding a job in a nation confounded with death and hostility."

He gazed again to the heavens in tormenting pounding agony. "Ah… ha… I will be cunning and keep on heading my bike in the direction of Hamburg. I recall Max Schmeling and his wife Anny Ondra lived there." Rudi recalled with hope, "I still remember the long friendship our family had with Anny and Max."

On the side road to Hamburg, Rudi remembered he had not seen the Schmelings for some time. Pensively, he wondered if he could locate the couple. Once in the city, it took him some time, and then he was impressed when, after inquiring in several sports houses, the men in charge were kind enough to aid him in locating the couple. Directions in hand, he postponed his arrival long enough to make a polite phone call to alert his mother's friends.

On his arrival at their home, the three friends embraced. Anny offered him the best chair in their home. Before long, she suggested it would be beneficial for Rudi to remove his saturated jacket and place it with his soaked shoes near the heated stove. Once they sat comfortably by the open fireplace, Anny offered Rudi a hot cup of substitute coffee and a warm roll. Rudi had an extensive, enjoyable visit with the famous German couple. They had a good time reminiscing about Rudi's mother, whom they affectionately called "Tante Dolo" and the fabulous seasonal hunting party gatherings held at Klein Pobloth.

"I must say, while sitting here, I can sense all three of us have to hold back tears about times long since gone. Most of Germany's people are seeking a fresh beginning."

To Osnabrück

"Why, if there is anything in the world I could do, I would be keen to help." Max flattered Rudi with his kind words. "Nonetheless, Anny and I cannot help you because we have nothing. Our home was bombed, so like you, we lost everything and live in this small apartment. As you know, we cannot return to Ponickel, our beloved estate in Pommern," he bemoaned. "Can you tell me about your dear mother?"

"Max and Anny, we have tried for months to learn what could have happened at Klein Pobloth. The only report we have heard was about Pinnow, the night watchman who rang the alarm a few hours before the Russians pushed into the village. From my understanding, this allowed many residents to take refuge in the fields or wherever they decided would be the safest place.

"Unfortunately, I have no idea what happened to my mother or the other workers still in the village. My heart is broken not to know what has happened to my mother. Ruth and Anneliese were able to flee with the children three days before the Russians attacked the community and the Gutshaus of Klein Pobloth. Ruth explained how my mother would not escape with them. She and Herr Risch were determined they'd be safe if they stayed behind. You probably remember Risch, who was the manager at Klein Pobloth. From how my wife described their argument with my mother, Dolores fleeing with Ruth and Anneliese would not occur. Herr Risch convinced my mother the Russians were no threat for she was an elderly woman, and they would not harm her."

"That does not seem logical to me," Max insisted.

"Why, Rudi, you know as well as I do the Russians could never be trusted. Could it be possible Herr Risch had some connection with the Nazi Party?" Anny questioned.

"The way I understand the past few years at Klein Pobloth, Risch had his sticky fingers in every pot to make himself wealthy and feel elevated. I remember Ruth telling me during one hunting party that Risch was bent on inviting Hermann Göring to several hunting parties. Thank the good Lord that my mother had enough sense not to allow that devil onto our property."

"You knew Hitler was bound and determined to give me the most difficult time he could dish out for not joining the Nazi Party by placing me in harm's way as a paratrooper," Max told Rudi.

"Yes, Ruth told me about your sad situation. As always, luck was on your side, Max. The most unusual turn of events occurred when our neighbour Horst Schumann found his way to live with Ruth and Anneliese. My sister's family and Schumann have moved elsewhere, but one of our workmen lives with us. You probably remember Albert Westphal because he worked with the horses and helped with the hunts. We make a nice little family. Though he has not found his own family. We are keeping our fingers crossed he will locate them soon."

Dislodging a tattered handkerchief from his threadbare trousers to rub his eyes, Rudi slid the handkerchief down to his dripping nose, stuffed the small damp cloth into his pants, and then excused himself. "Dear Max and Anny, I must be on my way because I must find a job. The pressure is weighing heavy on my shoulders. My family needs a new way of life and a home that will be warmer than the beach house we are living in now."

Rudi unconsciously swept his fingers through his thinning hair as he flung his leg over his bike. *What the heck of a mess did I get myself into this time? Life is not supposed to turn out this way. The world has become so brutal.*

When Rudi spotted a train temporarily halted by the road he had taken, he slung the battered bike over his shoulder to hitchhike on the freight train. It was travelling to the area he had visited for a few days with a fellow soldier during the war before everything turned sour for the German army. The train provided his transportation to the area around Osnabrück, where his unit had been stationed for several months. He enjoyed the region and remembered plenty of farms in this area. Perhaps luck would finally be on his side, and he could find work somewhere.

The surrounding area seemed familiar, so Rudi descended at the next train stop with his bike in tow. The name of the village did not come to mind, but he felt it was where he had visited a woodland range with one of his lieutenants.

As he went from village to village, he could not resist being captivated by the fascinating landscape, becoming aware of a vast swampy area. Gazing over the land, he noticed a peat factory nearby, abutting the peat fields. He saw they used horses to work on the peat farm. As he passed the factory, he saw the empty houses their workers had used before the war. Many families were living together throughout Germany and Europe in one room or on the streets while these houses remained empty. He could not imagine how such a thing could happen.

The factory's foreman informed Rudi that he needed to speak to the mayor of Bohmte since this municipality was responsible for the peat fields. Rudi asked around how to locate the mayor's office. Without hesitation, he turned his bike toward the small, paved road and peddled to the small rural community of Schwege, to the empty houses.

Rudi was not going to be put off. Due to his abrupt, persistent manner, the mayor's office assistant in Bohmte recognised that Rudi was the type to camp at their doorstep until the mayor took the time to see this strong-minded, middle-aged man.

After making him wait for an hour and a half, the mayor finally made himself available to Rudi. The mayor came meandering up to Rudi as if he had all the time in the world. The weary middle-aged man's anger was already at its highest level. Swallowing his rage, Rudi attempted to be the ever-pleasant gentleman. His ploy worked. The two men spoke briefly. Rudi introduced himself and explained his family's plight.

"Why are these houses empty?" he asked the mayor.

"Oh, these houses belonged to Polish men working at the peat factory. Since the war was over, they needed to return to Poland. We are eager to find someone who can work in the peat fields, but they must have a horse," the mayor mockingly said. "I can see from your sad situation that you have neither. If you had a horse hitched to our fencepost, you could have a job and a house."

With a chuckle, Rudi beamed with delight. With joy, Rudi did not realise he still possessed he said, "Here I am. I am your worker. Plus, I have two horses and a wonderful hefty wagon."

"Ja, if you have two horses, you have the job. That is yours for sure."

Enthusiastically, Rudi spoke up, "Well, of course. I also have one more man, my wife, and three children."

The mayor shoved several papers in Rudi's direction. Before the mayor could change his mind about the number of people, Rudi signed the documents without hesitation. As he signed, the mayor promised to hold the house for them for fourteen days. Rudi immediately sent a telegram to his family from the mayor's office, informing them of his good fortune. He sent a cable notifying the adults they should pack what little they had and be ready to leave as soon as he arrived in Vorrade.

Wasting no time, he hitchhiked on a freight train with his bike in tow back to Lübeck, arriving at the beach house in three days.

Everyone breathed with relief when Rudi parked his bike beside the front door. As it turned out, he arrived a day before the government officers were to seize the horses. Everyone was delighted with his news.

Chapter 36

FROM VILLAGE TO VILLAGE

With the weather distinguishably more overcast than when Rudi rode his bike earlier that month, Ruth and Rudi's family endured the move to their new location in the wet, cold autumn weather. The unconventional and clumsy move needed to happen quickly. The lengthy meandering back and forth through essentially a street-less area with their wagon ended in their travelling some 500 kilometres.

The adults understood if they made it to Osnabrück, it would be an exceptional achievement to pull off such a feat. Adding to their apprehension, it was knowing that the valuable horses were easy prey for someone to steal which instantly would place the group in a vulnerable position. One of the men settled the horses to avoid catastrophe while the other adults walked beside the wagon and begged for food. The threat was heightened since so many refugees were on the road. The family was suspicious of all of them. Ruth and Rudi's family constantly shifted their tactics so the thieves lurking in the area could not overtake them.

Secured by a rusty hook and chain, the wobbly, unstable bicycle hung on the back of the wagon. Rudi and Westphal shared the responsibility of riding the bike each day and proceeded cautiously to the farms, begging for food.

The refugees from the east going westward swamped the reluctant, overtaxed farmers who continuously provided food for those who found themselves as vagrants. When Ruth's family arrived, the farmers slowly grumbled when asked for a handout, although most farmers proved to be understanding. In contrast, others made the beggar scramble for cover under the nearest shrub when a pair of rigid, plump farmhands cried out with raised fists.

Exhausted from peddling from farm to farm, Rudi was elated to see a plump farm couple bent over their well-tended vegetable garden. As he approached, he detected several milk cows bellowing in an un-damaged barn. It appeared that he was the first person who was a prospective beggar on this well-appointed farm. With great anticipation, he pushed his way and peddled rapidly to set his bike beside them and pose his question. To his dismay, the overweight couple had added rocks to border their beautiful vegetable garden. Before he could pose the question, the man turned on him and hurled the intended rocks in his direction, with his wife following suit. One of the sharp-edged stones struck Rudi's left kidney area.

From Village to Village

Determined not to show them the satisfaction of being struck, he did not cry out in agony, but his breathing became painful, and with his left hand holding the struck area, he steered the black, chipped handlebars back the best he could to where the lane began. Regretting his choice of farms to beg from and peddling his bike at lightning speed until the nearest clearing appeared, he stopped and flopped down, bike and all, onto a grassy meadow – scattering a group of refugees who were about to approach the same farm where he had been a few moments earlier, cautioning the group.

After Rudi's experience with the irate farmer, their anxiety about finding food to quench their hunger rose considerably. Still, Ruth's family cluster created a unique self-contained environment within the wagon.

Several refugee groups travelled in the same direction to make life easier for the farmers and minimise their burden. When they arrived at a prospective farm, two men in the group tossed a coin to decide which family would have the opportunity to ask the farmer for help. In this way, they placed some space between them.

The national laws directive read that everyone was to be off the streets by dusk. The authority posted the ruling on every rural road, fencepost and byway to maintain law and order. The government mandate read, "Local citizens must indicate whether travelers could reach their desired destination by curfew."

While the adults were sitting around the campfire, the children were snuggled fast asleep in the wagon. Ruth took a quick inventory of their belongings. "We do not have any money to buy food to feed the family. I can't help noticing how everyone took to Dorlies – with her flushed, rosy complexion, blue eyes, curly blond straw hair, her tender age of two and a half years old now, she is the essence of what a beautiful German child should look like. With her blue eyes combined with her charming smile, she can melt the hardest of hearts. She delights at the thought of being a big girl and wants to help contribute to our needs. I could not help seeing her irrepressible eagerness when I casually suggested she could assist by asking the farmers for milk."

Acknowledging the torrent of hunger pains, Rudi listened intently, eager as Ruth to find a way to feed the family and keep everyone healthy.

Ruth continued her explanation, "Rudi, we have this little milk can," she pointed at the small tin container. "With the help of the older children, Dorlies can help collect enough milk, so then we can transfer the small cup into the bigger container we have on the wagon. I don't particularly appreciate using her this way. However, I think it is for the good of the whole family. So, if we can get a little milk at a time, it will go into the bigger container."

"We have learned to be aggressive in our quest for food because we have a long, risky journey ahead of us. Under the best conditions, a piece of bread or half a potato for each person is the only thing we might have to eat on this never-ending journey."

Chapter 37

THE ENORMOUS UNDERTAKING

Putting the family in for shelter at nearby villages or farms became a tremendous challenge. It was much more ambitious than anyone in Ruth and Rudi's family cluster could have anticipated. These small villages or farmers did not lose anything, but they did not want to help the refugees. They would belittle them while continually remaining entirely indifferent to their needs.

As twilight came, a newly acquired old lantern was lit inside the wagon, and storytelling began to entertain the occupants in their wagon. Inventive games were used during times like this and were enjoyable for the family. Fear and hunger haunted them during the inky night when sleep would not come since their stomachs growled, yearning to be filled.

One man was assigned to guard the horses, keeping them calm with a little food to feed them. The children were in the wagon while the adults hiked beside them as they travelled from Lübeck to Osnabrück. From there, they still needed to find their way to the township of Bohmte and then to Schwege-Hunteburg.

Before the curfew was enforced, potential danger lurked everywhere. No maps showed the cluster's way to the next farms or villages, and even if there were maps, they would not be accurate because of the countryside's destruction.

At dawn, Rudi took a turn riding the bike in front of the wagon in hopes of locating prospective farms. He returned to the wooden wagon with his report, "I am on fire with rage. One of the farms where I stopped dared ask, 'Why do you come to our area?' The farmer and his wife stared at me as if I were their enemy. They did not want me to interrupt their way of life, did not care to have me in their farmyard, and would not let us use their barns."

Rudi angrily rambled, "This was a terrible day to be on the road. The people have become bullheaded because they do not want us to have anything or interrupt their lives in the villages. One village elder assured me he would let us cook and live with the pigs in the barn. I am ashamed to admit that this is the best offer I have had all day. It is the one we must take whether we like it or not."

Grumbles of disappointment could be heard coming from under the adults' breaths.

For their safety, the refugees traveled together and after some time, many of the refugees became a close-knit group. Few men were around anymore since many

The Enormous Undertaking

had been lost in the war. When one of the men lit a cigarette, he took a puff and shared it until it travelled around the barn, and everyone could get a whiff.

The November howling winds made their journey even more unpleasant. Flurries of snow began to appear regularly. The children were delighted to see the snowflakes. If they could have read the trepidation in the adults' eyes, they would have feared what lay ahead of them.

The government ordered the refugees off the streets at dusk and to be in a town an hour before curfew. With this restriction, the villages were ordered to give the refugees sleeping quarters and food for twenty-four hours. Various towns accommodated and provided a schoolroom, a big barn or a public hall as an overnight resting place for the refugees.

Ruth's family preferred to sleep in a barn to keep an eye on their horses, which, at this point, would have been stolen from them right under their noses. So, they slept with their horses and often among the cows that happened to be in the barn.

Rudi and Westphal enjoyed the scent of the hay in their nostrils and heard the mooing of the cows as they settled down for the evening. Strangely, the animals made them more comfortable by being in their presence than the strangers in the unwelcoming villages.

The family's travel to the township of Bohmte by Schwege-Hunteburg became more difficult than Rudi had ever imagined. The necessity of being on the move required everyone's cooperation for seven days.

Bursting into thunderous anger after his return on the bike, Ruth raged at her husband, "Rudi, I cannot imagine we have been turned into little less than nomads."

Listening to his wife's warning words bit him to the core. Rudi placed his hands behind his back and then strode to and fro. "My dearest, I am doing the best I know how. I inquired at every village and farm I passed, humbling myself into begging for the last morsel of food the villagers might have."

Sputtering, Ruth spoke in anguish, "I am sorry you must keep up your brave efforts. It is horrible to see Hans-Georg's stomach swollen from hunger while Dorlies is weeping, tugging at my skirts for attention. I have no more energy to give her the little love she asks of me. Susanne, well, she keeps herself busy while playing with some creature she has befriended. She asked me to take a stray hedgehog today. I had to tell her no since we did not have enough food to feed ourselves.

"As people from the eastern part of the country, we have a rigid sense of morality in supporting anyone needing aid. The inhabitants of Klein Pobloth and the countless other estates extended a helping hand to anyone who came through their rural community. Now, it feels to me like we are being punished for our kindness. Particularly when we came to a farmhouse, stepped out of the wagon, crossed the courtyard, and could smell the freshly baked loaves of bread cooling on the windowsill.

"The tantalising fragrance still lingers in my nostrils," Ruth added with bitterness. "If you remember, the farmer and his wife implied we were not welcome in their home. He and his plump wife would not give us one bite. It almost made me sick because the whole yard smelled tantalisingly of freshly baked bread. It was demoralising to endure seeing little Hans-Georg's sad glance hiding his tears. I realise his unhappiness is from hunger."

Rudi's disappointment in his fellow man rumbled deep. "We didn't receive anything from the farmer or his fat wife. I do not intend to criticise, but to add insult to injury, we had to sleep in their foul-smelling pig barn at night without anything to eat. After our stay in the barn, the farmer indicated he and his wife were concerned about our lingering longer than we should. The fire in my belly came to a boiling point. I resentfully asked him if he had been drafted into the war effort. He answered me, 'Oh no, I have a medical impairment. The forces excused me from all military service.' My heart beat faster out of rage, so I could not look at this extremely healthy man. With my right foot, I kicked the nearest stone into the air, missing the kitchen window where, minutes before, the aroma of fresh bread wafted toward the wagon. All I wanted to do was put as much distance between that fool and us as possible and then quickly make our way to the main road."

Murmurs of displaced anger erupted from the couple as they embraced in silent comfort. "I am sure you will make things work out in the peat factory. The house you found for us will truly be a blessing." Ruth kissed her husband tenderly and patted his slender shoulders for encouragement.

Chapter 38

EATING CHICKEN

The country byways carrying the family to the west became grinding gullies, jarring the buckboard as an oppressive, freezing gale blew from the northeast when the wind beat against the thick wooden planking, posing a tense danger for the family.

Despite the perception of danger always awaiting them, Ruth was full of joy, anticipating their new home. The afternoon soon turned into mayhem when a sizeable English convoy of soldiers, who had supremacy over the roads, forced the family to stop their wagon on the side of the road. The impressionable children were told to remain on the buckboard while the adults rested their aching bodies on the hard-frozen field to observe the troops.

The adults suddenly marvelled at the unmistakable miracle that took place just a few feet from where they stood. Their burning hunger still not squelched, they had no misgivings when they saw the convoy hit a chicken as it attempted to run across the road. It ran under one of the trucks, which inadvertently clipped the hen enough to kill it but not crush it.

A yell of "Hallelujah" erupted from the group.

With a clever glee and infectious chuckle, Rudi beamed, "You do not need to point out that we must act quickly in grabbing the dead chicken."

Quick to joke, Westphal leaped to his feet, "I will dash to the bird so no one questions us about my deed and hide our bounty under some dirty old blankets."

A gaze of joy crossed Ruth. "After the convoy passed by us, the truck delivered the chicken so timely. Meat has been such a scarcity. My mind has a vision of a roasted chicken, causing me to salivate at the thought. Rudi, how shall we prepare this wonderful hen?"

Westphal confessed, "I can't help but notice that every one of us had an odd feeling. Not a pang of guilt among us for being so greedy in seizing the chicken without seeing if anyone watched us so they can say it belongs to a nearby farmer."

A gasp of unwelcome consternation erupted from Rudi, who watched at the back of the wagon. "The bike... where is our bike... no more bike..." was his cry.

The family's bike had hung on a rusty nail from a chain on the back of the wagon. It did not occur to them that the bike might be stolen or the nail and chain might not hold. "The nail must have turned, so the bike tumbled off. Or perhaps someone could have snatched it. We have lost so much already. I do not care anymore." Rudi kicked at the wagon wheel.

"At any rate, the convoy has delivered a chicken to us," Westphal teased.

"I do not have the energy to cry about what we have lost now. We must march on with no fear controlling us, for we feel like defiled animals, eating anything we find, even the hen killed by the truck," Ruth proclaimed.

"No," Rudi insisted. "The world around us has gone mad."

Towards nightfall, the travellers saw a group of flickering yellow lights seeming to shine together out of one large building. As they went closer, they saw a small guesthouse surrounded by a small settlement. Hoping for their hospitality, they felt it would be a minor infraction to ask one of the families to cook their chicken for supper in one of the kitchens.

Ruth listened to Rudi's appeal to the farmer's wife with much interest, for, after all, she had a chicken to roast for the family. A perplexing glance came over Ruth when her husband approached her with a disillusioned growl, one she knew only too well.

"It served no purpose to speak to them any further," Ruth's attempt at comforting her husband was of no avail.

"Is there no decency left in this world? It is as though all our lives have been merged into one mass of disappointment after another. The equality we had before with our own countrymen has been stripped away by the war. The woman I approached hurled insults at our family. Then she asked, with her short, hostile gaze, if we were seeking a haven. Her rebuff provoked such anger in me that it alarmed me. I only asked the woman if we could cook our chicken on her stove. I knew she assumed we stole the hen from how she stared at me. I wasted my time defending the meal. 'We truly found it,' I informed her, even though the hen was one of the only things we did not pilfer." Rudi shuffled his feet out of shame to admit such deeds openly.

Gazing back at the house, Rudi stood chatting with his wife, "By no means are we out of the woman's view. I can see her rapidly stiffening, pondering where we got the milk and the chicken."

Wisely, the group kept themselves isolated from the owner of the guesthouse and his inquisitive wife.

The last rays of winter sun gleamed on their campfire. While roasting the hen over the open pit, the wafting aroma filled their surroundings, announcing the meal of the decade. Ruth pulled the golden-brown bird from its iron dagger and served the ravenous family. The chicken and a big pot of milk soup comforted them and warmed their bellies.

Chapter 39

OVER THE BRIDGE

At every phase of their travels, a new challenge arose. The gullies in the well-worn road took Ruth's family cluster to one of the tributaries of the Elbe River, feeding the North Sea. Thus, crossing with the two horses and the heavy wagon would be a significant undertaking. They were not surprised when they saw the tremendous challenge lying before them.

The bridge they would have crossed had been bombed during the last months of the war. To make their situation more dangerous, the group had no other choice but to take the only available crossing to the other side which was a temporary pontoon bridge. A cruel warning hit Ruth, Rudi and Westphal of the task lying ahead of them.

They thought the crossing would become much more hazardous with the heavy dark clouds looming overhead, bringing thunderstorms to frighten the horses. The horses would already be spooked by the noise of the unstable metal and wooden bridge, combined with the sizzling of lightning rumbling through the air, which meant they could quickly get out of control. As they discussed the possibility of a furious rainstorm, the morning turned into a race against the elements. Within minutes, the temperature dropped, and it began to sleet, turning into snow.

The men attempted to cross the bridge. Westphal struggled to manoeuvre the horses and wagon nearer to the entrance. Abruptly, they were halted by British guards securing access. In a stubborn tone of authority, the guards informed them they only had half an hour to cross the bridge. It must be now or never. A significant British convoy was coming from the opposite direction and would take up the entire connection. The guards also informed the men that the temporary bridge would be destroyed after the convoy passed in preparation for a permanent one.

Holding a quick conference, they felt confident they could cross the bridge in the time allotted. They became relentless in their quest and did not give in to the soldiers' warnings. Irritated, the soldiers finally gave their permission. Displeasure could be seen in the guards' uneasy stance.

The adults recognised they were taking a dreadful risk, yet advancing was their only option, so they swiftly rejected the thought of not trying. Returning to where they came from would be admitting defeat, and their bellies would be full of disappointments, so they would not stand down.

Initially, the horses were unwilling to cross the vast body of water. When it seemed unlikely the horses were up to the task, Westphal quickly judged the problem and stepped back a few paces to assess the situation. His expertise in handling domestic animals was second to none, he realised the significance of covering the horse's eyes to remove their fear of the turbulent waters. Once the task was done, the two horses trotted onto the edge of the swaying pontoon bridge. Rudi and Ruth squeezed onto the bridge, flanking on either side. Westphal seized their bridles, encouraging them ever so softly with his gentle voice and calming the two horses down into a dazed state until, at last, he lured them onto the wooden planks.

A stiff breeze with sleet caused the icy cold river to lap the bridge. The tan horse's ears jerked in terror as the horse flung its large head forward at the unfamiliar sound and pawed in an unruly state at the freezing water. The horse's yanking of the wagon and the wet wooden bridge caused the wagon to jerk uncontrollably. As it trembled, the children cried out. Immediately sensing the danger, the black horse instinctively yanked his head and began to paw his footing, testing the wooden bridge. The wagon jerked again, causing the three children inside to scream hysterically.

Regrettably, the heavy wagon and the horses crossed the bridge only halfway. Unexpectedly, the iron rim of the wagon wheel split. The weight of the buckboard caused the rim to be torn asunder, giving it time to strike the wooden wheel and triggering it to crash into the bridge. The weight of the buckboard ploughed into the wet lumber of the bridge and dug a furrow, which caused the iron wheel's rim to form a cavity. Danger loomed with the possibility that the whole group could tumble into the rapidly flowing torrents.

The wagon tipped even further with the next gust. In an instant, the whole cluster – the buckboard, two horses, three children and the three adults – seemed doomed. Their most significant concern was that if this were to occur, the heavy wagon's force with the horses would hurl everyone into the freezing, rapidly flowing water.

The men quickly assessed the damage. On closer inspection, they discovered that the rough knocking about caused by the hazardous swaying movement on the bridge had shattered the left rear wheel.

Instinctively, Ruth turned her attention to the inside of the wagon to see the children recoil with profound hysteria and latch onto each other.

Rudi turned his attention to the outside of the wagon just in time to see Westphal clinging onto the horses. The heavy wagon staggered heavily. Out of sheer panic, the horses bolted up several times and hurled him off his feet with one foot dangling in the fast-moving current. Miraculously, Westphal regained his strength and found his footing enough to jerk the horses back into submission.

As Rudi drew in a quick breath to regain his composure, the breeze suddenly became a relentless wind and hurled him onto the edge of the swaying bridge.

Over the Bridge

His previously twice-injured knee hit the timber on the solid wooden edge. Out of excruciating agony, he unleashed a haunting cry of anguish, and his knee felt as if it had been pierced with sharp spikes.

Walking beside the wagon, Ruth attempted to regain her footing as the bridge swung back and forth. Filled with terror, she clung to the wagon for dear life. Westphal heard Rudi, although he could not help. Turning his head, he swiftly saw Rudi regain his footing despite his pain.

Rudi could only imagine what was happening on the inside of the buckboard. Out of terror, he screamed in the hope Ruth could hear him. Both made their way to inspect the back of the wagon. "Our children must be feeling mortal horror," Rudi yelled.

With the high surge of water surrounding them, they stood beside the wagon and pondered their options.

Rudi was in too much agony to make any decisions. "What the heck, this is a fine situation. How and in what possible way can we cross the bridge now? We have at least a quarter of the bridge left to go. Westphal, do you have any answers?"

"We have a spare axe with us," Westphal reminded Rudi. "The weather conditions are not as treacherous as earlier this morning. With the sleet stopping, it will make it easier on all of us."

After deliberation, Ruth suggested, "I will stay with the children to protect them along with the wagon."

"The pain in my knee has diminished. I am pleased I have not broken it for the third time." Rudi glanced down to inspect his injury further. "It is beginning to turn purple, but I can tolerate the pain."

After their quick examination, Westphal and Rudi dashed across the bridge on foot for the other side of the tributary, where they noticed a patch of mature trees and selected the correct size. With an axe, rope and chain in hand, they hastened to chop down two trees to prepare a toboggan bound together by belts, torn pieces of rope, and the chains they hauled from the wagon's rear.

Once the two were back, they quickly tied the logs to the buckboard.

After completing the makeshift wagon repair, it was challenging to make the children understand that if they held on to each other, they would be safe to cross to the other side of the bridge. Ruth tucked Dorlies under one arm, pulled her daughter to her breast, and held onto the wagon with her free hand for dear life.

After being instructed to stare straight ahead and not look down into the rushing water, the children were gravely reluctant, but when they found their footing and clasped hands, their confidence heightened. They all grasped onto the side of the wagon to ensure it stayed in the well-worn furrows caused by the weight of the many types of military equipment long passed by. Susanne became the leader, and Hans-Georg brought up the rear.

Escaping the Russian Onslaught

The horses were still blindfolded, so Westphal guided them by the harness to the bank for safety. When the horses were securely tied to the trees, the children waited on the grass for safety.

The three adults rushed back to the wagon. Pierced by the cold weather, yet sweaty, weak, and with raw nerves, they finally moved the heavy wagon to the damp ground on the west side of the tributary. They hauled their possessions to the other side of the bridge just as the British convoy came into view. Their crossing had been just shy of being a miracle. If the family had not crossed in time, they knew full well that the caravan would not have stopped for them. Instead, they would have quickly thrust them off and out of their way. Hardihood had turned many British soldiers from compassion to anger. Hence, countless military members could have eagerly pushed the wagon into the torrents for no reason other than to make an example to prove their might over the Germans. After the war, the British military's actions toward the German civilians were an indication of how badly the German people were treated.

Everyone suffered during the terrible ordeal. Ruth was mired in her thoughts of the danger in which the military had placed the children.

To expedite the replacement of a new rim, Westphal and Rudi grabbed the metal rim of the broken wheel and each grabbed a side. Undone, they stumbled onto a rural road, hurrying to the nearest settlement about a quarter of a mile away. The owner was not there when they arrived at the wagon repair shop. Only his labourer could assist them.

Rudi approached the young man with enormous hope. He asked him kindly, "I realise it is Saturday afternoon. The spokes of our wagon wheel must be reworked. We know this will not take much of your time. Can you please help us out?"

The young man turned away with a frown, sneering under his breath. "No… I will not… it – it is almost time for me to go home. Besides, it is Saturday afternoon, and my sweetheart is waiting for me."

His oafish comment stimulated further resentment in both men. Rudi's hopes quickly dwindled. Rudi snapped at him, "I have never seen a person who is more of a lazy klutz than you. I am sorely tempted to hit you over the head with the iron rim even though you are a young oaf."

The two older men paced the gritty wooden floor of the shop. The young man's laughter grated on Rudi. "We have our families out there, and we have nowhere to go. The curfew hours are upon us. We must be off the streets. You must help us," Rudi added in a fury. "At this point, even if it is the last thing I ever do, I want the satisfaction of striking you!"

"No, it is Saturday afternoon. My working hours were over at one o'clock. I will not help," the labourer said rudely.

A bored yawn was thrown directly at Rudi's scowl. Then, the oaf lazily covered his mouth several times. The young man's look of unconcern caused Rudi and Westphal's tempers to flare once more.

Over the Bridge

Rudi pleaded, "We have our family who we are responsible for waiting for us on the other side of the bridge."

"Obviously, he is not going to help," Westphal spat. He grabbed a piece of timber and was about to hit the young fool over the head with it.

"Do not submit yourself to his callousness. All they will do is put us in jail. Then where will we be?" Rudi cautioned.

Westphal added with enormous irritation, "I am so eager to be rid of these cruel people who are our own countrymen. We should leave this shop and quickly return to the street. We can watch for someone else who might be able to assist us."

Without striking him, it took a combined effort to escape the oaf. The iron frame clattered as it hit the cobblestone street. The banging caught a woman's attention. Within seconds, they spotted her standing on the sidewalk, gazing toward them where she had heard the clatter of the rim.

"No one else is in view, so the woman over there is our last hope. She appears to be a kind person. We should walk over to her and ask if she knows someone who can help us," Westphal suggested.

After hearing the clang, the woman motioned the men closer. As the men drew nearer, she noted their uneasy gaze. Once on the sidewalk and standing at the lady's side, Rudi advised her of their plight.

In a friendly, well-meaning voice, she replied, "There is a blacksmith around the corner. Perhaps he can help you."

"Thank you. Thank you, my dear woman. This is our last chance. This is all we have, one last chance."

They made their way to the blacksmith to see if he could help. "We have no money. We want to pay you or give you something, but we have nothing to give you."

The blacksmith smiled compassionately, "I do not care to haggle over such small things. I will repair the iron frame so you can get going. Your family is waiting. Show me your old wheel, and I will see how big it is." The actions of this one kind man spoke volumes.

The blacksmith dug around in his junk pile. He found a frame that was a bit heavier than their frame, and the form was about a quarter-inch shorter. Nonetheless, it was a frame for a wheel. The blacksmith worked the bushing out of the old wheel and then put it on the new one. He did everything in his power to help, but the new one was so much bigger, they would have to make it work.

They discovered the wheel was too heavy to carry, so Rudi and Westphal took turns rolling it. They placed the wheel onto the buckboard, and although it was a little lopsided, it worked.

Once safely underway, the family still gave into the desire to laugh when they stopped to ask a man where the town of Hoya was located. "Oh, you go this way to Ho-o-o-o-h-ya," he stuttered. His blue eyes stared back at the men with an empty haziness over them.

"He must have been drunk!" Westphal said as he nudged his friend.

"It is so amusing that we have to laugh so hard that now we have tears in our eyes," Rudi added with his infectious hearty chuckle.

"It is just one funny thing that happened among all the disastrous things going on around us," Ruth interjected as she hung onto the side of the rolling wagon for dear life.

"As hard as times are and as many indignities heaped upon us as fleeing Germans, I am glad we have been able to hold on to our humour," Rudi added.

With a lopsided wagon, they travelled westward. Within a few days, the group was only a one-day journey out of Osnabrück. Now, the family realised their travels should go well from this point on.

The same afternoon, they turned around a bend, coming upon a British jeep stuck in a ditch. It would have been impossible for the jeep to continue without assistance. The three adults, two horses and the chain link they kept in the back of the wagon assisted in hauling the vehicle out of the ditch. The driver was grateful for their assistance and gave the guys three cigars and two packages of cigarettes to show their appreciation.

Chapter 40

BEAUTIFUL BATHROOM

With the bike still on hand in earlier weeks, they could have had one of the men travel ahead of the wagon to secure housing. As it was now, the men hitched a ride or walked to the next location to find lodging for the night. For the second time this week, Rudi volunteered to hike in hopes of finding shelter. He enjoyed the delightful rustling of nature about him, the dry leaves crushing underfoot, the greenery mixed with gold on each side of him. A small flicker of hope crossed his face. Rudi pulled a large cloth out of his back pocket, swooping it into the fresh air and wiping the sweat from his face as he trudged to find housing for the night.

Rudi was ready to give up, but his feet kept him moving. He had been hiking for some time when he approached a beautifully tended dairy farm. He stopped in contemplation, as had been his habit since childhood, rubbing his left eyebrow until it danced. One more step, well, perhaps two, and soon, his concentration carried him onward.

After his long absence, Rudi related his story to the family. "If you remember, a dusting of snowfall chilled the wagon during the first wee hours of dawn. Dishevelled as I was, I braved the cold. I started on my daily hunt for our food and lodging. When I returned to the wagon, you were worried about my tardiness, which seemed like hours. I wish to tell you about our wonderful invitation to spend the night on the most delightful farm I have seen in some time."

Listening carefully, everyone studied him.

"After seeing the charming farm, I finally summoned the courage to walk down the path, where I spotted an attractive farmhouse nestled among an outcropping of pine trees. It appeared welcoming. Ruth, these people are so privileged with a great deal of kindness and reflecting the beauty of their farm in their compassion. They asked me into their house for a warm cup of tea and a slice of good German rye bread covered with farm butter. After visiting for some time, they invited us to spend the evening with them."

"We have no time for such frivolities. Just thinking about a beautiful life brings back painful recollections that sear my heart like a knife being held over hot coals."

"Ruth, I recognise you always have the family's safety at the front of your mind. Sometimes, it is good for our children to see the beautiful things in life.

We need not miss this opportunity. The folks at the farm told me we are welcome as soon as we can get our wagon into their farmyard."

Quickly finding his way back to the lane Rudi had used earlier that morning, he led the wagon to the small village and past an unwelcoming marketplace. However, when the buckboard pulled into the farmyard, Herr and Frau Miller had kerosene lanterns glowing.

Frau Miller approached Ruth and stretched out her hand to introduce herself: "Guten Abend." She lifted a kerosene lantern high enough to study Ruth's expression and gazed at the other party members. Frau Miller smiled kindly at Ruth and said, "My dear, you and your family appear to have suffered greatly. The distress of your losses shows in all of you. Please come make yourselves at home as best you can."

Ruth trusted no one by now, so she had become aloof toward outsiders. However, something different about this woman caused Ruth to let her guard down. She felt she could fall into this warm, friendly woman's arms and cling to her as she wished to with her mother. Unfortunately, this type of tenderness from her mother had never materialised. The painful memories caused tears to swell in Ruth's eyes as she nibbled at the side of her lips. *I will not let them drop or let them fall – no – not now.* "It is a generous gift you are extending to our family, Frau Miller, something we will never forget."

"Perhaps you and the children can rest comfortably in our empty bedrooms. You see, we had two sons, both lost in the war, and it would give me great pleasure to have your family use the rooms. The men might possibly sleep in the barn to watch the horses. There have been so many refugees who have become nothing more than thieves and vagrants. Someone like you must carry a high burden with such a large group to care for. It would give me pleasure to welcome you into our home."

"Your farm is impeccably beautiful, and you and your husband are equally so," Ruth acknowledged.

Frustrated by her inability to speak correctly at age two and a half, Dorlies struggled to tell her mother that she needed to relieve herself. Dorlies murmured something to her mother. Ruth stooped to hear what her timid daughter was struggling to whisper into her ear.

The woman guessed what the little blond, curly-locked girl needed. "I give you my permission to take your little girl into the house to use the lavatory."

Dorlies tugged at her mother's tattered skirt, questioning her with a stutter, "Mutti, the toilet is in the house?"

"Why yes, this time, we do not need to go in the bushes, as usual. When we go into the house, we must be as quiet as if we are invisible, creeping through the house little by little. We must not disturb anyone or anything when you use the bathroom."

Beautiful Bathroom

The woman of the house showed them the way. Dorlies' blue eyes grew big with wonder as they flitted through the house, not missing a single detail of the beauty she saw around her. As they entered the bathroom, Dorlies glanced about eagerly, speaking with all the seriousness her little frame could muster, and uttered to her mother, "Oh, just see Mutti. They have a beautifully clean, sparkling white bathroom."

Once out of the beautiful bathroom, Frau Miller, smiling, approached Ruth and said, "I am genuinely touched by your young daughter's astonishment."

"I must admit, her words made my heart sink to the ground because, before the war, we had an estate we were proud to call ours. Now, my own little daughter is already aware of the adjustments the war has brought into our lives. I am deeply distressed that her father and I can no longer provide a simple bathroom for our children, and I am pleased she is so delighted with your beautiful bathroom."

"I was moved when I noticed your daughter, at her tender age, can recognise the difference in her surroundings. I also am astounded that such a tiny little girl is sensitive to what makes life comfortable and beautiful," Frau Miller added.

Ruth and the children spent the night in the lovely farmhouse as promised while the men guarded their treasured horses and caught a bit of sleep in the barn.

It was November, so it was uncomfortably cold outside. Westphal and Rudi had their British cigars that they could not smoke in the horse barn, so they moved through the milk barn and stepped outside to enjoy the fresh air and the sounds of a farmyard they missed. As they smoked, the two men spoke about bygone days. There was a sudden silence. Westphal became dizzy and then slightly nauseated. He shed his jacket as sweat drenched his forehead. Then, he passed out.

Westphal knocked a few empty milk cans, waiting for delivery, onto the damp, cement floor as he fell. Rudi grabbed onto a piece of his clothing to keep his friend from injuring himself. Having not smoked for such a long time, they did not realise that smoking once again would affect them in this unforeseen manner.

Westphal soon returned to a sitting position. Rudi waited until Westphal felt well enough to make his way back to their horses. Following the experience beside the milk barn, the men had a well-deserved night of restful sleep.

The following morning, the sky was brilliantly blue, and the world appeared brighter. "*Liebe Frau Miller*, this is an experience our family will never forget. *auf Wiedersehen,*" Ruth said as she bid farewell to the Millers.

Frau and Herr Miller embraced the family before the horses pulled the heavy wagon out of the farmyard. Ruth's family waved vigorously, wearing big smiles of satisfaction after a peaceful night's sleep. For a few hours, their hunger had been satisfied.

Chapter 41

SCHWEGE-HUNTEBURG

The family's zigzagging 500-kilometre journey was relentless and took much longer than expected, yet excitement enforced their resolve to push on. Rudi had a passionate belief that travelling the distance to their new job was their only option. The sizeable bleeding blisters on their feet were only a minor irritation. The additional weight the adults lost walking the many kilometres were ones they hoped to regain by the expected better meals when the men had permanent jobs.

Ruth and her family were eager to find the little hamlet of Hunteburg. Driving their wagon through Osnabrück, the largest town in the area, they discovered that the village was so small it was not listed on a map. No one knew or had heard anything about the tiny village when they asked people on the street the location of the hamlet. Perplexed about the whereabouts of the little settlement, Rudi had tried to locate Hunteburg for two weeks and he had been in every small settlement from Lübeck to Osnabrück as he traversed his way across the countryside. Rudi sighed a heavy sigh of relief when the landmarks surrounding him finally became familiar. If he did not get his family to the factory when the management required him, all would be lost again.

The earth shook as heavy machinery pushed across the cold ground. The children descended from the wagon to observe the steady manoeuvres of British troops marching by. Soon, there was a traffic jam. Many of the flaps from the truck flew open, and the heads of young men popped out, with several men jumping off the vehicle with their rifles slung over their shoulders. Securing himself onto his mother, Hans-Georg whimpered, "*Nein Mutti*... please, no guns – please – please, *Mutti*." Her small son trembled behind his mother.

"I understand a little English, but please speak slowly. Where is Hunteburg or Schwege?" Rudi addressed one of the men in uniform.

"I grasp a bit of Deutsch," a young man volunteered. Nevertheless, in English, he said, "Come follow us. We have our camp very close to the village."

Soon after, several men grabbed chocolate bars and other foodstuffs from the back of their truck and pitched them toward the gaunt family. The children flew onto the unfamiliar bars, clasping them to claim them as their own, while the adults dashed for the most stable foodstuffs.

"Look! Just look at what they threw our way. Can you imagine? I have a whole bag of sugar!" Westphal cried out.

Schwege-Hunteburg

"I do not know if yours is better than the one I could grab. I have a cloth sack." Ruth sniffed. "It smells like white flour," Ruth sputtered joyfully. "I also have a container. If I can make out the spelling, it is much like our spelling of butter. Yes, I believe the writing on the can says butter on it. Just think what a find."

Rudi observed his wife in delight. "Ruth, when we find our house and get things cleaned up, you can bake us a Kuchen. What do you say?" Rudi winked at the children. His gaze caught the enormous smiles all around, and the beams of joy the children brought forth were heart-warming. At present, it seemed like a never-ending journey, and they were exhausted beyond all comprehension. They were overjoyed when they finally arrived in Schwege-Hunteburg. Ruth's husband smiled with a hint of pride. "This is where our jobs await us in the peat field. The adjacent factory processes the peat into heating fuel. I was given instructions by our new employer that we must advise the mayor of our arrival. The manager will notify us about our new jobs and obtain the proper instructions for our house in the New Colony. It was built for the factory workers, and we will now be part of it."

The family felt reassured they would be comfortable when the horses pulled their wagon into the lane at house Number Ten. The new home was in the New Colony in Schwege in the county of Wittlage.

Relieved that their journey had ended, Ruth teased her husband, "Why Rudi, you did not tell us the house was going to be so large. I can hardly believe my own eyes. Just think of the huge size of this house to live in. Rudi, I am overjoyed by your wonderful lucky find. It feels like home already."

Once they entered the house, they noticed it was divided into three small units. The management preferred to call them apartments, but he failed to mention that to Rudi before they arrived at their new location.

Somewhat deflated yet overjoyed, Ruth dropped to the ground, exhausted and thankful at the sight of the house their family would occupy. Unshed, grateful tears welled in Ruth's eyes as her husband took her elbow to support her to her feet. "I cannot believe this is going to be our house," she said. Since it was just a bit larger than the other areas, Onkel Westphal lived in their quarters on the first floor with the Meissner's. The Fischer family occupied one of the other apartments. Westphal enjoyed helping Ruth with the children because he missed the loving comfort of his own family, who had not been located. His most painful moments were when he drifted into deep thought, realising he did not know if his wife Ida or daughter Hilda were still alive.

Ruth scrubbed the grimy floors with a brush. The children could play there when it was too cold to play outdoors.

After cleaning the floor, she used one of her only pieces of clothing to wipe down the walls. The coating on them was so dense from years of burning brown peat that she could imagine the grime as teardrops from the weary, hungry families who had occupied the house over the years.

Escaping the Russian Onslaught

The family table for the first few days was an old door Rudi and Westphal found in a pile of debris. After Ruth gave it a good scrubbing, the two men turned it into a table and sat on wooden stumps pilfered from the nearby woods. The two men also laid a long plank supported by stumps in front of one of the only windows in the apartment so Ruth could use it as a countertop while watching the children happily play in the gravel yard.

Rudi rummaged through the neighbourhood. Soon, he found a tin barrel and shaped it into a bathtub, doubling as a washbasin for Ruth to wash the few clothes they owned. When time allowed, he whittled spoons, kitchen tools, sizeable wooden serving trays, smaller trays for plates and sizeable bowls to hold oatmeal. The horses would never miss the few oats Ruth cooked for the family's breakfast. This was the one meal the children disliked the most. Before eating the oats, they were required to use makeshift sieves with some wired mesh he discovered on the same debris pile where he and Westphal had unearthed their table.

Ruth snitched some of the oats meant for the horses, but they were still in whole pieces. A tool found on the debris pile was used to open the shells. Then, the screens were used to separate the large parts from the smaller edible pieces of the oats. While Ruth and the children were busily doing this job, it was not uncommon to find brown mouse droppings, forcing them to discard faeces using their fingers. Ruth was nauseated by the thought of the many illnesses the family could pick up from the droppings. She boiled the oats in salt water to kill the bacteria, so she had no choice but to cook them long enough until she was satisfied that it was safe to eat.

The morning after moving into the house, one room was converted into a bedroom with straw on the floor, and one corner was made into a cosy area for Westphal. After a long day's work on the peat farm, Rudi placed iron and bricks together to build a stove that doubled as a heating source for the apartment. Furniture for their home would have to wait until later when Rudi could build chairs out of the logs.

While the village lay in slumber, Rudi pilfered from the nearby woods one piece at a time. The one-hole outhouse at the back of the house was used for the three families. The acceptability of their surroundings came from their toil and extreme cleverness during intolerable times.

By late November of 1945, Ruth and Rudi had spent little time together as a married couple. The busy time the couple spent together during the first part of their married life became a distant fantasy. One of the first issues the middle-aged couple agreed to resolve was restoring and strengthening their family's lives.

During Rudi's prolonged absence, the children knew their father was in the war. Now, they did not recognise the person on the inside and did not appreciate his charming character. At every turn, the children rebuffed him, for as a father, he did not gain their trust or the affection he deserved. He understood only the rough tactics required of him from years of being a soldier, which was not to his liking. Much to his chagrin, Hans-Georg and Dorlies trembled at his very presence and would not warm up to him. Instead, Westphal had been with the children longer, so he was the man the children turned to for his affectionate nature.

Ruth did not begrudge Rudi's rough behaviour, knowing only too well how difficult it had been for her to balance fleeing and protecting her children from the onslaught of the outside world. The couple felt guilty for their desperate plight. Ignoring their pain, they focused their energy on finding a happy life for their three children.

The couple's children, displaying a resilience that even their parents had underestimated, momentarily set aside their hunger and instead found joy in exploring their new surroundings. In front of the house, the children's creative spirits were unleashed as they drew figures of animals on the gravel, a testament to their adaptability and resilience.

Two days after their arrival, the children discovered an endless sandpit a few metres away from the house. The trees beyond the house provided a secure hiding place for the children to construct fortresses from twigs and long grasses. Their father responded to the children's pleas, skillfully whittled digging devices, creating open tunnels that served as their playhouse and a secure place to spend their time. This act of love and care from their parents further enriched the children's experience in their new home.

Ruth was grateful because it was also a perfect playground where she could keep an ever-watchful eye on them. She was delighted in their hours of amusement, for it was a time-consuming project. Nevertheless, the idea frightened her not to see their every move. Trust was not yet built into her nature after knowing many incidences where children vanished into thin air. These children were pulled away by some unknown, lonely parents who had lost their own children. But Ruth remembered her childhood, and out in this rural area, life seemed tranquil, so she could not deny the children the happiness of being able to run free.

As the year drew to a close, Ruth's family prepared to spend their first Christmas away from their beloved Klein Pobloth. After the harrowing ordeals everyone within house number ten had endured over the last year, their new home, with its warm hearth and familiar scents, had transformed into a welcoming haven, a place of solace and comfort.

Amidst the children, the news of Christmas approaching spread like wildfire, filling the air with a palpable sense of anticipation and joy.

As Rudi and Westphal hurried home from work, they fetched as many pine branches as possible from the surrounding woods. After the children went to bed, the adults crafted an Advent Wreath that would hang from a cord over the kitchen table in a few days, creating a delightful fragrance in the home. Four tiny white candles were placed on the wreath to be lit, one each Saturday night.

Everyone waited for the magical hour of 4.30 pm. Just when twilight began to show the glimmering of the bright north star, the festivities were to begin. Ruth was honoured to light the first candle while the children's eyes twinkled in wonder.

On the first Saturday of Advent, Ruth and Rudi asked the children to place one of their wooden shoes on the windowsill.

"*Nein... nein... bitte, No... no... please,*" Dorlies whimpered.

Dorlies' big brother Hans-Georg rushed to her side, "Mutti, Vati, why is Dorlies crying?"

"We want to tell her about placing her shoe onto the windowsill so St Nickolas can put some sweets into them during the night," Ruth explained.

"What if he steals our shoe? I would rather have my shoes than a sweet. I do not want to put one of our shoes on the windowsill either. Please do not make us." He pleaded and then began to cry. "Mutti, I do not know why we must give up one of our shoes. I only have this one pair. If I give one of them away, I must walk around in the cold with one bare foot."

Dorlies sputtered, in her fragmented speech, "Mutti, will you wrap old rags around my feet?"

Ruth pulled her daughter onto her lap, "Oh, my dearest daughter, I forgot you and your brother can't remember one of the wonderful Christmases we had at Klein Pobloth."

"You see," her father began, "there is a wonderful old man named St Nickolas who visits homes every Saturday during the nights of the Advent Season. Ever so quietly, this lovely old man comes into the house when you are asleep, brings you sweets, and places them into your shoe that you left in the window so you will have a wonderful surprise to wake up to in the morning." To study Dorlies' teary eyes, her father lifted her chin. Rudi asked, "Can you smile now?" The two younger children sent him frowns of mistrust.

"Now, what do we do?" Rudi asked Ruth with a perplexed expression.

"Vati and I will not make you do anything you do not wish to do. Susanne remembers these fun times. If she places her shoe on the ledge, you can see how wonderful it will be in the morning. Perhaps St Nickolas will leave you something near her shoe, especially for you and your brother."

After much convincing, the three children placed one of their shoes into the window.

Before retiring, the children's parents lovingly prepared their shoes with little handmade gifts. The following morning, the three children rushed to the window ledge to see if St Nickolas had been in their home during the night. Their eyes sparkled with astonishment that turned into delight when they saw, as promised, that St Nickolas had placed a small, green pine branch along with a twig of dried berries to add a touch of colour around the shoes, which were filled with several homemade cookies and colourful bonbons into their shoes.

As the weeks passed, the children's joy of anticipation grew when it was time to light the other candles on the remaining Saturday Advent evenings, and the children cheerfully placed their shoes on the window ledge.

Schwege-Hunteburg

Ruth's resourcefulness saved the day when she exchanged a two-carat diamond ring given to her by her mother for a few pieces of bedding for the children and three adults. A few Marks were left over to spend on the Christmas sweets.

To prepare for Christmas Eve, Ruth strolled to a charming, empathetic proprietor who owned a modest store in Hunteburg, the hamlet next to Schwege. She entered the shop to speak with the owner. With high hopes, she said, "I do not have much money, really none or enough to speak of."

To her surprise, the proprietor said, "I know your circumstances, so I am willing to work with you. I know you are an honest family."

Ruth held her hands to her mouth and whispered, "Wunderbar," as her eyes swelled with tears that she would not allow to spill over.

"Now, Frau Meissner, which wonderful gifts can I show you?" the shopkeeper asked eagerly.

"Oh, Herr Meyer, how can I possibly choose? It has been such a long time since I could shop for my family." Ruth strolled around the shop as if it were her first time shopping. Rubbing her hands nervously, Ruth knew there was no room for error. Everyone needed to receive the perfect gift yet not exceed the supply of coins remaining in her pocket.

"Sensational. Here is a pipe for our dear Albert Westphal, who we consider part of our family. Even though there is no tobacco, we can be inventive by drying herbs and weeds for basic filler and roasting them to get some flavour into his pipe. And a wonderful small used Swiss army knife for my resourceful husband, Hans-Rudolf."

Ruth squealed joyfully, "I can see you have a black slate tablet, like a chalkboard used in a schoolroom. It is hanging on the wall, which you, as the store owner, use to advertise your weekly special buys. When I saw it, I almost jumped for joy."

"I see your unbridled emotions," Herr Meyer said.

"I'm so delighted," Ruth swiftly inquired. "Can I have the chalkboard for my three children? They need it so badly to help them learn their arithmetic lessons along with their reading and writing?"

"Frau Meissner, I will give you the board for your children. I can order another from my supplier. I will do one more thing, but it might take some time. All children need the opportunity to learn to read and write. I will try to find some books for your children."

"Outstanding. For the time being, I will homeschool the children. I will be forever obligated to you, my good man."

Ruth left the store with tears streaming down her face. She spoke as if speaking to the heavens, "I have tears… I have tears running down my face. My first tears since? *Here I go again, breaking my promise many years ago. No, a lifetime ago.* Oh, I do not want to think about that now. I am delighted with the beautiful Christmas gifts I have found. My father was correct when telling me that good things come to those who wait."

On her return home, the rising moon cast ribbons of dim light on the dusting of snow on the path. Rudi opened the door for his wife. "I became far too vulnerable when Herr Meyer gifted the chalkboard to me. I began to let my tears drop for joy." She dropped into a chair, allowing the brown-wrapped bundles to lay where they fell, and placed her hands to cover her anger at her weakness.

Although a Christmas tree was not possible this year, the family hoped a real tree might be available next year. Adhering to the traditions of Kempen and Klein Pobloth, the couple warmed the mood of their small apartment.

Ruth decorated their comfortable chair with a small white cloth laden with a small amount of silver tinsel, three bright, shiny oranges, one for each child, and a few acorns mixed with hazelnuts that grew in the area. The few gifts everyone would receive were carefully placed between the trimmings. By 4.30pm when darkness was about to fall, the winter skies were filled with the promise of snow, and everything was ready for St Nickolas's magic bell to ring.

On the evening of 24 December at 4.30pm sharp, the children were bathed and dressed in the only finery they owned. Onkel Westphal kept the youngsters entertained while Ruth and Rudi played St Nicholas. When he heard the magic bell ring, Onkel knew it was time to line up the children, the eldest in the back, while Dorlies, the youngest, stood in the front. Their parents, along with Onkel, brought up the rear. Onkel Westphal was happy to have the honour of lighting the largest candle in the centre of the wreath, creating a warm golden glow on the few gifts lying decoratively on the chair.

The children cried out with glee, overjoyed at the delightful display in front of them.

"Hush, children, listen to your mother. She has an important story of a wondrous birth to tell you about."

As per tradition, Ruth read the story of Christ's birth aloud. No matter if she had read the story so often during the previous Christmas she could recite the story from memory. After a round of *"O Tannenbaum* plus *"Stille Nacht, Heilige Nacht"* everyone was excitedly awaiting the moment they could see what gifts were brought to them for Christmas.

Onkel Westphal was seen in the faint light with tears of overwhelming joy flowing down his pale, gaunt cheeks when he discovered his new pipe. When they saw the children's eyes beam, grins erupted. Ruth's and Rudi's hearts were filled with joy as the children gently fingered their new belongings.

As the couple hoped, this Christmas would be one of the most memorable times the family had spent in years. The parents' endeavours genuinely blessed everyone. Rudi's skinny body clung onto his slender wife as if this were their first Christmas together. Ruth gazed up into Rudi's azure, blue eyes as the couple stood together, celebrating their magnificent gifts of being reunited once more.

Chapter 42

JANUARY 1946

The winter of 1946 was so extraordinarily cold that it made time stand still. As challenging as times were for the Meissner family, a sense of humour lifted their spirits whenever the occasion presented itself. At least, the family saw amusement in a roundabout way in the entertaining things occurring while living in house number ten in the New Colony of Schwege. The Fischer family, who lived in the other apartment, was included in the family cluster. Herr Fischer appeared to be a sort of know-it-all man. Living so close, their families were as friendly as possible. Fischer also worked at the peat bog, where Rudi and Westphal worked at the factory, and they walked back and forth to work together.

On their way home one day, Rudi and Westphal repeatedly failed to hide their snickers about what had occurred on the way to the bog. After returning home, Rudi stuck his head into the entryway. Still chuckling with his infectious laughter, he said, "Ruth!" His chuckle turned into yelling, "Come join Westphal and me. We must tell you a hilarious story that is not for the children's ears."

Ruth flung her tattered dishtowel to the side and rushed to her husband as requested. "These days, a laugh is all we can afford and is something we need to keep ourselves going."

"First, we need to step outside because this is a story I do not believe Herr Fischer would like the children to repeat to his family."

Rudi bent close to the others to begin. "The three of us rushed to work this morning. Herr Fischer's stomach was upset, so he needed to use the nearest bushes to do his business, fumbling about, exploring for something to wipe his hind end. You know how cold it was this morning since there was still frost on the ground when we started off for work."

Rudi nudged Westphal's shoulder, and both burst out in hysterical amusement. Both let out an enormous chuckle, knowing what Rudi would reveal to Ruth. "Well, you can imagine, there is not one weed around or any bushes with leaves. Panicked, Fischer groped about for something white in his reach and nabbed the fluffy white stuff to clean himself. Little did he realise the white fluffy material was glass wool that would render scratches and cut him, creating a lot of small lesions on his hind end."

"Oh, guys, what have I done?" Herr Fischer yelled in agonising pain as he pulled up his trousers.

Westphal interjected, "I must admit we did not treat him very kindly. Don't you agree, my friend?"

"Well, I can't say I am proud of our actions, but with his bold remarks, Herr Fischer had it coming to him. We disregarded his protesting moans even though we could see he had a tough time walking the rest of the way to work. The two of us busted out in laughter so hard it made the day go much faster. Not only was Herr Fischer annoyed at himself for being so foolish, but the glass wool had achieved much humiliation."

Rudi's mischievous smile played on his face once more. "As I can imagine, to make matters tougher for him, his dilemma became more painful once we returned home. As you know, none of us have a bathtub or a basin large enough for a man of his size to cleanse himself appropriately nor do we have any ointment to ease his pain."

Westphal was eager to add, "I do believe in the end his pride was hurt more than his hind end."

"Right as rain." Rudi began to chuckle once again.

The entire household was a happier place for a few hours. Or until the pangs of hunger struck once again.

Nevertheless, the house had intelligent, clever, resourceful men living under one roof who worked at the peat factory. Handily, they could slip a few pieces of broken peat fuel under their jackets from time to time to make their family's winter a bit more tolerable.

Undeniably everyone in the house looked forward to spring arriving with the warmth their bodies craved from the lack of enough fuel to heat the apartments. Susanne cared for her siblings, while Ruth enjoyed walking to Hunteburg to use the few food stamps available to the family. She enjoyed seeing the graceful, small snowdrops popping their fragile heads through the fertile black earth. Soon, the daffodils and the primroses completed their winter slumber under the brown ground. A few weeks later, the purple lilac bushes growing in the farmer's garden took her breath away.

Sadly, the food lines persisted as usual, causing Ruth's temper to spark when she walked home with the little food the family was allotted. Yet, hope was again heightened when she spotted new colonies of wild asparagus and nettle plants bursting through the ground. The family would have fresh greens if Ruth rose before daybreak and found the plants before anyone else arrived. Better yet, if she were shrewd and stood in line long enough to get hold of milk, Ruth would make soup from her find, thereby giving the entire family a nourishing meal.

During the snowy days of spring, the children sketched plans on their new chalkboard about how their building project would be laid out. Their excitement grew as the weather improved. Ruth was eager to get the children out from under her feet when the summer months came.

January 1946

In Schwege-Hunteburg, the topography was a layer of sandy soil deposited remarkably close to the area of the peat bog. Ruth was thankful that an area of sand was near the house. The area became a favourite playground for the neighbourhood children. Finally, it was warm enough to dig ditches and tunnels and build a clubhouse from weeds and scraps of discarded lumber from the woodpile.

Frau Fischer was in her apartment busily doing her household duties while her youngster, a one-and-a-half-year-old, copper-haired son, played happily outside with the three children.

A kind British soldier brought each of the children a handful of colourful bright balloons of red, blue and yellow. Such gorgeous colours had not been a part of the children's lives for as long as they could remember. Ruth was thrilled to see the children have something new to colour their world. First, the children needed to know what the brightly coloured, funny-shaped things were and what could be done with them. The young soldier helped them blow up their fascinating new toy. As all children do, they used them, batting them from here to yonder, becoming more enchanted with every stroke, making the balloons bounce high into the sky.

Fischer's toddler soon popped his balloon, causing him to be disinterested in what the others were doing. His mother had left a small wash pan in the front of the house, intending to throw the water out when she finished her household duties. Even though the other children were all playing out in the yard, the little boy became lodged in the bucket for some unknown reason and could not get his head back out. The adorable young child drowned in less than seven inches of water.

The children realised something was amiss and ran over to fetch the lad. None of them could say how or when it happened. Frau Fischer heard the children's blood-curdling screams and dashed to the front door. Within seconds of hearing the children's cries, she saw her son's limp body lying lifeless in the bucket.

Wailing the whole while, she claimed, "Oh! No! You horrible children! Why didn't you watch him? Why didn't you watch him?"

At this moment, Ruth rushed out of her apartment to spot the wretchedness besetting the gravel yard. The older three children were sobbing when suddenly Ruth stood her ground. "It is not the children's responsibility. Besides, they do not know how this terrible thing occurred," Ruth claimed gently but firmly. "The accident must have happened so quickly. Only God in his mercy can explain why such a sweet copper-haired angel should be taken so early in life."

The loss weighed heavily on all the folks who lived in house number ten in the New Colony in Schwege. It was one more life snuffed out unnecessarily and without reason.

To rid herself of the depressing atmosphere of the Colony, Ruth began her stroll to stand in line. The warmth of the summer sun made its way through the heavy thunderclouds, and a new promise of growth was seen in every meadow. The fresh, brilliant mantle of yellow primroses and daffodils combined with the glorious purple lilac bushes were combined with blooming fruit trees everywhere the eye could see. Many of the refugees were still so destitute that they had nothing, only a few scraps. They gathered anything by begging from the many farmers who lived in the surrounding area. Being a part of a small community allowed the Meissner family to observe almost everything and everyone who scuttled their way.

Rudi's storytelling was well known to the others in the house. When the youngsters were finally tucked into bed, the adults made it a ritual to wait in the Meissners' apartment to enjoy their entertainment for the day.

On this summer's evening, Rudi took a deep breath before beginning the story he was about to share, eager to mesmerise the rest of the family with his tale. "It was a fine summer's morning when the four of us walked to work. On our way, we saw something so humorous we wish to tell you about this scene that we happened upon." The men had difficulty not snickering while beginning to account for what they had witnessed earlier in the morning. "We had a good laugh at the expense of one woman. You know the one I am talking about? Her large farm is right on the way to the peat bogs. The woman is blond, short and has a wayward tongue. By the appearance of her robust round figure, she has more food in her cupboard than she and her husband could ever wish for. The couple has many chickens, geese and a storage room for potatoes in their cellar. The bounty this couple has is incredible.

"As you probably remember, the woman is very hefty, or at least, we could tell she ate well. Earlier, when we had pleaded with her for help, she harshly replied, pressing her lips together and not holding back her anger, 'You irresponsible refugees, get away from my property. I have had enough of all of you. I refuse to help any of the refugees any longer!'

"Well, this morning, when we walked by her house as we do every morning on our way to work, a hullabaloo broke out, causing us to glance back in her direction. Her unsteady actions became hysterical. At first, her screaming was unexplainable, but soon we became aware of her problem. She was working in her garden when a beehive had erupted under her long skirt. As you know, in this part of the rural country, many farm women wear no undergarments beneath their long dresses. As many farm women do, she considered them a useless impediment. This made it possible for the bees to attack her private parts.

"The whole time we were walking past her farmyard, she called for her husband, 'August – August – come – come – help me!'

"No wonder the unfortunate woman was crying out. As she yelled for his help and moaned, her sweaty-beaded brow reminded us of a big, fat, pink pig being taken to slaughter." Rudi slapped his knee and howled in laughter until tears flooded his five o'clock stubble. His boyish, hardy chuckle made it difficult to continue the story.

January 1946

Westphal took over where his friend left off. "Then she jumped on a small shaggy hedge that impaled her by the sheer force of her weight and scuttled her bottom while riding it half on and half off to brush the bees from under her skirt.

"We scratched the top of our heads and stood there, questioning whether to help the unfortunate woman. Then, we thought it would be better not to interfere at such a delicate moment. Besides, her husband might not like the idea. Instead, as we hurried to work, we laughed out loud."

Chuckling again with a tinge of mockery, Rudi joked, "We could not wait to come home to relate our hilarious story to you, Ruth." He ran his fingers through his thinning hair. "We all need a good laugh, along with the comforting thought that the woman's greediness seemed to end up in the proper place. Now, we are getting a laugh at her expense. The woman's plight helped to restore a sense of stability to our everyday lives. Laughter gives us back our strength to help support our hungry bodies and sustain the disappointments of our everyday lives."

Not much had changed, but the children and the adults in house number ten grew stronger with each passing day. For the time being, working at the peat factory gave them an adequate income, especially when it was generally difficult to find work. The only way they could keep their position in life continued to be with the two able horses and the wagon the two women had obtained near Lübeck back in 1945 on the meadow. Ruth and Anneliese's story had become famous in the colony by this time.

It was now mid-summer 1946 and Ruth and Rudi gained some weight back, strengthening their desires. A peaceful Sunday afternoon gave Westphal time to tend to the horses and groom them well. While the children played in their sandy tunnels located far enough away from the house, Rudi felt safe to give in his desire, firing up to a point he had not recognised for some time. As his passion grew, he sought his wife for a little fling on their straw bed. Privacy was rare in a three-room apartment with three children and three adults. Thus, the couple had a few moments of afternoon bliss to get to know one another intimately again.

A few weeks after their lovemaking, Ruth realised she had missed her time of the month in the first few weeks of September. After Ruth's first fleeting thought of the problem, the day's activities distracted from any consideration of how her body would change, dismissed by the end of the day any further thoughts of carrying a child.

Formulating a plan for educating her children was foremost on Ruth's mind. The overpowering problem of how her children were to be educated nagged her night and day. Her children also needed to feel secure and something beautiful in their lives to make them light-hearted again instead of being fearful at every turn.

In her third month, Ruth could no longer put off telling her husband about their new addition to the family. Sitting huddled together on the makeshift straw bed, she broke the news to Rudi. A mischievous smile of satisfaction played on her husband's face, for he loved the idea of playing with a baby, something he did not get to enjoy with their first three children.

In 1939, when they were newly married, he had more time for Susanne, and life was completely different. When Rudi came home on furlough two different times, Ruth heard the maids chattering with gossiping to follow, "I wonder if he had left a bundle of a baby in Ruth's belly." Twice, the maids were correct. With the couple's later children, Hans-Georg in 1941 and Dorlies in 1943, Rudi received leave again but had to return to his military duties a few days after their birth.

Torrential rain poured and penetrated into the family's chilly bones and persisted through the last days of November 1946. Under these conditions, pushing the horses through their agonising work was too difficult, causing them to often get stuck in the mucky peat. The boss at the factory ordered everyone to stay home for several days until it became cold enough for the earth to freeze. Work would begin again when conditions were right.

Soon after the Christmas Bells echoed freely in every nearby rural church steeple, Ruth beamed with delight. "Now, I have more joyful news. I am pleased to hear about my mother's whereabouts from the Red Cross, detailing how I could get a letter to her. She has been living at the home of our Schläger relatives in Peine by Hanover." Ruth clasped Rudi's hand for reassurance. "Sadly, after receiving the letter, I did not have a piece of paper or a pencil to post her a Christmas greeting. I walked down to the shopkeeper who had befriended me. I begged for a sheet of paper and an envelope." Tears began to swell in Ruth's eyes, but she willed them not to drop. "Herr Meyer's unending kindness never faltered, for within a moment, he offered me the only sheet of grey paper in his shop, and then he added a matching envelope, insisting I keep the pencil for my children. At that moment, he suggested I could use his countertop to pen my letter. To my mortification, Herr Meyer must have seen my expression and brought out the necessary stamp from behind his counter. I moistened it with my embarrassingly dry lips, I told him that I could work in his shop as repayment. He said, 'No…no…no need, my dear woman.' As I dropped the letter into the postal box, I thought how grateful I was to hear my mother was alive."

Ruth was enthusiastic about deciding to see her mother. It had been such a long time since they had seen one another. Ruth asked a neighbour to keep the children during the day for her while she made a quick visit to Peine.

Chapter 43

RUTH VISITS HER MOTHER

Anxiety grew when Ruth could not gather enough money to make the trip to visit her mother on her birthday, 11 February 1947. Every Mark Ruth placed in the hidden container above the kitchen window was needed whenever an emergency arose. Being heavy with her fourth child made it particularly grim to work as a helping hand for neighbours who might be able to use her for ironing, washing the floors or caring for sick children while their mothers worked in the few shops beginning to open again.

Due to the lack of proper nutrition, desperately important for the mother and growing baby but unavailable, Ruth's health was becoming stressed. The family's diet of potatoes and cabbage seven days a week merely satisfied their hunger, but they lacked necessary vitamins.

With much more scrimping than usual, bit by bit, the train fare accumulated. If Ruth brought along a lunch to eat while travelling to Peine, if nothing went awry, then the trip would not cost much money. As the day for Ruth's journey grew closer, she felt she could pull it off. Ruth would travel on one of the only trains available to her. She knew the hours of gruelling travel to see her mother for the first time after the war would be overwhelming. To see her mother on her birthday, the journey was worth placing herself in harm's way, even while carrying a baby. Besides, she had lost a great deal of weight after fleeing Klein Pobloth, so it was not noticed that she was heavy with child. Her concern for the new baby was overridden by the wish to see her mother, whom she had not seen for four years.

Ruth was very hesitant since her mother was a person who had never lived in the reality of what the war had done. When Ruth stepped from the arduous train trip to Peine, she tenderly embraced her mother and then lovingly placed her in front of herself to study Luise Schläger's expression. To Ruth's surprise, her mother appeared not as she remembered her. Instead, she seemed much older than Ruth could ever have imagined. Her mother's beautiful, thick hair had thinned a great deal and was snow white. However, she still wore it in a bun on the top of her head. She appeared frailer than Ruth expected, and her hands shook as she spoke softly, placidly. Her ankles were swollen to the point that her mother walked cumbersomely. Ruth tucked her arm under her mother to support the woman she loved, although she had not been the kindest of mothers to her.

The trip did not go as Ruth had hoped. During her visit, her Tante Louise Schläger trampled upon her heart. Attempting to shed her cloak of grief proved more difficult than Ruth could shoulder. Perhaps her emotions ran too high because of her vulnerable condition. On the other hand, were her expectations too lofty? It did not matter. Ruth wished to return to her loving family in Schwege on the next train to let her off in Bohmte.

Turning on her heels, Ruth entered the train, where she took her seat alongside the window. She turned to wave her tattered handkerchief in case her mother was in sight, knowing her mother was not eager to say goodbye to her. Ruth laid her head back on the headrest and closed her watery eyes to the rhythm of the clattering. *Just put your head back in hopes of ignoring the unpleasantness of the entire experience. Yes, my home is small, but at least there is kindness mixed with an abundance of love between the four walls of our small apartment.*

Ruth frowned at the terrible ordeal of the past few days, unable to push the events to the back of her mind. Her fretfulness grew with every whistle-stop the train made. The baby in her must have sensed her anxiety and then revolted at the stress being sent in its direction. A few moments later, the baby began to move, jabbing from within, nudging at her ribs, and pushing against her belly until Ruth felt the child would penetrate her skin. She placed her warm hand on her bulge and then massaged it in a circular motion. The baby would not be comforted. "Oh my, you are a strong-minded little one," she murmured. "There is no one else in the compartment, so perhaps if I can get my worries off my mind, I will tell you all my troubles. Hopefully, you will not think too unkindly of me for being too overwrought."

"You see, it is like this," Ruth began to talk to the child while tenderly massaging her belly. "As a special surprise, I baked *Streusel Kuchen* to bring with me. I baked it in the oven Rudi built for me at our new little home. I was so proud to give my mother and Tante Louise something exceptional. Perhaps I baked the cake because it reminds me of my mother and Kempen."

Ruth paused for a moment before continuing to talk to her unborn child. "It was the wonderful crumcake my mother brought to me while I was pregnant and living in Berlin before I married your father. Yes, your father was not the first man in my life. When I discovered that I was pregnant, naturally, I sobbed for weeks on end, enough tears to cascade until they caused the Rhein Falls to create the colossal Rhein River.

"When I informed my parents that I would be an unwed mother, they sent me to live at a home for girls in my dilemma. After the birth of my beautiful baby girl, I visited my parents, hoping they would accept my baby girl along with me back into the fold of my family.

Ruth Visits Her Mother

"After they rejected my tiny Annerose, I contracted scarlet fever while on my return trip to Berlin. The doctor who saw to my health and a neighbourhood pastor maintained I was too sick to keep my child. I had to give her up for adoption. You see, being an unwed mother in August 1933 was unacceptable. Both my parents placed dreadful shame and heartache on me. From then on, I could not cry any longer.

"However, I have never stopped thinking about my darling little girl. I do not know if she is dead or alive. Perhaps one day, God will see fit to reveal an answer. I will cry if I do not change the subject of my visit.

"We sat on the edge of Tante Louise Schläger's divan. I studied my mother, who was quite thankful. Tante Lousie invited my mother's old girlfriends, the elegant ladies who were her friends before she and my father moved to our Kempen Estate. The afternoon coffee hour began promptly at four o'clock. Still, even with the kindest of intentions on my part, Tante Louise did not care for the cake I brought.

"Regrettably, Tante Louise voiced that the bit of baking I brought was not up to her standards, not delectable enough for her guests. Without my knowledge, before the ladies arrived, my aunt disappeared into the kitchen to cut the bottom half off and then threw away the lower portion of the cake. From what I gather, Tante Louise felt the underside of the Kuchen had too much dough and was not sweet enough. When she returned to join my mother and me, the cake seemed entirely unlike the one I had given my mother. When the other ladies came, she only served the upper portion of the Kuchen.

"Her actions stabbed me deeply since she discarded food that could have fed my family. Tante Louise had been spoiled her whole life by her family and then later by her husband. Now, her daughter was a war widow. She dates a British officer she intends to marry in a few months. The officer could give them what they desired. Consequently, my little offering was not good enough.

"After the ladies left Tante Louise's home, my mother and I had a tender mother-daughter chat. I intently hung on to every word while my mother related her experiences during the last four years.

"When I inquired how my mother had stayed alive, Mutti told me she had spent a few weeks with friends in Kolberg. Her friends had warned her that the Red Cross had infiltrated Pomerania's frontier and that no one would stay alive when the Russians broke through the German border. When the Russians penetrated the German stronghold and then thrust towards Pomerania, her friend insisted she board the next train to Hanover. When onboard, her friends warned that from then on, my mother should not get off and, most of all, ignore anyone who tried to change her plans. She took their advice. My mother placed her jewellery inside the handheld box where her beautiful, expensive diamond brooches were housed, then placed her suitcases on the rack above her.

"My mother told me that luck was with her as she travelled. Fortunately, the journey only took her several hours. She had all her suitable clothing and personal belongings with her. She had her favourite gold, hand-forged stickpin which contained the teeth of the first red deer your grandfather, Georg, bagged at the Kempen Estate, given to her before my brother Joachim was born.

"She kept everything in her travelling bag tightly clutched on her lap for security. Can you imagine she could get on the train and escape the chaos without trouble? As I remember, the trains were still travelling to their intended destinations. She had to go beyond Berlin. Directly before everything in Germany collapsed and the air attacks on the city. Astonishingly, the train made its way safely through Berlin. Since then, she has lived in Peine with our Schläger relatives.

"I told Mutti I was so pleased she could return to the area where she and my father had grown up and lived after they first married."

Ruth rubbed her stomach again. "Well, you dear little thing, you have been so tolerant in listening to me. It must be helping me to talk to you about all my problems because you seem more relaxed now. And so am I. There are some more troubling things I need to get off my mind before I get back to our family.

"My dear baby, I did not wish for my mother to see how hurt I was when I left the train station in Hanover. My mother saw my beautiful lambskin leather fawn-coloured suit from the clothes I had with me. She felt it needed to be cleaned. Tante Louise has a sister-in-law who owns a dry-cleaning establishment. I brought this beautiful suit, professionally tailored for me, under my coat when I fled. The fawn-coloured suit was incredibly special to me and not practical for my escape, yet we expected to only be away from Klein Pobloth for two weeks, at best three. The supple lambskin was especially fine and velvety to the touch, the ultimate luxury. Something incredibly special to me because my father had given me the leather for the beautiful suit. I loved it very much because he is no longer with us.

"I left the suit at the cleaners. The dry cleaner was supposedly broken into at night, and my suit was one of the few stolen pieces. I loved this suit. It was one of the only good pieces I could flee with and still have after the war. I gave the suit to the cleaners, sad – sad..." Tears welled up in Ruth's eyes, "I will not cry. I cannot cry now.

"Many goods throughout Germany, Pomerania and other parts of Europe were also stolen and undoubtedly sold on the black market. 'I will never get anything back for it,' I said tearfully to my Tante.

"Disillusion with life drifted through my heart when Tante Louise gave me an apron to replace the luxurious lambskin suit. Giving me the apron almost hurt me more than receiving nothing. You see, my aunt and my cousin could keep all their belongings. They did not lose one thing during the war. This suit and my few clothes were the only things I could call my own. The gall that my own relatives could behave unconscionably to buy me off by giving me an apron stabbed me deeply. I felt this defined Tante's character.

"This is how a lot of issues happen. I have learned that one can live without certain people because in bad times and in times of need, people learn who their friends are, which people are reasonable, and which people are selfish beyond comprehension.

"Tension in the house grew the few days after I arrived at the Schlägers' home. Warding off their unnecessary, cruel remarks about my mother, I soon recognised their attempt to intimidate me, so I decided to have my mother live with us. My mother's eccentricities were too much for the Schlägers, and my mother had become an object of ridicule. My own family did not have anything in this blighted Germany, yet some people could keep everything. The strain on my family would be heightened, but I will adjust to their requirements.

"I found it bizarre that these people who could keep their belongings would not share them with those who had lost everything. My parents' home was in the country, but their relatives were from the city. It was understood that the relatives, even if they were only remotely related, came to Kempen or Klein Pobloth on their vacations at our expense.

"When the war broke out, they wrote to the families living in the country, complaining the winters were too unbearable in the metropolitan areas. Often, they requested a helping hand to get them through these brutal times. My parents and I always packaged up mounds of food and sent them with a large turkey and a ham or two, including all types of canned vegetables and fruits, so that they could have a wonderful holiday. Most packages included the best coffee still available. The boxes contained sugar and flour to satisfy their appetite for sweets. Also, my parents continually went out of their way to be cordial to one and all.

"When I stepped onto the train's platform, my tante pushed a spool of thread into my palm as she said goodbye. 'Here is something wonderful to take home to your family.' Now, when the tables are turned, and the Meissner family and my mother need help, they cannot find it in their hearts to give us anything, only a spool of thread. Now, these same people are ignoring those who lost everything. People such as this dare to look past us. This is something I will never forgive.

"To satisfy the Schlägers' selfish desires, I decided I would no longer have my mother live with Tante Louise. Despite my family's housing limitations, I left my mother and Tante Louise with the understanding that, somehow, I would arrange my mother's travels so she could live with us. She will bring endless hours of comfort to me and a feeling of warmth that will embrace my whole family.

"Now, baby, that you and I have had an opportunity to get to know one another, our visit needs to end because the train is pulling into my destination. Just think, sometime during the beginning of April, you and I can have another heartfelt conversation. After the war, you might not always feel welcome in this trying world." With her head held high, "Nonetheless, in Rudi's and my hearts, we think you will bring cheerfulness to the household, which is sorely lacking."

There would be no reprieve for now: dealing with the loss of Pomerania and the many losses of life. After an agonising journey, Ruth's tenacity had brought her family to safety. If her husband had managed to survive the war unscathed, and during the Great War, her mother-in-law, Dolores, had escorted a railroad car of supplies to the German front in Lithuania, Ruth could carry on into the unknown future. As she stepped from the train, Ruth's eyes glistened in the sun with hope. "I can mask my distress and will not flinch at being the custodian of our family's future."

EPILOGUE

The Allies had cheered wildly as the bitter blow came, and Germany was defeated. They hunted and captured thousands of German soldiers and men. With no questions asked, they ordered the young boys and the older men to be arrested, blasted the landscape, lashed out at the Germans, and ended their freedom abruptly by corralling every male lurking in their path. The act of finger-pointing would never be complete. The wrath of the victors was upon Germany. It was said that the Russians were an encounter like no other. Without intervention, they captured three million males for forced labour, ultimately sending many to their deaths.

After the war, the United Kingdom requested the United States' help in housing 175,000 prisoners of war. Seven hundred POW camps were set up across the United States. The United States was unprepared to house this many soldiers. Per the Geneva Conventions, the government was required to provide humane treatment to all POWs.

Racked with anger and seeking revenge, the United Kingdom sent 400,000 German males to the United Kingdom. The British leaders placed the men into 1,000 camps to teach Germany that they had won despite the costs. German males were transported to Poland, Czechoslovakia, Norway and France to work as hard labourers.

According to the latest news reports, the number of ethnically cleansed or displaced people in Pommern totalled some 12 million lives to countries such as Russia, the United Kingdom, the United States and France.

By now, the German people were beyond all consolation. Above all else, this period was dreadful for Ruth's family cluster and the rest of Germany. Thus, it would forever alter Europe, if not world history. It is safe to say the events during this time would modify the course and circumstances of world history, instigating controversies lasting for years regarding how, who and why such events occurred.

1945 and 1946 were horrific for those in Pommern when the East and West were cleansed of their ethnic German population by the so-called Allied victors, the Polish and the Russians. The plundering of these parts was unfathomable. After they did their dirty work, they handed the area of Pommern, including the Klein Pobloth Estate, over to Russia and Poland, displacing millions of Germans from their homes and then relocating the outsiders to the area along the Baltic Sea, including the Klein Pobloth Estate.

The Western powers were silent on the issue of the ethnic cleansing of Pommern and Eastern Germany, resulting in approximately 12 million German refugees being challenged to find food and housing. This was the most significant influx of refugees to be deprived of their homeland since the beginning of recorded time.

Ruth and her family witnessed the destruction of their home country during the First and Second World Wars. During this time, Germany lost much of its history and cultural pride. The people were broken and defeated. Many wondered if their home country could ever overcome the shame and humiliation of war. After the war, Germans suffered the ire of the Allies and other nations. These scars would be worn by her family for generations to come. However, Ruth and Anneliese were among the stalwart women who belonged among the countless fearless women of the world's history.

Between 1941 and 1953, the United States admitted 400,000 Displaced Persons from Eastern Europe.

GERMAN WORDS AND DEFINITIONS

1. Absender: R. Meissner: sent by R. Meissner
2. auf Wiedersehen: goodbye
3. bitte: please
4. Danke schön: thank you
5. Dummkopf: stupid
6. Dorf: village
7. Feldpost: Field Post
8. Für Hans-Rudolf Meissner Wiesbaden: For Hans-Rudolf Meissner Wiesbaden
9. gnädige Frau: my lady
10. Guten Abend: good evening
11. Gott im Himmel: God in heaven
12. Gott im Himmel, nein danke: God in heaven, no thank you
13. Gutshaus: Manor house
14. Ja: yes
15. Fallschirmjäger: Parachute Major
16. Kuchen: cake
17. Luftwaffe: Air Force
18. Mark: dollar
19. Mutti: mother
20. Onkel: uncle
21. Rosenblüte auf dem Heidegrab: Roses Blume on the Heide Grave
22. Pommern: Pomerania
23. Schloss Prützen be Güstrow: Castle Prützen be Güstrow
24. "Stille Nacht, Heilige Nacht": "Silent Night Holy Night"
25. Streusel Kuchen: a cake with a sugar topping
26. Tante: aunt
27. Vati: daddy

GERMAN TOWN NAMES AFTER 1945 POLISH TOWN NAMES

The province of Pommern-Pomerania

Belgard: Białogard

Berlin: Berlin

Bütow: Bytow

Danzig: Gdansk

Gross Jestin: Gościno

Kempen: Kepno

Klein Pobloth: Poblocie-Male

Kolberg: Kolobrzeg

Königsberg: Chojna

Körlin: Karlino

Köslin: Koszalin

Ostsee: Baltic Sea

Schönebeck: Dzwonowo

Stargard: Szczeciński

Stettin: Szczecin

Stolp: Slupsk

Trampke: Trabki

Uchtenhagen: Krzywnica

Dear Reader,

We hope you have enjoyed this book, but why not share your views on social media? You can also follow our pages to see more about our other products: facebook.com/penandswordbooks or follow us on X @penswordbooks

You can also view our products at www.pen-and-sword.co.uk (UK and ROW) or www.penandswordbooks.com (North America).

To keep up to date with our latest releases and online catalogues, please sign up to our newsletter at: www.pen-and-sword.co.uk/newsletter

If you would like a printed catalogue with our latest books, then please email: enquiries@pen-and-sword.co.uk or telephone: 01226 734555 (UK and ROW) or email: uspen-and-sword@casematepublishers.com or telephone: (610) 853-9131 (North America).

We respect your privacy and we will only use personal information to send you information about our products.

Thank you!